Recent Progress and Challenges of Artificial Intelligence in Bioinformatics and New Medicine

Recent Progress and Challenges of Artificial Intelligence in Bioinformatics and New Medicine

Guest Editors

Tao Wang
Jiajie Peng
Yongtian Wang

MDPI

Basel • Beijing • Wuhan • Barcelona • Belgrade • Novi Sad • Cluj • Manchester

Guest Editors

Tao Wang
School of Computer Science
Northwestern Polytechnical
University
Xi'an
China

Jiajie Peng
School of Computer Science
Northwestern Polytechnical
University
Xi'an
China

Yongtian Wang
School of Computer Science
Northwestern Polytechnical
University
Xi'an
China

Editorial Office
MDPI AG
Grosspeteranlage 5
4052 Basel, Switzerland

This is a reprint of the Special Issue, published open access by the journal *Applied Sciences* (ISSN 2076-3417), freely accessible at: https://www.mdpi.com/journal/applsci/special_issues/MCNN50PGBK.

For citation purposes, cite each article independently as indicated on the article page online and as indicated below:

Lastname, A.A.; Lastname, B.B. Article Title. *Journal Name* **Year**, *Volume Number*, Page Range.

ISBN 978-3-7258-5185-0 (Hbk)
ISBN 978-3-7258-5186-7 (PDF)
https://doi.org/10.3390/books978-3-7258-5186-7

Contents

About the Editors

Tao Wang

Tao Wang is an Associate Professor at the School of Computer Science, Northwestern Polytechnical University, focusing his research on bioinformatics, computational biology, and the application of artificial intelligence to biomedical big data. He currently holds editorial positions for several SCI-indexed journals including *BMC Bioinformatics* and *Scientific Reports*.

Jiajie Peng

Jiajie Peng is a Professor at the School of Computer Science, Northwestern Polytechnical University, where he also serves as the Assistant to the Dean and Director of the Scientific Intelligence Interdisciplinary Research Center. His research spans large model agents, intelligent drug design, and bioinformatics, with particular interest in deep learning, explainable AI, and their applications in single-cell biology, network biology, and brain diseases.

Yongtian Wang

Yongtian Wang is an Associate Professor at the School of Computer Science, Northwestern Polytechnical University, conducting research in bioinformatics, data mining, artificial intelligence, and drug/vaccine design. He currently chairs the IEEE BIBM BiOK international conference and serves as an Editor or Guest Editor for several international journals such as *BMC Bioinformatics*.

Preface

The rapid expansion of big data in biology, medical science, and public health has ushered in a new era of scientific discovery and technological innovation. This growth is profoundly reshaping the landscape of life sciences and translational medicine, accelerating the development of what we now term "new medicine." In this context, the cross-integration of life sciences, medical research, and information science has become a critical engine driving progress.

Artificial intelligence (AI), with its remarkable capabilities in pattern recognition, predictive modeling, and multi-scale data integration, is playing an increasingly vital role in bioinformatics and modern medicine. From deciphering complex biological mechanisms to enabling early diagnosis and personalized treatment strategies, AI continues to demonstrate tremendous potential. Nevertheless, these advances are accompanied by significant challenges, including handling heterogeneous and high-dimensional data, integrating multi-omics information—particularly in single-cell contexts—and extracting meaningful insights from limited sample sizes.

This Special Issue aims to present cutting-edge research and comprehensive reviews that highlight the transformative impacts of AI methodologies in bioinformatics and new medicine. Topics range from deep learning and network modeling to cancer genomics, disease risk exploration, and the development of new computational tools and databases. We hope this collection not only reflects the current state of the art but also inspires further innovation and collaboration across disciplines.

We are delighted to introduce this curated selection of articles. It is our sincere hope that this issue will serve as a valuable resource for researchers, clinicians, and engineers working at the intersection of computation and biology.

Tao Wang, Jiajie Peng, and Yongtian Wang
Guest Editors

applied sciences

MDPI

Editorial

Recent Progress and Challenges of Artificial Intelligence in Bioinformatics and New Medicine

Tao Wang [1,2,*], Xuchao Zhang [1,2], Yongtian Wang [1,2,*] and Jiajie Peng [1,2,*]

1 School of Computer Science, Northwestern Polytechnical University, 1 Dongxiang Rd., Xi'an 710072, China
2 Key Laboratory of Big Data Storage and Management, Ministry of Industry and Information Technology, Northwestern Polytechnical University, 1 Dongxiang Rd., Xi'an 710072, China
* Correspondence: twang@nwpu.edu.cn (T.W.); wangyt@nwpu.edu.cn (Y.W.); jiajiepeng@nwpu.edu.cn (J.P.)

1. Introduction

The exponential growth of big data in biology, medical science, and public health is fundamentally transforming the landscape of biomedical research and therapeutic development [1]. This data-driven revolution, accelerated by disruptive technologies in life and health sciences, has positioned artificial intelligence (AI) as a strategic cornerstone for advancing novel medicine and understanding complex disease mechanisms [2,3]. Cross-disciplinary convergence—spanning life sciences, clinical medicine, and computational informatics—is catalyzing unprecedented innovations in bioinformatics and translational research [4–7].

Significant progress has been made in leveraging AI for critical biomedical challenges. Deep learning architectures now enable precise analysis of multi-modal biological data [8], while network-based approaches decode intricate gene interactions underlying pathologies like cancer [9–11]. Recent advances include in silico modeling of cellular processes [12], AI-enhanced histopathological quantification [13], and personalized health monitoring through wearable biosignal interpretation [14]. Concurrently, large-scale omics integration—particularly single-cell sequencing—has unveiled unprecedented resolution of cellular heterogeneity and microenvironment dynamics [15–17].

However, this rapid progression faces persistent challenges. Key among these are the complexities of multi-omics data integration, the curse of dimensionality in high-feature/small-sample scenarios, and the demand for clinically interpretable AI solutions [18–20]. Data modality heterogeneity (e.g., genomic, imaging, wearable biosensors) further complicates model generalizability [21]. In histopathology, subjective manual analysis remains burdensome despite computer vision advancements [22], while in genomics, feature selection instability across omics layers undermines biomarker reliability [23]. Translational hurdles also persist, particularly in scaling advanced therapies like cell/gene treatments through constrained clinical infrastructures [24].

Addressing these frontiers necessitates the development of advanced computational methodologies that integrate innovation with tangible biomedical impact. Recent advances demonstrate how tailored AI frameworks—including ensemble deep learning architectures, self-supervised personalization techniques, and novel network algorithms—are overcoming domain-specific barriers by enabling transformative capabilities across multiple dimensions. These approaches facilitate the discovery of molecular biomarkers through integrative multi-omics analysis, automate the transformation of complex histopathological patterns into quantitative diagnostic criteria, enhance interpretation of multimodal physiological signals for personalized health monitoring, and optimize generative models for scalable biological simulation. Collectively, these methodologies exemplify AI's capacity to distill actionable insights from biomedical complexity, driving innovations across diagnostics, therapeutic development, and precision intervention strategies. This paradigm shift is fundamentally reshaping computational medicine workflows while establishing robust pipelines for clinical translation.

2. An Overview of Published Articles

Recent research highlights significant advancements in artificial intelligence across diverse biomedical domains, enhancing precision, efficiency, and inclusivity.

In the critical field of cancer prognostics, Xu et al. introduced a significant advance with EP-WGCNA [25]. This weighted gene co-expression network employs a novel Euclidean-Pearson approach to identify key ferroptosis-related genes (FRGs) associated with gastric cancer. Their resulting prognostic model demonstrated substantially improved survival prediction capabilities compared to conventional methods. The clinical relevance of these identified biomarkers was further supported by experimental validation and pathway enrichment analysis.

When investigating challenges in biomarker stability, Łukaszuk et al. analyzed feature selection consistency in multi-omics data for TP53 mutation prediction—mutations associated with poor clinical outcomes in cancer [26]. Using three classifiers with L1 regularization and five-fold cross-validation across 15 TCGA datasets, they measured stability via the Nogueira metric. Their findings revealed that higher regularization strength consistently produced optimal stability across all classifiers and omics layers. Significantly, miRNA data layers exhibited the highest overall stability. In contrast, mutation and RNA expression layers showed substantially lower stability, particularly when regularization was weak. This research underscores the critical impact of data type, regularization strength, and careful analytical validation on the reliability of biomarker discovery in high-dimensional multi-omics data.

Advancing reproductive medicine, Raudonis et al. [27] developed an ensemble AI framework (UNet++, UNet, ResNet34-UNet) to determine the receptivity stage of the endometrium in HE-stained histology images. Their technique integrated image segmentation with statistical analysis of stromal nuclear feature evolution. Demonstrating superior segmentation performance (Dice: 0.95, IoU: 0.90), the approach revealed statistically significant differences in nuclear count and stromal tissue size across pre-receptive, receptive, and post-receptive stages. This demonstrates promising potential to enhance fertility treatments through objective endometrial tissue analysis.

Advancing personalized health monitoring, Islam et al. [28] leveraged wearable technology for stress prediction. Their approach employs self-supervised pre-training on 1D CNNs to develop personalized models using electrodermal activity data. Remarkably, on the WESAD dataset, their method achieves baseline performance with less than 30% labeled data, enabling real-time precision health interventions despite the inherent challenges of subjective biosignals.

In the field of computer vision, Wang et al. introduced SSSGAN, a generative approach that significantly enhances computational efficiency in semantic image composition by utilizing a single-generator design [29]. This method overcomes the scalability limitation of traditional multi-generator approaches, reducing the number of required generators to a constant while maintaining competitive performance. Complementing advancements in medical image analysis, Gonciar et al. developed a semi-automatic method for quantifying myocardial fibrosis in cardiac histopathology using objective digital color analysis

(CIELAB-based methods) [30]. This approach minimizes subjectivity inherent in visual assessment and demonstrates comparable performance to established analytical techniques like stereology and ImageJ (version 1.54).

Separately, Kim et al. applied an ensemble of VGGish and YAMNet to Speech Emotion Recognition (SER) [31]. Using STFT preprocessing, speech was converted to spectrograms, segmented, and represented as Gaussian distributions, with data quality assessed by correlation coefficients. This reduced data scale and minimized uncertainty. Explanatory techniques (Grad CAM, LIME, and occlusion sensitivity) provided interpretable insights. The ensemble model achieved 87% accuracy across three datasets, outperforming individual models and showing adaptability to diverse environments. Key emotional areas identified by Grad CAM were converted to audio for analysis, enhancing reliability and explainability.

Similarly employing a comprehensive approach to complex system optimization, Aguilar-Gallardo et al. examined hospital-integrated GMP facilities for advanced therapies (ATMPs) [32]. While presenting promising treatment options, this integration demands significant adaptation within constrained healthcare infrastructures. Their analysis outlines critical implementation strategies, emphasizing enabling technologies like PAT, continuous manufacturing, and AI-driven process control. Success demands tailored quality systems prioritizing product quality over compliance alone; substantial investment; and sustained multidisciplinary collaboration bridging research and clinical impact.

Collectively, these diverse studies powerfully illustrate AI's transformative role in driving precision, efficiency, and inclusivity across the biomedical landscape. Navigating the accompanying ethical and translational hurdles will require sustained collaborative validation efforts to maximize the clinical impact of these innovations and ultimately improve patient outcomes.

3. Conclusions

These studies highlight significant advancements in biomedical artificial intelligence, particularly in precision diagnostics, personalized health monitoring, and therapeutic innovation. Breakthroughs in computational methodologies—such as gene co-expression networks, self-supervised learning for biosignals, GAN-based architectures, and ensemble models for histopathology—demonstrate potential to enhance precision, scalability, and efficiency in tackling complex biomedical challenges. These findings underscore the necessity of interdisciplinary convergence to navigate data heterogeneity, ensure biomarker stability, and achieve robust clinical translation.

Future research should prioritize ethical frameworks, validation across diverse populations, and infrastructure investments to address challenges in data integration, model interpretability, and clinical implementation.

Author Contributions: T.W. and X.Z.: writing—original draft preparation; T.W., Y.W. and J.P.: writing—review and editing. All authors have read and agreed to the published version of the manuscript.

Funding: This work has been supported by the National Natural Science Foundation of China (grant number: 62102319).

Conflicts of Interest: The authors declare no conflicts of interest.

References

1. Ashley, E.A. Towards precision medicine. *Nat. Rev. Genet.* **2016**, *17*, 507–522. [CrossRef]

2. He, J.; Baxter, S.L.; Xu, J.; Xu, J.; Zhou, X.; Zhang, K. The practical implementation of artificial intelligence technologies in medicine. *Nat. Med.* **2019**, *25*, 30–36. [CrossRef]
3. Zhou, H.Y.; Li, Y.; Li, J.; Meng, J.; Wu, A. Unleashing the potential of artificial intelligence in infectious diseases. *Natl. Sci. Rev.* **2025**, *12*, nwaf004. [CrossRef]
4. Patel, A.U.; Gu, Q.; Esper, R.; Maeser, D.; Maeser, N. The crucial role of interdisciplinary conferences in advancing explainable AI in healthcare. *BioMedInformatics* **2024**, *4*, 1363–1383. [CrossRef]
5. Wang, T.; Luo, Z. Large language models transform biological research: From architecture to utilization. *Sci. China Inf. Sci.* **2025**, *68*, 170101. [CrossRef]
6. Jiang, T.; Cao, S.; Liu, Y.; Zhang, Z.; Liu, B.; Luo, R.; Wang, G.; Wang, Y. cuteFC: Regenotyping structural variants through an accurate and efficient force-calling method. *Genome Biol.* **2025**, *26*, 166. [CrossRef] [PubMed]
7. Wang, H.; Yang, Y.; Huang, Y.; Zang, T.; Liu, Y. TDLM: A Diffusion Language Model for TCR Sequence Exploration and Generation. In Proceedings of the 2024 IEEE International Conference on Bioinformatics and Biomedicine (BIBM), Lisboa, Portugal, 3–6 December 2024; pp. 113–120.
8. Acosta, J.N.; Falcone, G.J.; Rajpurkar, P.; Topol, E.J. Multimodal biomedical AI. *Nat. Med.* **2022**, *28*, 1773–1784. [CrossRef]
9. Ranea, J.A.G.; Perkins, J.; Chagoyen, M.; Díaz-Santiago, E.; Pazos, F. Network-based methods for approaching human pathologies from a phenotypic point of view. *Genes* **2022**, *13*, 1081. [CrossRef] [PubMed]
10. Zhang, L.; Wang, S.; Wang, Y.; Zhao, T.; Wren, J. HBFormer: A single-stream framework based on hybrid attention mechanism for identification of human-virus protein–protein interactions. *Bioinformatics* **2024**, *40*, btae724. [CrossRef] [PubMed]
11. Song, W.; Xu, L.; Han, C.; Tian, Z.; Zou, Q.; Gao, X. Drug–target interaction predictions with multi-view similarity network fusion strategy and deep interactive attention mechanism. *Bioinformatics* **2024**, *40*, btae346. [CrossRef]
12. Barh, D.; Yiannakopoulou, E.C.; Salawu, E.O.; Bhattacharjee, A.; Chowbina, S.; Nalluri, J.J.; Ghosh, P.; Azevedo, V. In silico disease model: From simple networks to complex diseases. In *Animal Biotechnology*; Academic Press: Cambridge, MA, USA, 2020; pp. 441–460.
13. Ma, Y.; Jamdade, S.; Konduri, L.; Sailem, H. AI in Histopathology Explorer for comprehensive analysis of the evolving AI landscape in histopathology. *npj Digit. Med.* **2025**, *8*, 156. [CrossRef]
14. Vaghasiya, J.V.; Mayorga-Martinez, C.C.; Pumera, M. Wearable sensors for telehealth based on emerging materials and nanoarchitectonics. *npj Flex. Electron.* **2023**, *7*, 26. [CrossRef]
15. Wu, X.; Yang, X.; Dai, Y.; Zhao, Z.; Zhu, J.; Guo, H.; Yang, R. Single-cell sequencing to multi-omics: Technologies and applications. *Biomark. Res.* **2024**, *12*, 110. [CrossRef]
16. Chen, C.; Wang, J.; Pan, D.; Wang, X.; Xu, Y.; Yan, J.; Wang, L.; Yang, X.; Yang, M.; Liu, G. Applications of multi-omics analysis in human diseases. *MedComm* **2023**, *4*, e315. [CrossRef]
17. Zhu, P.; Shu, H.; Wang, Y.; Wang, X.; Zhao, Y.; Hu, J.; Peng, J.; Shang, X.; Tian, Z.; Chen, J.; et al. MAEST: Accurately spatial domain detection in spatial transcriptomics with graph masked autoencoder. *Brief. Bioinform.* **2025**, *26*, bbaf086. [CrossRef]
18. Ballard, J.L.; Wang, Z.; Li, W.; Shen, L.; Long, Q. Deep learning-based approaches for multi-omics data integration and analysis. *BioData Min.* **2024**, *17*, 38. [CrossRef] [PubMed]
19. Hagos, D.H.; Aryal, S.K.; Ymele-Leki, P.; Burge, L.L. AI-driven multimodal colorimetric analytics for biomedical and behavioral health diagnostics. *Comput. Struct. Biotechnol. J.* **2025**, *27*, 2219–2232. [CrossRef] [PubMed]
20. Zhang, X.; Chen, J.; Wang, Y.; Wang, X.; Hu, J.; Peng, J.; Shang, X.; Wang, Y.; Wang, T. cfMethylPre: Deep transfer learning enhances cancer detection based on circulating cell-free DNA methylation profiling. *Brief. Bioinform.* **2025**, *26*, bbaf303. [CrossRef] [PubMed]
21. Mezei, T.; Kolcsár, M.; Joó, A.; Gurzu, S. Image analysis in histopathology and cytopathology: From early days to current perspectives. *J. Imaging* **2024**, *10*, 252. [CrossRef]
22. Ma, D.; Fan, C.; Sano, T.; Kawabata, K.; Nishikubo, H.; Imanishi, D.; Sakuma, T.; Maruo, K.; Yamamoto, Y.; Matsuoka, T.; et al. Beyond Biomarkers: Machine Learning-Driven Multiomics for Personalized Medicine in Gastric Cancer. *J. Pers. Med.* **2025**, *15*, 166. [CrossRef]
23. Austin, C.P. Opportunities and challenges in translational science. *Clin. Transl. Sci.* **2021**, *14*, 1629–1647. [CrossRef]
24. Luo, X.; Wang, Y.; Zou, Q.; Xu, L.; Ioshikhes, I. Recall DNA methylation levels at low coverage sites using a CNN model in WGBS. *PLoS Comput. Biol.* **2023**, *19*, e1011205. [CrossRef]
25. Xu, Y.; Zhang, H.; Cao, D.; Ning, Z.; Zhu, L.; Liu, X. A Novel Prognostic Model for Gastric Cancer with EP_Dis-Based Co-Expression Network Analysis. *Appl. Sci.* **2023**, *13*, 7108. [CrossRef]
26. Łukaszuk, T.; Krawczuk, J.; Żyła, K.; Kęsik, J. Stability of Feature Selection in Multi-Omics Data Analysis. *Appl. Sci.* **2024**, *14*, 11103. [CrossRef]

27. Raudonis, V.; Bartasiene, R.; Minajeva, A.; Saare, M.; Drejeriene, E.; Kozlovskaja-Gumbriene, A.; Salumets, A. Towards metric-driven difference detection between receptive and nonreceptive endometrial samples using automatic histology image analysis. *Appl. Sci.* **2024**, *14*, 5715. [CrossRef]
28. Islam, T.; Washington, P. Individualized stress mobile sensing using self-supervised pre-training. *Appl. Sci.* **2023**, *13*, 12035. [CrossRef]
29. Wang, Z.; Liu, Z. Unlocking Efficiency in Fine-Grained Compositional Image Synthesis: A Single-Generator Approach. *Appl. Sci.* **2023**, *13*, 7587. [CrossRef]
30. Gonciar, D.; Berciu, A.G.; Danku, A.E.; Lorenzovici, N.; Dulf, E.-H.; Mocan, T.; Nicula, S.-M.; Agoston-Coldea, L. The Quantification of Myocardial Fibrosis on Human Histopathology Images by a Semi-Automatic Algorithm. *Appl. Sci.* **2024**, *14*, 7696. [CrossRef]
31. Kim, T.W.; Kwak, K.C. Speech emotion recognition using deep learning transfer models and explainable techniques. *Appl. Sci.* **2024**, *14*, 1553. [CrossRef]
32. Aguilar-Gallardo, C.; Bonora-Centelles, A. Integrating artificial intelligence for academic advanced therapy medicinal products: Challenges and opportunities. *Appl. Sci.* **2024**, *14*, 1303. [CrossRef]

applied sciences

MDPI

Article

Unlocking Efficiency in Fine-Grained Compositional Image Synthesis: A Single-Generator Approach

Zongtao Wang and Zhiming Liu *

School of Computer & Information Science, Southwest University, Chongqing 400715, China; wztdream@email.swu.edu.cn
* Correspondence: zhimingliu88@swu.edu.cn

Abstract: The use of Generative Adversarial Networks (GANs) has led to significant advancements in the field of compositional image synthesis. In particular, recent progress has focused on achieving synthesis at the semantic part level. However, to enhance performance at this level, existing approaches in the literature tend to prioritize performance over efficiency, utilizing separate local generators for each semantic part. This approach leads to a linear increase in the number of local generators, posing a fundamental challenge for large-scale compositional image synthesis at the semantic part level. In this paper, we introduce a novel model called Single-Generator Semantic-Style GAN (SSSGAN) to improve efficiency in this context. SSSGAN utilizes a single generator to synthesize all semantic parts, thereby reducing the required number of local generators to a constant value. Our experiments demonstrate that SSSGAN achieves superior efficiency while maintaining a minimal impact on performance.

Keywords: compositional learning; generative adversarial network; image synthesis; disentanglement; efficiency

1. Introduction

There has been significant progress in the field of digital signal processing [1–7]. With the advancement of deep learning, researchers have increasingly focused on processing digital information using neural networks, including the synthesis of images through generative models. Our world, with its diverse range of objects and scenes, is inherently compositional. Compositionality emphasizes that complex entities are composed of simpler parts or components [8,9]. In the realm of generative models for image synthesis, it is crucial to embrace this fundamental principle that underlies the fabric of our reality. By considering objects as compositions of semantic parts, we can generate images that not only possess visual appeal but also exhibit a deeper level of interpretability. This approach grants us greater control over the generation process and facilitates the creation of highly customizable and meaningful images. Unfortunately, much of the existing literature has overlooked this principle, focusing solely on visual appeal or layout manipulation without leveraging compositionality. A limited number of recent works have proposed models based on compositionality, but these studies often neglect an important factor: efficiency. Real images or scenes typically involve a significant number of semantic parts and, without taking efficiency into consideration, the generative model becomes non-scalable and impractical. Hence, it is imperative to address both compositionality and efficiency when developing generative models for image synthesis.

Generative Adversarial Networks (GANs) have emerged as the dominant approach for image generation, primarily due to their superior performance in generating high-fidelity, visually appealing images. A typical example is the style-based GAN [10], where a noise code drawn from a Gaussian distribution is mapped to a latent space. This latent code is then used to modulate each layer of the model. Although this method can generate high-fidelity images efficiently, the generation process lacks semantic meaning. This limitation arises from the use of a single latent code to modulate the generation of the entire image, without the ability to represent the semantic meanings of its components. In our work, we propose to utilize a set of latent codes, each of which represents a specific semantic meaning, to generate images. These latent codes encode both the individual components and their relationships, allowing for the formation of complete images based on the compositional principle.

Another line of research focuses on the mapping from layout to image, exemplified by SPADE [11]. Such an approach utilizes the layout as a content latent code to modulate the style of the image. While efficient and capable of achieving semantic control, these methods require the layout as a conditional input for image generation and cannot generate images from scratch. As the semantic meaning is provided by the user—rather than learned by the model—there is no explicit modeling of semantic parts and the model lacks compositionality.

One promising new model, called SemanticStyleGAN, has recently been proposed by Yichun et al. [12]. This model utilizes one latent code to modulate a set of local generators, with each local generator representing a semantic component. Following the compositional principle, these components are combined to form the complete object. However, a significant limitation of their model lies in the need for substantial local generators to represent each semantic part, resulting in linear growth in the number of local generators. This limitation makes their model non-scalable and inefficient. In contrast, our approach goes in the opposite direction: instead of using a single latent code to modulate multiple heavy local generators, we employ a set of latent codes to modulate a single local generator. This results in an efficient model that reduces the required number of local generators to a constant.

The limitations of the discussed models can be summarized based on three criteria: whether they are semantic-aware, compositional and efficient (see Table 1). It is evident that those models proposed in the existing literature either lack semantic awareness, compositionality or efficiency. In this paper, we introduce SSSGAN to address these limitations. The primary contribution of our work is a novel method that addresses the challenging task of generating all parts using a single local generator. This innovation is crucial, due to the inherent difficulties posed by strong entanglement and mode collapse problems associated with the generation of semantic parts using a shared generator. These challenges are further elaborated on in Section 3. The resulting model is both semantic-aware and compositional, while maintaining high efficiency. We conducted a comprehensive comparative analysis between SSSGAN and a state-of-the-art model, clearly demonstrating that SSSGAN excels in efficiency while making only minimal compromises in compositional performance. Our contributions are summarized as follows:

1. We propose a novel method that enables the generation of all semantic parts using a single local generator. This method effectively addresses the efficiency challenge encountered in large-scale compositional image-synthesis tasks.
2. We introduce SSSGAN, a model that is semantic-aware, compositional and efficient. It addresses the gap in existing works by meeting all three of these criteria simultaneously.
3. We conduct extensive experiments to evaluate the performance of SSSGAN, examining its compositional properties and the characteristics of its latent space.
4. We investigate the entanglement mechanism between semantic parts and devise a method to control the intensity of this entanglement.

Table 1. Comparison of representative models with the proposed model.

Model	Semantic-Aware	Compositional	Efficient
StyleGAN [10]	✗	✗	✓
SPADE [11]	✓	✗	✓
SemanticStyleGAN [12]	✓	✓	✗
Ours	✓	✓	✓

In the following sections, we delve deeper into the topic of compositional image generation. Section 2 provides a comprehensive review of the related literature, highlighting the existing approaches and their limitations. In Section 3, we present our proposed model, SSSGAN, detailing its architecture and key components. The experimental setup and results are presented in Section 4, and we evaluate the performance and efficiency of SSSGAN against a state-of-the-art model. Finally, in Section 5, we conclude the paper by summarizing our contributions, discussing the limitations faced and outlining future research directions in this field.

2. Related Work

Here, we review the related works in three areas: Disentanglement in generative models, compositional image synthesis and layout-to-image generation. It is worth noting that disentanglement and composition are inter-related and a work may be relevant to both aspects. To ensure clarity, we categorize the models that involve a compositional step into the compositional group, and those that do not into the disentanglement group. To enhance comprehension, the reviewed works are summarized in Table 2.

Disentanglement in Generative Models. Disentanglement refers to the property of a learned representation being sensitive to changes in one generating factor while being relatively insensitive to changes in other factors [13]. Some studies promote disentanglement by regularizing the distribution of latent codes to be factorized or independent [14,15]. This regularization encourages the latent code to control specific attributes of the generated image. Other studies introduce additional information loss to enhance the influence of factorized latent codes [16,17]. However, due to the lack of explicit inductive bias, the disentanglement achieved by these models is not predictable and the phenomenon is often not apparent. In contrast, our model incorporates an explicit inductive bias that considers an object as a composition of several parts, with each part defined in a supervised manner and assigned a semantic meaning. As a result, our model achieves significantly improved disentanglement, compared to these existing models.

Some studies have focused on achieving disentanglement between specific attribute pairs, such as style and content [18,19], identity and pose [19], identity and domain [20], shape and physical attribute [21] and appearance and geometry [22–27]. In contrast, our model aims to disentangle semantic parts defined by humans. Another line of research aims to disentangle representations in the hierarchy dimension by incorporating structure priors into the model [28–31] or by utilizing structured noise codes [32]. However, as the disentanglement in these models is achieved without supervision, the resulting disentangled factors may not align well with human understanding. In contrast, the disentangled factors in our model align closely with human conception.

Compositional Image Synthesis. Composition reflects the concept that an object is composed of its components and the goal of compositional learning is to explicitly model these components and their interactions [33]. Some researchers have directly performed compositional image synthesis in pixel space [34–36]. However, these models often generate floating objects over the background or are only effective on simple datasets, due to the limited representational power of the pixel space. In contrast, our model achieves high-fidelity image synthesis on real-image datasets.

It is important to note that our world is inherently three-dimensional. Several models with a 3D prior have recently been proposed in the literature [37–44]. These models typically encode a 3D prior by incorporating explicit 3D operations such as camera view direction, rotation and translation. However, these models are still designed to decompose the image at the object level and are unable to fully capture the fine-grained part-level decomposition.

Table 2. Analysis and summary of relevant research.

References	Achievement	Disadvantage	Comparison with Our Model
[14,15]	Increased disentanglement by encouraging latent codes to be factorized	Non-obvious, non-predictable disentanglement	Disentanglement factor has semantic meaning
[16,17]	Use of mutual information loss to boost factorized latent codes for improved disentanglement	Non-obvious, non-predictable disentanglement	Disentanglement factor has semantic meaning
[18,19]	Style–content disentanglement	Not fine-grained	Part-level disentanglement
[19]	Identity–pose disentanglement	Not fine-grained	Part-level disentanglement
[20]	Identity–domain disentanglement	Not fine-grained	Part-level disentanglement
[21]	Shape and physical attribute disentanglement	Not fine-grained	Part-level disentanglement
[22–27]	Appearance–geometry disentanglement	Not fine-grained	Part-level disentanglement
[28–31]	Structure disentanglement by customizing model architecture, unsupervised	Disentanglement factor does not align well with human conception	Disentanglement factor aligns with human conception
[32]	Structure disentanglement by use of structured noise codes, unsupervised	Disentanglement factor does not align well with human conception	Disentanglement factor aligns with human conception
[34–36]	Compositional image synthesis in pixel space	Floating object over background or feasible on simple dataset	Composition in hidden space, high quality on real-image dataset
[37–44]	3D-aware compositional image synthesis	Decomposes images into object and background, not fine-grained	Part-level compositional image synthesis
[45,46]	Decomposes image into foreground shape, foreground appearance and background	Not fine-grained	Part-level compositional image synthesis
[47]	Part-level compositionality, unsupervised	Decomposition quality is low	With supervision, high-quality decomposition
[12]	Part-level compositionality, high-quality for image and decomposition	Need substantial amount of heavy local generators, inefficient	Uses single local-generator, efficient
[48–54]	Sketch-to-image mapping	Semantic-agnostic, need sketches as input	Semantic-aware, no need for input
[11,55–58]	Semantic layout-to-image mapping, semantic aware	Object-level, need semantic layout as input	Part-level, no need for input, generation from scratch
[59,60]	Semantic layout-to-image mapping, part-level	Need layout as input	No need for input, generation from scratch
[60–62]	Semantic layout-to-image mapping, supports both part- or object-level layout	Needs layout as input	No need for input, generation from scratch
[55,62,63]	Semantic layout-to-image mapping, utilizing multi-scale methods to better encode semantic component	Needs layout as input	No need for input, generation from scratch

Some studies have explored compositional learning by decomposing objects into shape and appearance representations [45,46]; however, these are still not as fine-grained as that in our model. To the best of our knowledge, only a limited number of studies have achieved compositional learning at the semantic part level [12,47]. Among them, SemanticStyleGAN [12] stands out for its high-quality compositional image synthesis ability. However, SemanticStyleGAN sacrifices efficiency for performance by employing separate local generators for each semantic part. Additionally, it requires explicit factorization of the latent code into base, shape and texture codes, resulting in a complex and inefficient model. In contrast, our model overcomes these limitations by using a single local generator for all parts and eliminates the need for latent code factorization, making it more efficient and simple.

Layout-to-Image Generation. Many studies have focused on mapping layouts to realistic images, which is valuable for controllable image editing and creation. Some studies have utilized sketches as input, which lack semantic meaning [48–54]. Other studies have employed segmentation masks. The granularity of the semantic component varies from object level [11,55–58] to part level [59,60]. Certain models support both object- and part-level semantic layouts [60–62]. Some researchers have utilized multi-scale methods during training to capture the varying granularity of semantic components [55,62,63]. While these models achieve high-fidelity image synthesis and provide control over the semantic component(s), they share a common drawback, when compared to our model: they require a layout as input. As a result, they are unable to generate images from scratch and their models are not compositional.

3. Methods

Our method is based upon SemanticStyleGAN. In order to understand the proposed approach in this work and the reason why SemanticStyleGAN sacrifices efficiency for performance, it is necessary to comprehend the challenges involved in image composition at the semantic part level. These challenges can be identified in two aspects. First, at the part level, the components are typically strongly entangled with each other, making it difficult to achieve compositional learning, necessitating the disentanglement of the parts as a prerequisite. Second, the parts themselves are usually heterogeneous objects originating from different distributions, posing a challenge for GANs to model due to the notorious mode collapse problem [64]. So, how does SemanticStyleGAN address these challenges and what is the trade-off? At the core of SemanticStyleGAN is a set of local generators responsible for generating the corresponding features for each semantic part—in other words, it utilizes a separate generator for each semantic part. This design naturally resolves the second difficulty mentioned earlier, as each local generator only needs to generate one semantic part from a single distribution. Moreover, this design also aids in addressing the first challenge, as there is no interaction between the parts within the local generator, given that each local generator has its own parameters. While SemanticStyleGAN has good performance, the drawback of this design is apparent: as it requires a dedicated local generator for each semantic part, the number of local generators increases linearly with the number of semantic parts, making the model impractical when dealing with a large number of semantic parts. Therefore, addressing this issue is crucial for achieving large-scale compositional image synthesis at the semantic part level.

So, the following question arises: can we achieve similar performance with SemanticStyleGAN by using fewer generators or even a single local generator? To do so, we face the same challenges mentioned above. To tackle these challenges, we drew inspiration from the auto-regressive model [65], in which the image is generated in a pixel-by-pixel manner, with each pixel being sampled conditioned on the previously sampled pixels. Our main idea is to apply a similar approach to model the relationships between the noise codes. By doing so, the sampled noise codes will contain the dependency information. Despite processing the noise codes with a shared local generator, it is possible for the GAN to utilize this dependency information to encode each part feature in its own distinct way. Therefore, this design has the potential to overcome the aforementioned challenges. The key distinction between the original auto-regressive model and our approach lies in the generation process. While the original auto-regressive model generates images pixel-by-pixel, our approach generates them part-by-part. Additionally, in the original auto-regressive model, no semantic meaning is assigned to each pixel. However, in our approach, our model learns the semantic meaning of each part's noise code during training. The necessity of the proposed approach is further examined in Section 4.2.4.

The architecture of SSSGAN is depicted in Figure 1. In particular, SSSGAN is built upon SemanticStyleGAN [12], consisting of three main modules: A set of local generators, a render network and a dual-branch discriminator. SSSGAN introduces modifications to SemanticStyleGAN in three key aspects. First, it incorporates a LSTM module to model the relationships between the parts and generate the noise codes. Second, it employs a single local generator for generating all the parts. Third, unlike SemanticStyleGAN—which factorizes the latent code into a base code, shape code, and texture code to enhance the encoding of part relationships—our model leverages the LSTM module to capture the part dependencies, rendering the manual factorization of latent codes unnecessary. Instead, we use a single latent code to modulate the local generator. To offer a comprehensive understanding of the information processing flow in SSSGAN, we provide brief descriptions of the modules inherited from SemanticStyleGAN as needed. For more detailed information, please refer to the original paper [12].

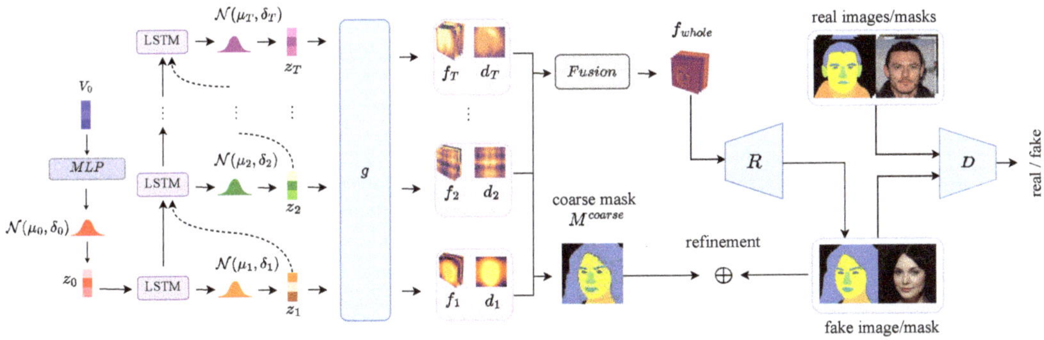

Figure 1. Overview of the SSSGAN architecture: The LSTM module models noise code relationships, the shared generator g generates part features, the *Fusion* module fuses part features, the render net R renders features to images and the discriminator D provides adversarial loss.

Noise Code Generation. As SSSGAN uses a single local generator for the generation of all parts, we need to explicitly model their joint distribution $P(\mathbf{q}_1, \mathbf{q}_2, \cdots, \mathbf{q}_K)$, where $\mathbf{q}_k$, $k = 1, \cdots, K$ is a random variable representing the kth part. Instead of directly modeling this joint distribution, inspired by the auto-regressive model [65], we factorize this joint distribution into the product of a sequence of conditional distributions, as defined below:

$$P(\mathbf{z}_1, \mathbf{z}_2, \cdots, \mathbf{z}_K) = \prod_{k=1}^{K} P(\mathbf{z}_k | \mathbf{z}_1, \cdots, \mathbf{z}_{k-1}). \tag{1}$$

We start the generation of the noise codes from a learnable constant vector V_0, which is mapped to a tuple $(\mu_0, \log var_0)$ by a two-layer MLP; here, μ_0 and var_0 represent the mean and variance of the Gaussian distribution, respectively. The logarithm operation is performed to ensure that the variance is a positive value. The initial input to the LSTM layer is sampled from the diagonal Gaussian $\mathcal{N}(\mu_0, \delta_0)$ using the re-parameterization trick:

$$z_0 = \epsilon_0 \odot \delta_0 + \mu_0, \tag{2}$$

where $\odot$ denotes element-wise product, $\epsilon_0 \sim \mathcal{N}(\mathbf{0}, \mathbf{I})$ and $\delta_0 = \sqrt{var_0}$. $\mathcal{N}(\mathbf{0}, \mathbf{I})$ represent the multivariate Gaussian distribution with zero mean $\mathbf{0}$ and identity covariance matrix $\mathbf{I}$.

At step t, the LSTM layer takes two vectors as input: one is the noise code z_{t-1} sampled at step $t-1$ and the other is the hidden state of the LSTM layer h_{t-1}, which aggregates the interaction of the parts up to step $t-1$. The output layer of the LSTM is a single linear layer that maps the hidden state h_t to a tuple $(\mu_t, \log var_t)$. Similarly, the noise code z_t is sampled from the diagonal Gaussian $\mathcal{N}(\mu_t, \delta_t)$ using the re-parameterization trick, defined as follows:

$$z_t = \epsilon_t \odot \delta_t + \mu_t, \tag{3}$$

where $\epsilon_t \sim \mathcal{N}(\mathbf{0}, \mathbf{I})$ and $\delta_t = \sqrt{var_t}$.

In our experiment, we set the maximum step T to the part count K, which means that we generate one part at each step.

Part Feature Generation and Composition. The noise codes $\{z_k\}_{k=1}^{K}$ are mapped to a set of latent codes $\{w_k\}_{k=1}^{K}$ by a group of equal linear layers [66]. As mentioned above, we do not factorize the latent code as in SemanticStyleGAN and use one latent code to modulate the generator; that is, SemanticStyleGAN uses a separate local generator for the generation of each part, while we use a shared local generator for the generation of all the parts. The architecture of the local generator is shown in Figure 2. The local generator is a stack of modulated convolutional layers [66] and the *toDepth* and *toFeat* modules are mainly single modulated convolutional layers with fixed style. The local generator g takes the Fourier feature p and the kth latent code w_k as input, then produces a pseudo depth map $d_k \in \mathbb{R}^{H_f \times W_f \times 1}$ and a feature map $f_k \in \mathbb{R}^{H_f \times W_f \times D_f}$, where H_f, W_f and D_f are the spatial height, spatial width and channel dimension, respectively. The mapping is defined as:

$$g : (p, w_k) \mapsto (f_k, d_k). \tag{4}$$

The main logic of the composition process is to use the pseudo depth map d_k as a weighting factor for the feature map f_k. Specifically, the depth maps are squeezed to a channel-wise probability function by the softmax function, defined as:

$$M_k^{coarse}(i,j) = \frac{exp(d_k(i,j)/\tau)}{\sum_{k'}^{K} exp(d_{k'}(i,j)/\tau)}, \tag{5}$$

where τ is a temperature hyper-parameter with default setting of 1. Then, the feature maps $\{f_k\}_{k=1}^{K}$ are fused using weighted summation, defined as follows:

$$f_{whole} = \sum_{k}^{K} M_k^{coarse} \odot f_k, \tag{6}$$

where $\odot$ represents element-wise multiplication.

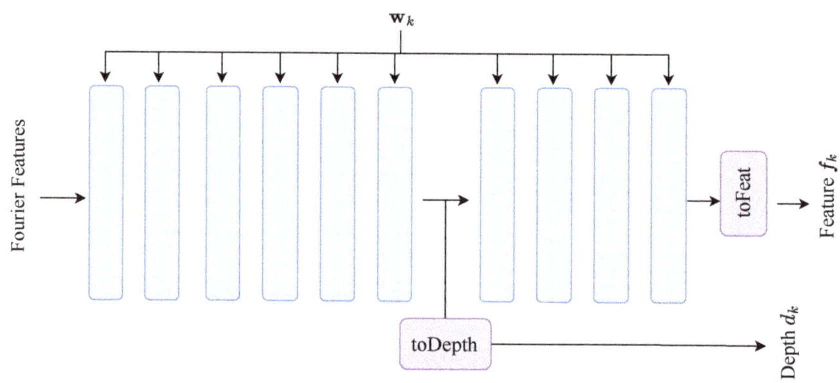

Figure 2. The architecture of the local generator. The blue blocks are modulated convolutional layers and the purple blocks are both a single modulated convolutional layer with fixed style.

Image Rendering. Following SemanticStyleGAN [12], the whole feature map f_{whole} is rendered into realistic images using a render net R. The render net R is actually the generator of StyleGAN [66]. As our goal is to render the feature and generate the image, R should only depend on the whole feature f_{whole}. To achieve this, the style of the generator is fixed. The render net is defined as follows:

$$R : f_{whole} \mapsto (\tilde{x}, M^{fine}), \tag{7}$$

where $\tilde{x} \in \mathbb{R}^{H \times W \times 3}$ and $M^{fine} \in [0,1]^{H \times W \times K}$ are the fake image and the fake segmentation mask, respectively; and H and W represent the image height and width, respectively.

The segmentation signal directly interacts with the fine mask M^{fine}, but only indirectly interacts with the coarse mask M^{coarse} through the pseudo depth maps. As M^{coarse} is crucial for decomposing the part features, a mask loss is used to strengthen the supervision signal over M^{coarse}, defined as:

$$\mathcal{L}_{mask} = \|upsample(M^{coarse}) - M^{fine}\|_2, \tag{8}$$

where *upsample* denotes the bilinear interpolation function.

Discriminator and Loss. As the output of the render net is a synthesized image and a segmentation mask, a dual branch discriminator D is used to enhance the regularization of the segmentation mask. This discriminator is a variation of the discriminator in StyleGAN [66], with the addition of a *toSeg* branch, which consists of a stack of equal convolution layers [66]. In the discriminator, the image feature and the segmentation feature are added for further processing. The benefit of this design is that a separate $R1$ regularization term [67] $\mathcal{L}_{R1_{seg}}$ can be applied specifically to the segmentation mask.

As there is no constraint on the values of the noise codes, we empirically observed that the values of the noise codes tend to grow very large during training, leading to training instability. To address this issue, we introduce a Kullback–Leibler divergence term, defined as follows:

$$\mathcal{L}_{KL} = \frac{1}{T}\sum_{t=1}^{T} -D_{KL}(P(\mathbf{z}_t|\mathbf{z}_1, \cdots, \mathbf{z}_{t-1})\|\mathcal{N}(\mathbf{0}, \mathbf{I})). \tag{9}$$

The final loss is

$$\mathcal{L}_{all} = \mathcal{L}_{stylegan2} + \mathcal{L}_{mask} + \mathcal{L}_{R1_{seg}} + \mathcal{L}_{KL}, \tag{10}$$

where $\mathcal{L}_{stylegan2}$ represents the loss used in StyleGAN2 [10].

4. Experiments and Results

4.1. Dataset and Training Method

Our main results were obtained using the CelebAMask-HQ dataset [68], which is a large-scale face image dataset consisting of 30,000 high-resolution images accompanied by fine-grained segmentation masks for facial attributes. This dataset is well-suited to our fine-grained compositional image synthesis task. To ensure a fair benchmark comparison with SemanticStyleGAN, we adopted the same pre-processing method. Specifically, we used the first 28,000 facial images and their corresponding segmentation masks for training. The segmentation masks include thirteen semantic parts: Background, skin, eyes, eyebrows, nose, mouth, ears, hair, neck, clothing, eyeglasses, hats and earrings. Prior to training, we resized both the images and segmentation masks to 256 $\times$ 256 pixels and normalized them within the range of $[-1, 1]$.

We also attempted to use the same optimization settings as SemanticStyleGAN, whenever possible, to ensure a fair comparison. For training, we employed the Adam optimizer with $\beta = (0, 0.99)$. In SemanticStyleGAN, a single learning rate of 0.002 was used. However, we observed that this value is too high when applied to the LSTM module with the Adam optimizer, as it leads to gradient spikes and disrupts the training process. Consequently, we introduced a separate learning rate of 0.0001 exclusively for the LSTM module to mitigate this issue.

To regularize the training process, we applied path regularization [10] on the generator and $R1$ regularization on the discriminator every 4 and 16 iterations, respectively. The weight factors for $\mathcal{L}_{mask}$ and $\mathcal{L}_{KL}$ were set to 100 and 0.0001, respectively. As we explicitly modeled the relationships between the parts using the LSTM module, we observed that style mixing had a detrimental effect on the training. This is expected, as style mixing assumes independent styles for the parts, which contradicts the function of the LSTM module. Therefore, we did not utilize style mixing during training.

Our model was trained using a single RTX3090 GPU, with a batch size of 16 and gradient accumulation every two iterations, resulting in an effective batch size of 32. We set the maximum number of training steps to 150,000, with each iteration taking approximately 4 s.

4.2. Results

4.2.1. Image Quality Evaluation

The quality of the generated images is a crucial aspect for a generative model. In Figure 3, we show some generated images produced with a resolution of 256 × 256 and with a truncation of 0.7. It is evident that these images have high perceptual quality and the corresponding segmentation masks accurately align with their intended semantic meanings. To quantitatively assess the image quality, two widely used metrics—namely, the Fréchet Inception Distance (FID) [69] and Inception Score (IS) [70]—were employed. A lower FID value or a higher IS value indicates higher image quality. The FID and IS scores are summarized in Table 3. Notably, SSSGAN achieved the lowest FID value of 6.19, albeit with a slightly lower IS value of 3.15. It should be acknowledged that quantitative evaluation of image quality remains an open problem; overall, based on the results, we can conclude that SSSGAN achieves comparable performance in generating high-quality images.

The semantic parts of a face exhibit strong correlations with each other. To generate a high-fidelity facial image, it is essential to arrange the latent codes for these parts in a cohesive manner. Our findings demonstrated that the LSTM module of SSSGAN effectively captures the relationships between the parts, enabling a single local generator to encode the facial images using these latent codes.

Table 3. Quantitative evaluation of the quality of the synthesized images.

Method	Data	Compositional	FID ↓	IS ↑
SemanticGAN [1]	img & seg	✗	7.50	3.51
SemanticStyleGAN [1]	img & seg	✓	6.42	3.21
SSSGAN	img & seg	✓	6.19	3.15

[1] These data are from [12].

Figure 3. Examples of images and segmentation masks generated by SSSGAN.

4.2.2. Compositional and Disentanglement Properties

Sequential Part Composition. Sequential Part Composition (SPC) is a task that involves sequentially adding components to an object for composition. This task serves as an intuitive demonstration of both the model's compositional ability and its disentanglement property. In terms of compositional property, a desirable model should accurately add each semantic part. Regarding the disentanglement property, there should be minimal interference with previously added components when a new component is introduced.

As SSSGAN utilizes a single local generator for all parts, it is possible that there are stronger interactions between the features of different parts, resulting in a higher degree of entanglement. The evaluation results for the SPC task are depicted in Figure 4. It is evident that SSSGAN successfully added the correct semantic part at each step, indicating its compositional ability. When comparing it with SemanticStyleGAN (Figure 4a), a stronger entanglement between the part features in SSSGAN can be observed; for example, in Figure 4b, the lip color and even the gender changed in the first and second samples, respectively. Furthermore, it can be observed that the most significant change occurred when the hair was added. This observation can be attributed to the fact that the hair is a prominent part of the human face, occupying a large portion of the image's pixels. Consequently, more neural activity is dedicated to representing its features. Given the limited resources, SSSGAN learned to exert greater control over facial attributes through interactions with the larger part (i.e., the hair).

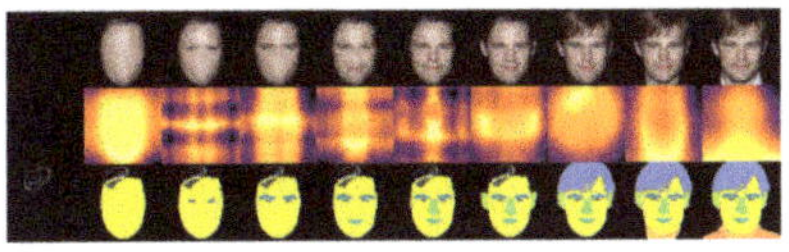

(**a**) SemanticStyleGAN

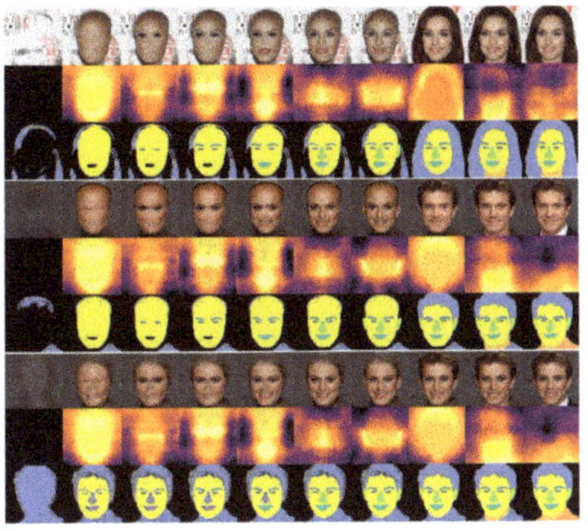

(**b**) SSSGAN

Figure 4. Sequential part composition: (**a**) SemanticStyleGAN, and (**b**) SSSGAN. Each sample consists of three rows: The synthesized image, the pseudo depth map and the segmentation mask.

Although there was entanglement between the parts in SSSGAN, it occurred in a coherent manner. For instance, consider the skin: while its appearance changes after the addition of hair, a shared coarse structure remains before and after the change, indicating that the coarse structure is disentangled. This aspect may initially seem like a drawback, in terms of image attribute editing; however, we argue that entanglement also offers an advantage, in terms of representation efficiency. This entanglement enables the model to re-use learned features to represent a wider range of attributes. This ability becomes particularly crucial under limited computational resources.

Entanglement Mechanism. The next question was the following: how does this entanglement occur? As we did not employ any style-mixing tricks during training, the only source of disentanglement came from the supervision of the segmentation mask. We speculate that information leakage occurred in the spatial dimension, from one part to another. Figure 5 illustrates the proposed mechanism of entanglement between the parts. The coarse mask in Equation (5) was computed using a softmax activation function. It is possible that SSSGAN learns to decrease the intensity of the pseudo depth map to create a softer mask. Taking the situation in Figure 5 as an example, when the temperature is higher, the segmentation mask becomes softer. As a result, the features of part B may leak to parts A and C, enabling part B to influence the attributes of parts A and C through their interaction.

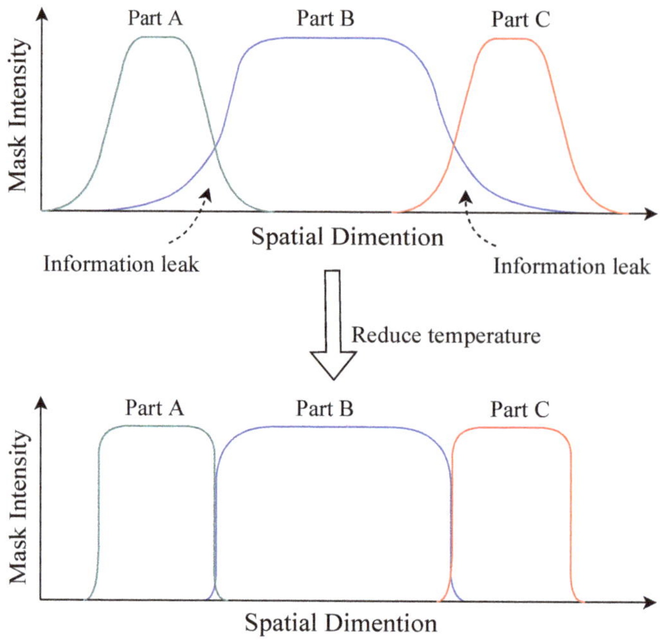

Figure 5. Illustration of the proposed entanglement mechanism.

Conversely, when we lower the temperature in Equation (5), the coarse mask becomes harder, making it more challenging for information to leak to neighboring parts. To validate our hypothesis, we decreased the temperature in Equation (5) from the default value of 1.0 to 0.01 and generated the second sample in Figure 4b again. The result is shown in the last sample of Figure 4b. It can be observed that, through the sequential composition process, there was minimal change in previous results when a new part was added and the gender of the individuals remained unchanged. While lowering the temperature can achieve better disentanglement, SSSGAN tended to generate femininity in males under lower temperatures. This outcome suggests a trade-off between disentanglement and diversity in SSSGAN, which can be controlled by the temperature variable. Higher temperatures increase the intensity of entanglement but yield more diverse images, while lower temperatures reduce entanglement intensity but also decrease the diversity of the generated images.

To quantitatively assess the level of disentanglement in the SPC task, we propose a metric called Sequential Mean Square Error (SMSE), as defined in Equation (11).

$$\mathrm{SMSE}_i = \frac{\sum_{h=1}^{H}\sum_{w=1}^{W}\left[\left(\sum_{j=1}^{i-1} M^i_{j,h,w}\right)\left(I^i_{h,w} - I^{i-1}_{h,w}\right)\right]^2}{\sum_{h=1}^{H}\sum_{w=1}^{W}\sum_{j=1}^{i-1} M^i_{j,h,w}}, \tag{11}$$

where h, w represent the spatial height and width indices, respectively; i denotes the sequence index; $M^i_{j,h,w} \in \{0,1\}$ represents the mask value at location (h,w) of the jth part in step i; and $I^i_{h,w}$ represents the pixel value at location (h,w) in step i. The SMSE metric quantifies the intensity of change in the original image when the ith part is added. A lower SMSE value indicates a better performance, in terms of disentanglement, meaning that the added part has a lesser impact on the rest of the image.

Figure 6 displays the quartiles of the SMSE values at different temperatures for each semantic part. For quantitative comparison, Table 4 presents the SMSE values and their corresponding standard deviations. Each row in the table corresponds to a specific part, while each column represents the SMSE values at different temperatures. The lowest SMSE value for each part is highlighted in bold font in the table. From Figure 6, it can be observed that the skin and hair exhibited relatively larger SMSE values, indicating higher entanglement for larger parts. Additionally, SSSGAN with the default temperature of 1.0 exhibited higher SMSE values, compared to SemanticStyleGAN. However, by reducing the temperature in Equation (5) for SSSGAN, the SMSE values were effectively reduced. For instance, as shown in Table 4, the skin's SMSE value for SSSGAN with a temperature of 0.01 was 0.022 ± 0.036, significantly lower than that for SemanticStyleGAN (0.078 ± 0.101). This result indicates that the level of entanglement can be significantly reduced by lowering the temperature. This finding is in alignment with the proposed entanglement mechanism illustrated in Figure 5.

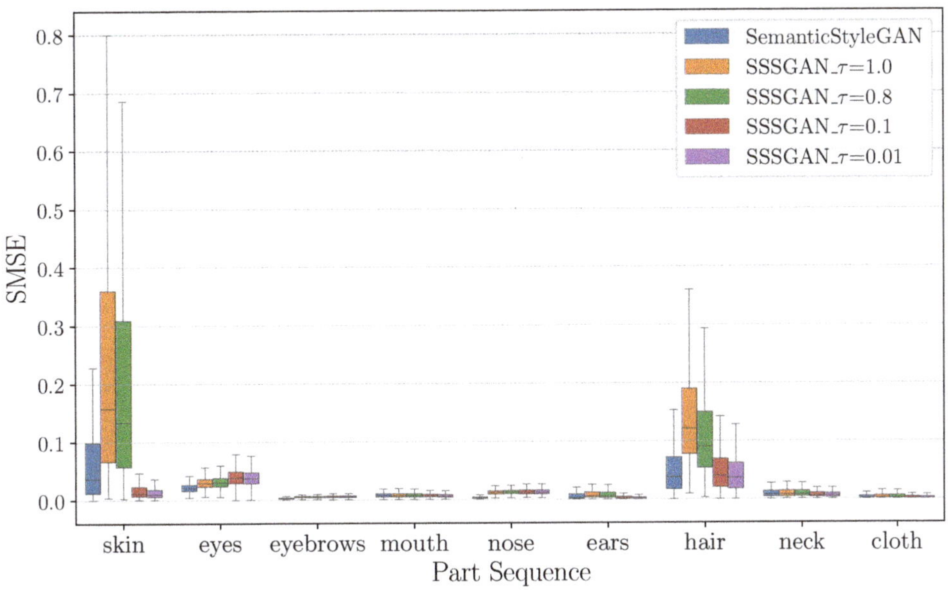

Figure 6. Quartiles of SMSE for the semantic parts. The statistical calculation is based on 10,000 samples.

Table 4. SMSE mean value and standard deviation for SemanticStyleGAN and SSSGAN at different temperatures.

Model	**SemanticStyleGAN**	**SSSGAN**			
Temperature	**1.0**	**1.0**	**0.8**	**0.1**	**0.01**
skin	0.078 ± 0.101	0.244 ± 0.232	0.214 ± 0.210	0.028 ± 0.044	**0.022 ± 0.036**
eyes	**0.022 ± 0.009**	0.031 ± 0.011	0.032 ± 0.012	0.041 ± 0.017	0.040 ± 0.016
eyebrows	**0.004 ± 0.002**	0.006 ± 0.003	0.006 ± 0.002	0.006 ± 0.002	0.006 ± 0.002
mouth	0.009 ± 0.006	0.009 ± 0.005	0.009 ± 0.005	**0.008 ± 0.004**	**0.008 ± 0.004**
nose	**0.004 ± 0.003**	0.013 ± 0.005	0.014 ± 0.005	0.014 ± 0.006	0.014 ± 0.007
ears	0.008 ± 0.012	0.012 ± 0.016	0.011 ± 0.016	0.005 ± 0.010	**0.004 ± 0.010**
hair	0.053 ± 0.051	0.149 ± 0.104	0.115 ± 0.090	0.052 ± 0.044	**0.046 ± 0.041**
neck	0.011 ± 0.012	0.013 ± 0.017	0.012 ± 0.016	0.008 ± 0.007	**0.008 ± 0.007**
cloth	0.004 ± 0.006	0.005 ± 0.009	0.005 ± 0.009	0.003 ± 0.005	**0.002 ± 0.004**

4.2.3. Noise and Latent Space Property

As SSSGAN utilizes a shared local generator for generating all the parts, we can analyze the properties of the noise codes and latent codes directly, without considering the local generator. In particular, we can visualize the noise codes and latent codes through low-dimensional embeddings. Figure 7 presents the two-dimensional embedding results using the t-SNE algorithm [71]. It can be observed that the noise codes were not well-separated, with clusters formed by the background, neck and clothes being close together. In contrast, the latent codes were well-grouped and did not overlap. These results suggest that the latent space of SSSGAN is flatter (or more linear) than the noise space. Consequently, the t-SNE algorithm finds it easier to separate the parts in the latent space, compared to the noise space. Furthermore, we noticed that the noise codes for consecutive semantic parts, such as the eyes, eyebrows and mouth, were closely grouped. This finding indicates that the LSTM module of SSSGAN can capture the relationships between these parts well.

Given that t-SNE is designed to capture local patterns within a distribution, we also examined the relationships between the noise codes and latent codes by measuring the pairwise cosine similarity. The results, illustrated in Figure 8, revealed a distinct pattern: the cosine similarity between parts was significantly stronger in the latent space, compared to the noise space. This suggests that the vectors representing the parts are more closely distributed, possibly forming a smoother manifold, in the latent space. In contrast, the distribution of part vectors in the noise space appeared to be less structured. Additionally, in the noise space, we observed slightly stronger cosine similarity between consecutive parts, indicating that the LSTM module can successfully capture the interdependence of adjacent parts, in line with our earlier analysis. Furthermore, in the latent space, we observed a stronger cosine similarity among facial components such as the eyes, eyebrows, mouth and nose. This observation indicates stronger correlations between these features, suggesting that they are distributed closer to each other in the manifold.

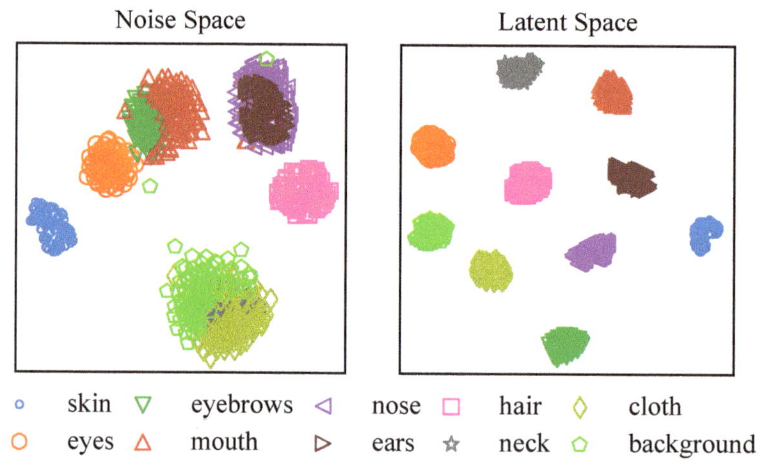

Figure 7. Noise code and latent code visualization using the t-SNE algorithm [71].

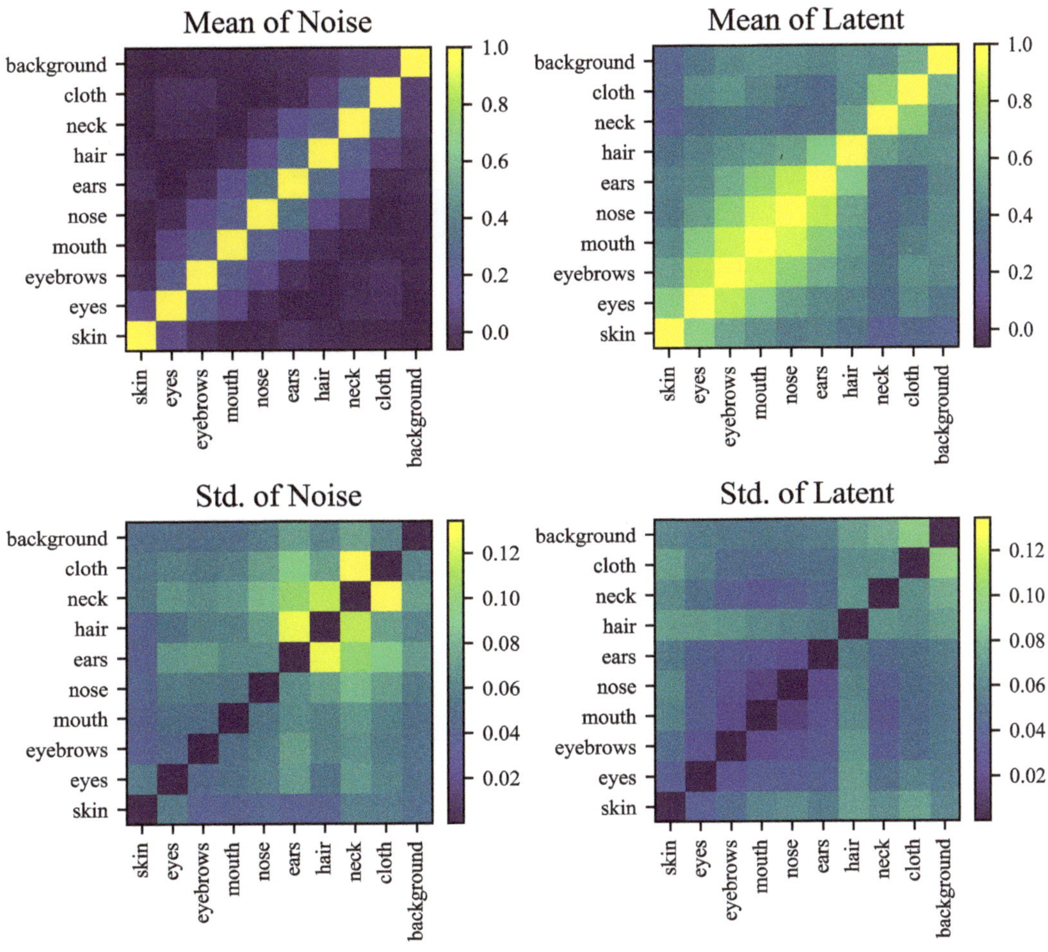

Figure 8. Correlation analysis between noise codes and latent codes using cosine similarity. The stochastic calculation is based on 10,000 samples.

4.2.4. Necessity of the LSTM Module

SSSGAN includes an LSTM module to explicitly capture the relationships between the noise codes, which plays a crucial role in the subsequent compositional synthesis steps. While GANs have the capability to generate diverse images, one might question the need for the LSTM module. Could SSSGAN achieve similar performance without modeling these relationships? To address this question, we conducted an ablation study by removing the LSTM module, resulting in a simplified version called SSSGAN-s. In SSSGAN-s, the noise codes for the parts were independently sampled from a Gaussian distribution, while other aspects remained the same as in SSSGAN. The experimental results on the CelebAMask-HQ dataset are presented in Figure 9, revealing that SSSGAN-s failed to generate the semantic mask, indicating a lack of awareness of the semantic part structure. To further examine how SSSGAN-s encodes the part noise code, we evaluated its performance on the sequential part composition task, as shown in Figure 10. It is evident that SSSGAN-s treated each part code as a whole face, completely disregarding the semantic meaning of each part. These findings clearly demonstrate the necessity of the LSTM module in SSSGAN, validating the effectiveness and novelty of our approach.

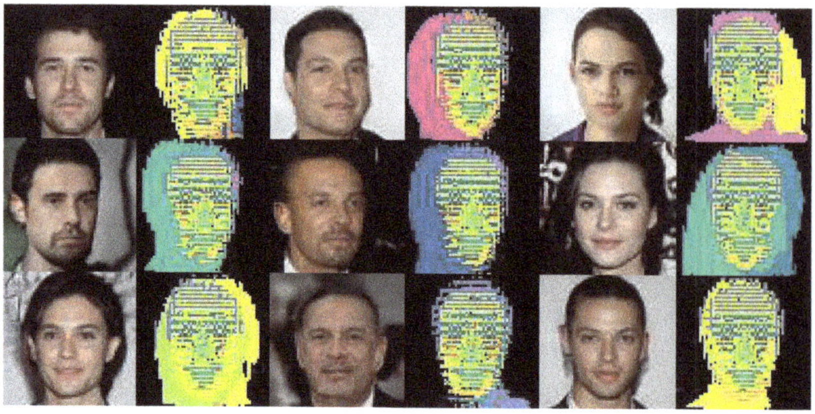

Figure 9. Images and segmentation masks generated by SSSGAN-s without the LSTM module.

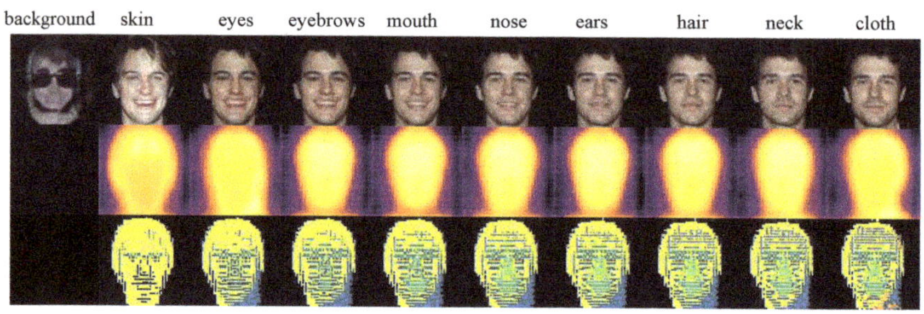

Figure 10. Sequential part composition results of SSSGAN-s without the LSTM module.

4.2.5. Performance on Other Domains

To demonstrate the versatility of our model beyond facial datasets, we conducted an evaluation on the DeepFashion dataset [72]. This dataset comprises 30,000 fashion images and we utilized the segmentation data provided in [60]. For supervision, we considered seven semantic parts; namely, background, skin, hair, face, upper clothes, pants and shoes. The experiment followed the same settings as our main results. The sequential part composition outcomes are presented in Figure 11. It is evident that the components were successfully combined one-by-one, starting from the background. At each step, the added part aligned with its semantic meaning and no apparent entanglement was observed. These results indicate that our model also demonstrated impressive performance on this dataset, in terms of compositional synthesis and disentanglement.

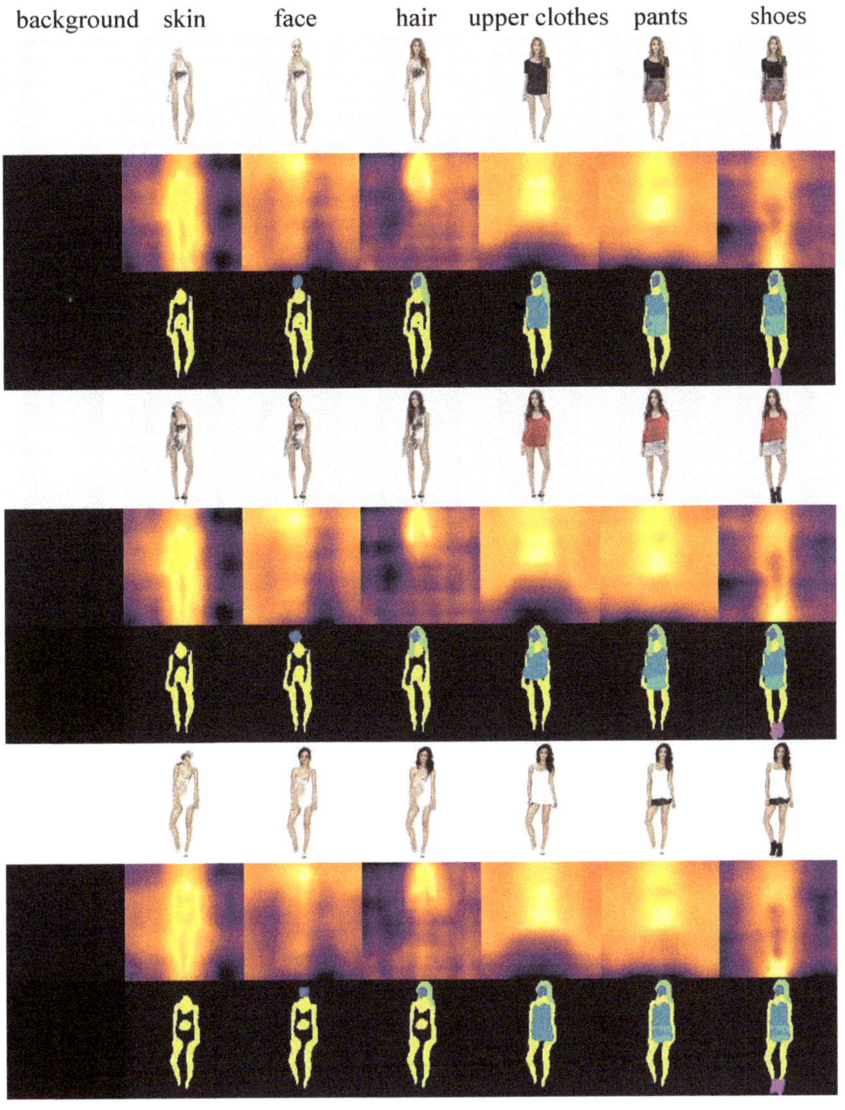

Figure 11. Sequential part composition results on DeepFashion dataset.

5. Conclusions

In this paper, we introduced SSSGAN, an efficient model for fine-grained compositional image synthesis. SSSGAN achieves improved efficiency by utilizing a shared generator to generate all of the semantic components. In order to accomplish this, we needed to address the challenges associated with entanglement and mode collapse. To overcome these challenges, we presented a novel method that explicitly models the relationships between the noise codes. Each noise code in SSSGAN controls the generation of a specific semantic part, which are then combined to form a complete object. Our model demonstrated impressive performance in generating high-quality images, providing a high level of control over the generation process for each semantic part, albeit with a slightly increased level of entanglement. We believe that efficiency is crucial for large-scale, fine-grained compositional image synthesis and our work presents a fundamental methodology for advancing this field. However, there are still several challenges that need to be addressed in future research. First, improving the disentanglement performance while maintaining image diversity is crucial. Incorporating style-mixing techniques into our method (which is currently incompatible) could potentially achieve this goal. Second, our current model supports the generation of images with a fixed component count. However, it is important to extend its capability to handle dynamic component counts, which are common in real-world objects and scenes. This can potentially be achieved by explicitly modeling the component count in the composition process. Finally, similar to SemanticStyleGAN, SSSGAN relies on full supervision, and so would be valuable for developing models with similar performance having lower supervision requirements.

Author Contributions: Conceptualization, Z.W. and Z.L.; methodology, Z.W.; software, Z.W.; validation, Z.W.; formal analysis, Z.W.; investigation, Z.W. and Z.L.; resources, Z.L.; data curation,Z.W.; writing—original draft preparation, Z.W.; writing—review and editing, Z.W. and Z.L.; visualization, Z.W.; supervision, Z.L.; project administration, Z.L.; funding acquisition, Z.L. All authors have read and agreed to the published version of the manuscript.

Funding: This research was funded in part by the National Natural Science Foundation of China grant number 62032019 and 61732019.

Institutional Review Board Statement: Not applicable.

Informed Consent Statement: Not applicable.

Data Availability Statement: The code will be made publicly available upon acceptance at https://gitee.com/zongtao_wang/sssgan-pytorch, accessed on 23 April 2023.

Acknowledgments: We would like to express our gratitude to the anonymous reviewers for their valuable feedback, which greatly contributed to improving our research paper. Additionally, we acknowledge the GPU support provided by the Center for Research and Innovation in Software Engineering (RISE).

Conflicts of Interest: The authors declare no conflict of interest. The funders had no role in the design of the study; in the collection, analyses or interpretation of data; in the writing of the manuscript; or in the decision to publish the results.

Abbreviations

The following abbreviations are used in this manuscript:

GAN	Generative Adversarial Network
MLP	Multi-Layer Perceptron
SSSGAN	Single-Generator SemanticStyleGAN
SPC	Sequential Part Composition
SMSE	Sequential Mean Square Error
LSTM	Long Short-Term Memory
FID	Fréchet Inception Distance
IS	Inception Score

References

1. Guido, R.C.; Pedroso, F.; Contreras, R.C.; Rodrigues, L.C.; Guariglia, E.; Neto, J.S. Introducing the Discrete Path Transform (DPT) and Its Applications in Signal Analysis, Artefact Removal and Spoken Word Recognition. *Digit. Signal Process.* **2021**, *117*, 103158. [CrossRef]
2. Guariglia, E.; Silvestrov, S. Fractional-Wavelet Analysis of Positive definite Distributions and Wavelets on $\mathcal{D}'(\mathbb{C})$. In *Engineering Mathematics II*; Springer Proceedings in Mathematics & Statistics Series; Springer: Berlin/Heidelberg, Germany, 2016; pp. 337–353.
3. Yang, L.; Sun, H.; Zhong, C.; Meng, Z.; Luo, H.; Li, X.; Tang, Y.Y.; Lu, Y. Hyperspectral image classification using wavelet transform-based smooth ordering. *Int. Wavelets Multiresolution Inf. Process.* **2019**, *17*, 1950050:1–1950050:18. [CrossRef]
4. Guariglia, E. Harmonic Sierpinski Gasket and Applications. *Entropy* **2018**, *20*, 714. [CrossRef] [PubMed]
5. Guariglia, E. Primality, Fractality and Image Analysis. *Entropy* **2019**, *21*, 304. [CrossRef] [PubMed]

6. Zheng, X.; Tang, Y.Y.; Zhou, J. A Framework of Adaptive Multiscale Wavelet Decomposition for Signals on Undirected Graphs. *IEEE Trans. Signal Process.* **2019**, *67*, 1696–1711. [CrossRef]
7. Berry, M.V.; Lewis, Z.V.; Nye, J.F. On the Weierstrass-Mandelbrot fractal function. *Proc. R. Soc. Lond. Math. Phys. Sci.* **1980**, *370*, 459–484.
8. Osherson, D.N.; Smith, E.E. On the Adequacy of Prototype Theory as a Theory of Concepts. *Cognition* **1981**, *9*, 35–58. [CrossRef]
9. Lake, B.M.; Ullman, T.D.; Tenenbaum, J.B.; Gershman, S.J. Building Machines That Learn and Think Like People. *Behav. Brain Sci.* **2017**, *40*, e253. [CrossRef]
10. Karras, T.; Laine, S.; Aittala, M.; Hellsten, J.; Lehtinen, J.; Aila, T. Analyzing and Improving the Image Quality of StyleGAN. In Proceedings of the IEEE Conference on Computer Vision and Pattern Recognition (CVPR), Seattle, WA, USA, 13–19 June 2020; pp. 8110–8119.
11. Park, T.; Liu, M.Y.; Wang, T.C.; Zhu, J.Y. Semantic Image Synthesis With Spatially-Adaptive Normalization. In Proceedings of the IEEE Conference on Computer Vision and Pattern Recognition (CVPR), Long Beach, CA, USA, 15–20 June 2019; pp. 2337–2346.
12. Shi, Y.; Yang, X.; Wan, Y.; Shen, X. SemanticStyleGAN: Learning Compositional Generative Priors for Controllable Image Synthesis and Editing. In Proceedings of the IEEE Conference on Computer Vision and Pattern Recognition (CVPR), New Orleans, LA, USA, 18–24 June 2022; pp. 11254–11264.
13. Bengio, Y.; Courville, A.; Vincent, P. Representation Learning: a Review and New Perspectives. *IEEE Trans. Pattern Anal. Mach. Intell.* **2013**, *35*, 1798–1828. [CrossRef]
14. Higgins, I.; Matthey, L.; Pal, A.; Burgess, C.; Glorot, X.; Botvinick, M.; Mohamed, S.; Lerchner, A. beta-VAE: Learning Basic Visual Concepts with a Constrained Variational Framework. In Proceedings of the International Conference on Learning Representations (ICLR), Toulon, France, 24–26 April 2017.
15. Kim, H.; Mnih, A. Disentangling by Factorising. In Proceedings of the International Conference on Machine Learning (ICML), Stockholm, Sweden, 10–15 July 2018; Volume 80, pp. 2649–2658.
16. Chen, X.; Duan, Y.; Houthooft, R.; Schulman, J.; Sutskever, I.; Abbeel, P. InfoGAN: Interpretable Representation Learning by Information Maximizing Generative Adversarial Nets. In Proceedings of the Advances in Neural Information Processing Systems (NIPS), Barcelona, Spain, 5–10 December 2016; Volume 29, pp. 2172–2180.
17. Lin, Z.; Thekumparampil, K.; Fanti, G.; Oh, S. InfoGAN-CR and ModelCentrality: Self-supervised Model Training and Selection for Disentangling GANs. In Proceedings of the International Conference on Machine Learning (ICML) 2020, Virtual, 13–18 July 2020; Volume 119, pp. 6127–6139.
18. Kazemi, H.; Iranmanesh, S.M.; Nasrabadi, N. Style and Content Disentanglement in Generative Adversarial Networks. In Proceedings of the IEEE Winter Conference on Applications of Computer Vision (WACV), Waikoloa, HI, USA, 7–11 January 2019; pp. 848–856.
19. Tran, L.; Yin, X.; Liu, X. Disentangled Representation Learning GAN for Pose-Invariant Face Recognition. In Proceedings of the IEEE Conference on Computer Vision and Pattern Recognition (CVPR), Honolulu, HI, USA, 21–26 July 2017; pp. 1415–1424.
20. Liu, A.H.; Liu, Y.C.; Yeh, Y.Y.; Wang, Y.C.F. A Unified Feature Disentangler for Multi-Domain Image Translation and Manipulation. In *Proceedings of the Advances in Neural Information Processing Systems (NIPS)*; NIPS: La Jolla, CA, USA, 2018; Volume 31, pp. 2595–2604.
21. Medin, S.C.; Egger, B.; Cherian, A.; Wang, Y.; Tenenbaum, J.B.; Liu, X.; Marks, T.K. MOST-GAN: 3D Morphable StyleGAN for Disentangled Face Image Manipulation. *AAAI Conf. Artif. Intell.* **2022**, *36*, 1962–1971. [CrossRef]
22. Skafte, N.; ren Hauberg, S. Explicit Disentanglement of Appearance and Perspective in Generative Models. In *Proceedings of the Advances in Neural Information Processing Systems (NIPS)*,; NIPS: La Jolla, CA, USA, 2019; Volume 32, pp. 1016–1026.
23. Lorenz, D.; Bereska, L.; Milbich, T.; Ommer, B. Unsupervised Part-Based Disentangling of Object Shape and Appearance. In Proceedings of the IEEE Conference on Computer Vision and Pattern Recognition (CVPR), Long Beach, CA, USA, 16–20 June 2019; pp. 10955–10964.
24. Xing, X.; Gao, R.; Han, T.; Zhu, S.C.; Wu, Y.N. Deformable Generator Networks: Unsupervised Disentanglement of Appearance and Geometry. *IEEE Trans. Pattern Anal. Mach. Intell.* **2022**, *44*, 1162–1179. [CrossRef] [PubMed]
25. Liu, L.; Jiang, X.; Saerbeck, M.; Dauwels, J. EAD-GAN: A Generative Adversarial Network for Disentangling Affine Transforms in Images. *IEEE Trans. Neural Netw. Learn. Syst.* **2022**, 1–11. [CrossRef] [PubMed]
26. Tewari, A.; R, M.B.; Pan, X.; Fried, O.; Agrawala, M.; Theobalt, C. Disentangled3D: Learning a 3D Generative Model with Disentangled Geometry and Appearance From Monocular Images. In Proceedings of the IEEE Conference on Computer Vision and Pattern Recognition (CVPR), New Orleans, LA, USA, 18–24 June 2022; pp. 1516–1525.
27. Nguyen-Phuoc, T.; Li, C.; Theis, L.; Richardt, C.; Yang, Y.L. HoloGAN: Unsupervised Learning of 3D Representations from Natural Images. In Proceedings of the IEEE Conference on Computer Vision and Pattern Recognition (CVPR), Long Beach, CA, USA, 15–20 June 2019; pp. 7588–7597.
28. Sønderby, C.K.; Raiko, T.; Maaløe, L.; Sønderby, S.R.K.; Winther, O. Ladder Variational Autoencoders. In *Proceedings of the Advances in Neural Information Processing Systems (NIPS)*; NIPS: La Jolla, CA, USA, 2016; Volume 29, pp. 3738–3746.
29. Zhao, S.; Song, J.; Ermon, S. Learning Hierarchical Features from Deep Generative Models. In Proceedings of the International Conference on Machine Learning (ICML), Sydney, Australia, 6–11 August 2017; Volume 70, pp. 4091–4099.
30. Li, Z.; Murkute, J.V.; Gyawali, P.K.; Wang, L. Progressive Learning and Disentanglement of Hierarchical Representations. In Proceedings of the International Conference on Learning Representations (ICLR), Addis Ababa, Ethiopia, 26–30 April 2020.

31. Kaneko, T.; Hiramatsu, K.; Kashino, K. Generative Adversarial Image Synthesis with Decision Tree Latent Controller. In Proceedings of the IEEE Conference on Computer Vision and Pattern Recognition (CVPR), Salt Lake City, UT, USA, 18–23 June 2018; pp. 6606–6615.
32. Alharbi, Y.; Wonka, P. Disentangled Image Generation through Structured Noise Injection. In Proceedings of the IEEE Conference on Computer Vision and Pattern Recognition (CVPR), New Orleans, LA, USA, 19–24 June 2020; pp. 5134–5142.
33. Goyal, A.; Bengio, Y. Inductive biases for deep learning of higher-level cognition. *R. Soc. Math. Phys. Eng. Sci.* **2022**, *478*, 20210068. [CrossRef]
34. Arandjelović, R.; Zisserman, A. Object Discovery with a Copy-Pasting GAN. *arXiv* **2019**, arXiv:cs/1905.11369.
35. Azadi, S.; Pathak, D.; Ebrahimi, S.; Darrell, T. Compositional GAN: Learning Image-Conditional Binary Composition. *Int. J. Comput. Vis.* **2020**, *128*, 2570–2585. [CrossRef]
36. Sbai, O.; Couprie, C.; Aubry, M. Surprising Image Compositions. In Proceedings of the IEEE Conference on Computer Vision and Pattern Recognition (CVPR), Nashville, TN, USA, 20–25 June 2021; pp. 3926–3930.
37. Burgess, C.P.; Matthey, L.; Watters, N.; Kabra, R.; Higgins, I.; Botvinick, M.; Lerchner, A. MONet: Unsupervised Scene Decomposition and Representation. *arXiv* **2019**, arXiv:cs/1901.11390
38. Greff, K.; Kaufman, R.L.; Kabra, R.; Watters, N.; Burgess, C.; Zoran, D.; Matthey, L.; Botvinick, M.; Lerchner, A. Multi-Object Representation Learning with Iterative Variational Inference. In Proceedings of the International Conference on Machine Learning (ICML), Long Beach, CA, USA, 10–15 June 2019; Volume 97, pp. 2424–2433.
39. Liao, Y.; Schwarz, K.; Mescheder, L.; Geiger, A. Towards Unsupervised Learning of Generative Models for 3D Controllable Image Synthesis. In Proceedings of the IEEE Conference on Computer Vision and Pattern Recognition (CVPR), Seattle, WA, USA, 13–19 June 2020; pp. 5871–5880.
40. Nguyen-Phuoc, T.H.; Richardt, C.; Mai, L.; Yang, Y.; Mitra, N. BlockGAN: Learning 3D Object-aware Scene Representations from Unlabelled Images. In *Proceedings of the Advances in Neural Information Processing Systems (NIPS)*; NIPS: La Jolla, CA, USA, 2020; Volume 33, pp. 6767–6778.
41. Niemeyer, M.; Geiger, A. GIRAFFE: Representing Scenes As Compositional Generative Neural Feature Fields. In Proceedings of the IEEE Conference on Computer Vision and Pattern Recognition (CVPR), Nashville, TN, USA, 20–25 June 2021; pp. 11453–11464.
42. Li, N.; Eastwood, C.; Fisher, R. Learning Object-Centric Representations of Multi-Object Scenes from Multiple Views. In *Proceedings of the Advances in Neural Information Processing Systems (NIPS)*; NIPS: La Jolla, CA, USA, 2020; Volume 33, pp. 5656–5666.
43. Anciukevicius, T.; Lampert, C.H.; Henderson, P. Object-Centric Image Generation with Factored Depths, Locations and Appearances. *arXiv* **2020**, arXiv:cs/2004.00642.
44. Henderson, P.; Lampert, C.H. Unsupervised Object-Centric Video Generation and Decomposition in 3D. In *Proceedings of the Advances in Neural Information Processing Systems (NIPS)*; NIPS: La Jolla, CA, USA, 2020; Volume 33, pp. 3106–3117.
45. Singh, K.K.; Ojha, U.; Lee, Y.J. FineGAN: Unsupervised Hierarchical Disentanglement for Fine-Grained Object Generation and Discovery. In Proceedings of the IEEE Conference on Computer Vision and Pattern Recognition (CVPR), Long Beach, CA, USA, 15–20 June 2019; pp. 6490–6499.
46. Schwarz, K.; Liao, Y.; Niemeyer, M.; Geiger, A. GRAF: Generative Radiance Fields for 3D-Aware Image Synthesis. In *Proceedings of the Advances in Neural Information Processing Systems (NIPS)*; NIPS: La Jolla, CA, USA, 2020; Volume 33, pp. 20154–20166.
47. Kwak, H.; Zhang, B.T. Generating Images Part by Part with Composite Generative Adversarial Networks. *arXiv* **2016**, arXiv:cs/1607.05387.
48. Chen, W.; Hays, J. SketchyGAN: Towards Diverse and Realistic Sketch to Image Synthesis. In Proceedings of the IEEE Conference on Computer Vision and Pattern Recognition (CVPR), Salt Lake City, UT, USA, 18–22 June 2018; pp. 9416–9425.
49. Lu, Y.; Wu, S.; Tai, Y.W.; Tang, C.K. Image Generation from Sketch Constraint Using Contextual GAN. In Proceedings of the European Conference on Computer Vision (ECCV), Salt Lake City, UT, USA, 18–22 June 2018; pp. 205–220.
50. Zhao, J.; Xie, X.; Wang, L.; Cao, M.; Zhang, M. Generating Photographic Faces From the Sketch Guided by Attribute Using GAN. *IEEE Access* **2019**, *7*, 23844–23851. [CrossRef]
51. Ghosh, A.; Zhang, R.; Dokania, P.K.; Wang, O.; Efros, A.A.; Torr, P.H.S.; Shechtman, E. Interactive Sketch & Fill: Multiclass Sketch-to-Image Translation. In Proceedings of the IEEE International Conference on Computer Vision (ICCV), Seoul, Republic of Korea, 27 October–2 November 2019; pp. 1171–1180.
52. Chen, S.Y.; Su, W.; Gao, L.; Xia, S.; Fu, H. DeepFaceDrawing: Deep Generation of Face Images from Sketches. *ACM Trans. Graph.* **2020**, *39*, 72:1–72:16. [CrossRef]
53. Richardson, E.; Alaluf, Y.; Patashnik, O.; Nitzan, Y.; Azar, Y.; Shapiro, S.; Cohen-Or, D. Encoding in Style: A StyleGAN Encoder for Image-to-Image Translation. In Proceedings of the IEEE Conference on Computer Vision and Pattern Recognition (CVPR), Nashville, TN, USA, 19–25 June 2021; pp. 2287–2296.
54. Wang, S.Y.; Bau, D.; Zhu, J.Y. Sketch Your Own GAN. In Proceedings of the IEEE International Conference on Computer Vision (ICCV), Montreal, BC, Canada, 11–17 October 2021; pp. 14050–14060.
55. Chen, Q.; Koltun, V. Photographic Image Synthesis with Cascaded Refinement Networks. In Proceedings of the IEEE International Conference on Computer Vision (ICCV), Venice, Italy, 22–29 October 2017; pp. 1511–1520.

56. Liu, X.; Yin, G.; Shao, J.; Wang, X.; Li, h. Learning to Predict Layout-to-image Conditional Convolutions for Semantic Image Synthesis. In *Proceedings of the Advances in Neural Information Processing Systems (NIPS)*; NIPS: La Jolla, CA, USA, 2019; Volume 32, pp. 568–578.
57. Isola, P.; Zhu, J.Y.; Zhou, T.; Efros, A.A. Image-To-Image Translation With Conditional Adversarial Networks. In Proceedings of the IEEE Conference on Computer Vision and Pattern Recognition (CVPR), Honolulu, HI, USA, 21–26 July 2017; pp. 1125–1134.
58. Tang, H.; Xu, D.; Sebe, N.; Wang, Y.; Corso, J.J.; Yan, Y. Multi-Channel Attention Selection GAN With Cascaded Semantic Guidance for Cross-View Image Translation. In Proceedings of the IEEE Conference on Computer Vision and Pattern Recognition (CVPR), Long Beach, CA, USA, 16–20 June 2019; pp. 2417–2426.
59. Wang, Y.; Qi, L.; Chen, Y.C.; Zhang, X.; Jia, J. Image Synthesis via Semantic Composition. In Proceedings of the IEEE/CVF International Conference on Computer Vision (ICCV), Montreal, Canada, 11–17 October 2021; pp. 13749–13758.
60. Zhu, Z.; Xu, Z.; You, A.; Bai, X. Semantically Multi-Modal Image Synthesis. In Proceedings of the IEEE Conference on Computer Vision and Pattern Recognition (CVPR), Seattle, WA, USA, 14–19 June 2020; pp. 5467–5476.
61. Zhu, P.; Abdal, R.; Qin, Y.; Wonka, P. SEAN: Image Synthesis With Semantic Region-Adaptive Normalization. In Proceedings of the IEEE Conference on Computer Vision and Pattern Recognition (CVPR), Seattle, WA, USA, 14–19 June 2020; pp. 5104–5113.
62. Wang, T.C.; Liu, M.Y.; Zhu, J.Y.; Tao, A.; Kautz, J.; Catanzaro, B. High-Resolution Image Synthesis and Semantic Manipulation with Conditional GANs. In Proceedings of the IEEE Conference on Computer Vision and Pattern Recognition (CVPR), Salt Lake City, UT, USA, 18–23 June 2018; pp. 8798–8807.
63. Chen, A.; Liu, R.; Xie, L.; Chen, Z.; Su, H.; Yu, J. SofGAN: A Portrait Image Generator with Dynamic Styling. *ACM Trans. Graph.* **2022**, *41*, 1–26. [CrossRef]
64. Thanh-Tung, H.; Tran, T. On Catastrophic Forgetting and Mode Collapse in Generative Adversarial Networks. *arXiv* **2020**, arXiv:cs/1807.04015.
65. van den Oord, A.; Kalchbrenner, N.; Kavukcuoglu, K. Pixel Recurrent Neural Networks. In Proceedings of the International Conference on Machine Learning (ICML), New York City, NY, USA, 19–24 June 2016; Volume 48, pp. 1747–1756.
66. Karras, T.; Laine, S.; Aila, T. A Style-Based Generator Architecture for Generative Adversarial Networks. In Proceedings of the IEEE Conference on Computer Vision and Pattern Recognition (CVPR), Long Beach, CA, USA, 16–20 June 2019; pp. 4401–4410.
67. Mescheder, L.M.; Geiger, A.; Nowozin, S. Which Training Methods for GANs do Actually Converge? In Proceedings of the International Conference on Machine Learning (ICML), Stockholm, Sweden, 10–15 July 2018; Volume 80, pp. 3478–3487.
68. Lee, C.; Liu, Z.; Wu, L.; Luo, P. MaskGAN: Towards Diverse and Interactive Facial Image Manipulation. In Proceedings of the IEEE Conference on Computer Vision and Pattern Recognition (CVPR), Seattle, Washington, USA, 14–19 June 2020; pp. 5548–5557.
69. Heusel, M.; Ramsauer, H.; Unterthiner, T.; Nessler, B.; Hochreiter, S. GANs Trained by a Two Time-Scale Update Rule Converge to a Local Nash Equilibrium. In *Proceedings of the Advances in Neural Information Processing Systems (NIPS)*; NIPS: La Jolla, CA, USA, 2017; Volume 30, pp. 6626–6637.
70. Salimans, T.; Goodfellow, I.; Zaremba, W.; Cheung, V.; Radford, A.; Chen, X.; Chen, X. Improved Techniques for Training GANs. In *Proceedings of the Advances in Neural Information Processing Systems (NIPS)*; NIPS: La Jolla, CA, USA, 2016; Volume 29, pp. 2226–2234.
71. Van der Maaten, L.; Hinton, G. Visualizing data using t-SNE. *J. Mach. Learn. Res.* **2008**, *9*, 2579–2605.
72. Liu, Z.; Luo, P.; Qiu, S.; Wang, X.; Tang, X. DeepFashion: Powering Robust Clothes Recognition and Retrieval with Rich Annotations. In Proceedings of the IEEE Conference on Computer Vision and Pattern Recognition (CVPR), Las Vegas, NV, USA, 27–30 June 2016; pp. 1096–1104.

applied sciences

MDPI

Article

Individualized Stress Mobile Sensing Using Self-Supervised Pre-Training

Tanvir Islam and Peter Washington *

Information and Computer Sciences, University of Hawaii at Manoa, Honolulu, HI 96822, USA; tislam@hawaii.edu
* Correspondence: pyw@hawaii.edu

Abstract: Stress is widely recognized as a major contributor to a variety of health issues. Stress prediction using biosignal data recorded by wearables is a key area of study in mobile sensing research because real-time stress prediction can enable digital interventions to immediately react at the onset of stress, helping to avoid many psychological and physiological symptoms such as heart rhythm irregularities. Electrodermal activity (EDA) is often used to measure stress. However, major challenges with the prediction of stress using machine learning include the subjectivity and sparseness of the labels, a large feature space, relatively few labels, and a complex nonlinear and subjective relationship between the features and outcomes. To tackle these issues, we examined the use of model personalization: training a separate stress prediction model for each user. To allow the neural network to learn the temporal dynamics of each individual's baseline biosignal patterns, thus enabling personalization with very few labels, we pre-trained a one-dimensional convolutional neural network (1D CNN) using self-supervised learning (SSL). We evaluated our method using the Wearable Stress and Affect Detection(WESAD) dataset. We fine-tuned the pre-trained networks to the stress-prediction task and compared against equivalent models without any self-supervised pre-training. We discovered that embeddings learned using our pre-training method outperformed the supervised baselines with significantly fewer labeled data points: the models trained with SSL required less than 30% of the labels to reach equivalent performance without personalized SSL. This personalized learning method can enable precision health systems that are tailored to each subject and require few annotations by the end user, thus allowing for the mobile sensing of increasingly complex, heterogeneous, and subjective outcomes such as stress.

Keywords: mobile sensing; affective computing; personalized machine learning; self-supervised learning; biosignals; stress prediction

1. Introduction

Chronic stress can drastically affect an individual's health across several dimensions. Continuous stress increases the risk of cardiovascular disease, hypertension, reduced immunity, and cancer [1]. Despite these detrimental physical effects, stress is often left unmanaged. A growing body of work in the field of human–computer interaction (HCI) is focusing on mobile sensing of stress using signals from wearable consumer devices [2]. Real-time detection of stress via wearable devices can enable stress interventions, which can provide therapeutic support via immediate prompting when stress is detected. Until recently, these mobile sensing methods of subjective outcomes have required large amounts of training data from each user, making the deployment of such models infeasible in practice. We present a novel methodology for personalizing mobile sensing models using a minimal number of human labels.

Consumer wearable devices offer a range of biosignal measurements, which may include, but are not limited to, electrodermal activity (EDA), electrocardiograms (ECGs), electromyography (EMG), respiration rate, and galvanic skin resistance (GSR). EDA is a physiological measurement of the electric current that flows through the skin. EDA is particularly sensitive to changes in skin ionic conductivity caused by even minor perspiration that is not visible on the surface of the skin [3]. In comparison to other physiological measurements like heart rate variations and blood pressure, EDA is a robust way to gauge physiological arousal and, by extension, the response to stress. In the field of affective computing, EDA is widely recognized as a key marker of physiological arousal and stress responses [4]. Therefore, an EDA-based stress quantification approach was the primary focus of this investigation.

Deep neural networks (DNNs) have been a driving force behind major machine learning progress in recent years [5]. DNNs are multi-layer computational models that may learn progressively complex and high-level representations of the input data to accomplish a prediction goal. DNNs are an especially promising solution for analyzing biosignals due to their ability to spot patterns and learn meaningful features from unprocessed data inputs without requiring extensive data preprocessing or manual feature engineering [6].

Creating a stress prediction model using biosignal data that is generalizable is impractical due to the varying physiological responses to stress among individuals. As a result, stress-monitoring systems must possess the flexibility to accommodate these differences [7]. Rather than building a one-size-fits-all stress-prediction model, we propose a novel approach aimed at developing individual-specific models, with the goal of achieving greater personalization. Such models can enable precision health mobile sensing systems to reach clinically useful performance.

A major hurdle in developing personalized mobile sensing models through biosignal data is the procurement of adequate supervisory data (i.e., ground truth labels) to train DNNs, which require large training sets for the training process to converge. Self-reported stress labels are often generated by laborious and faulty manual human labeling owing to human subjectivity and weariness [8].

Current research on EDA-based stress assessment tends to focus on supervised deep learning. Achieving clinically useful model performance is hindered, however, by the fact that traditional supervised learning does not make use of all of the unlabeled data that are available. Individuals who use wearable devices have copious amounts of unlabeled longitudinal body signal data, but only a few labels to indicate important health events. These labels are used for training machine learning models to recognize the events of interest.

To bridge this gap, we propose the use of self-supervised Learning (SSL) to learn neural network weights, which are optimized to make predictions about the baseline temporal dynamics of a user's biosignals. Such weights can then be efficiently fine-tuned to personalized prediction tasks using that user's biosignal data. We hypothesized that by utilizing self-supervised learning (SSL) on biosignal data from wearables, we can develop personalized stress prediction models that are more effective and efficient than traditional supervised learning models, even with limited labeled data. We implemented an instantiation of this SSL paradigm and, then, fine-tuned the resulting models to the stress-prediction task using EDA signals. In particular, we made the following contributions:

- We introduce a novel "personalized SSL" paradigm to address the common real-world situation of large datasets with few training labels. This solution enables mobile sensing systems to predict traditionally subjective classes such as stress. This interaction paradigm is similar to how Apple's Face ID works: once the face recognition system is provided with only a few examples provided by the end users, it can be used repeatedly to unlock the device. In this case, the labels are stress predictions, rather than identity predictions, and the model input is wearable biosignals, rather than a face image.
- We evaluated this novel mobile sensing methodology on a real-world biosignal dataset with stress labels: the Wearable Stress and Affect Detection (WESAD) dataset.

Once the model is calibrated, it can be used repeatedly to predict how stressed that person will be in different scenarios. The stress-prediction task requires less computing power because the model uses the model weights learned during the training process to efficiently fine-tune towards stress prediction. This reduced need for computing resources means that the model can be processed faster, making it easier to use in real-world settings.

The remainder of the paper is structured as follows: Section 2 explores contemporary SSL techniques with bio-signals. Section 3 outlines our proposed method and its implementation. Section 4 presents the model results and performance. Section 5 discusses the strengths, limitations, and future directions. Section 6 provides concluding remarks.

2. Related Work

2.1. Stress Assessment Using Biosignals

The hyperactivity of the nervous system is associated with chronic stress and is responsible for its wide range of adverse effects on health and behavior. Stress and brain activity are closely correlated [9]. Hannun et al. showed that single-lead ECGs can be used to identify rhythms using an end-to-end deep learning method. They demonstrated that the 1D CNN model architecture can be successfully applied towards making predictions from biosignal data without manual feature engineering and feature selection [6].

Variations in the skin's electrical characteristics are reflected by EDA, making it a helpful stress indicator for the nervous system. Sweating is a natural response to stressful situations and may further enhance the skin's conductivity [10]. Spathis et al. described a stress-prediction framework that enables consumers to receive feedback on their stress levels through speech-enabled consumer devices like smartphones and smart speakers [11]. EDA sensors are located on the hands, whereas ECG sensors are located on the chest. Data from the EDA sensors are wirelessly transferred to the ECG sensor through WiFi. This method attempts to improve stress prediction by capturing two EDA channels to eliminate motion artifacts. The designed sensor yields excellent linearity and jitter performance and exhibits minimal delays during wireless transmission. Zhu et al. studied the possibility of detecting stress using EDA data acquired from wearable sensors [12]. The study made use of two publicly accessible datasets: VerBIO [13] and WESAD [14], both of which comprise EDA signals from research-grade wearable sensors. The experimental results demonstrated that Random Forests differentiate stress from non-stress conditions with an accuracy of 85.7%, highlighting the potential for wearable devices with EDA sensors to anticipate stress. The study also evaluated the dependability of training with extracted statistical and EDA-related features from EDA signals, discovering no consistent trend between employing complete features and chosen features. The findings indicated the effectiveness of placing EDA sensors into wearable devices for stress prediction, instilling confidence that incorporating EDA sensors into smartwatches is a potential option for future product development.

In addition to research-grade equipment, EDA is also frequently measured using consumer wearable devices. Using low-resolution electrodermal activity (EDA) data from consumer-grade wearable devices, Ninh et al. explored the stress prediction capabilities of user-dependent and user-independent models [15]. This work revealed that stress-prediction models employing low-resolution EDA data from wrist-worn and finger-mounted sensors have high balanced accuracy scores (66.10% to 100%). This finding indicated that low-resolution EDA signals from consumer-grade devices may be used to efficiently create user-dependent stress-prediction models, enabling the collection of in-the-wild data for mental health tracking and analysis.

EDA is often used in conjunction with other biosignals. Eren et al. suggested a way to detect stress by using sensors from the Empatica E4 device used in the WESAD [14] dataset to measure blood volume pulse (BVP) and electrodermal activity (EDA) [16]. The suggested neural network model was 96.26% accurate. The study also called for more research to test the method's usefulness and general flexibility. Pakarinen et al. [17] explored the capacity of electrodermal activity (EDA) to precisely categorize mental states, including relaxation, arousal, and stress, in addition to self-perceived stress and arousal, utilizing a three-phase modified MIST test. The research demonstrated high levels of accuracy in identifying these mental states, indicating that EDA has the potential for long-term evaluation of stress and arousal in the workplace. They explored the utilization of machine learning models for stress detection and classification, employing features derived from physiological signals, including EDA and BVP. By achieving an F1-score of 0.71, the study highlighted the potential to create a seamless, real-world stress-monitoring system and promoted continued investigation through the integration of machine learning and signal-processing methodologies in a professional context. Kalimeri et al. proposed an advanced multimodal framework to assess the emotional and cognitive experiences of visually impaired individuals while navigating unknown indoor environments, leveraging mobile monitoring and the combination of EEG and EDA signals [18]. The goal was to identify the environmental factors that increase stress and cognitive load, thereby guiding the creation of emotionally intelligent mobility systems that can adapt to challenging environments using real-time biosensor information.

2.2. SSL on Biosignals

The field of SSL on biosignals is an emerging field of study. Two popular SSL approaches, SimCLR [19] and BOYL [20], are contrastive learning approaches, which rely on data augmentation. This methodology contains limitations such as invariance, which can obscure valuable detailed information necessary for specific downstream tasks. Additionally, predicting which augmentations will yield optimal benefits can prove to be challenging [21]. As a result, in our study, we excluded the use of data augmentation and chose instead to focus on pre-training and downstream tasks with raw data. Pöppelbaum et al. introduced a novel self-supervised learning approach for time series analysis using the SimCLR contrastive learning model, which was enhanced with new data augmentation techniques. The authors demonstrated improved fault classification accuracy [22]. Robert et al. offered a contrastive-learning-based stress-prediction system that uses modified EDA signals to classify stress and non-stress circumstances [23]. Nevertheless, the current project differs from this approach because it did not require any signal transformation. Instead of only stress vs. non-stress categorization, our presented study allowed for the learning of a wide range of stress levels. By using the temporal and spatial information included within ECG impulses, CLOCS uses contrastive learning to acquire unique representations of each patient [24]. This novel concept considers a positive pair as a representation of two changed occurrences that both correspond to an identical patient. As a result, the model automatically adjusts the learned representations to the specifics of every patient's case. Sarkar et al. offered a self-supervised method for learning ECG representations for the purpose of emotion classification [25]. Eldede et al. introduced a novel time series representation learning framework, TS-TCC, leveraging contrastive self-supervised learning for unlabeled data, focusing on temporal and contextual contrasting [26]. Additionally, they extended their model for semi-supervised settings and demonstrated its effectiveness through extensive real-world dataset experiments. Yang et al. proposed TimeCLR, a self-supervised representation learning framework tailored to univariate time series, which integrates the benefits from dynamic time warping (DTW) and InceptionTime, offering improved performance in scenarios with limited labeled data across various time series domains [27]. Sunmin et al. propose SIM-CNN, a self-supervised learning framework that improves stress recognition by training a personalized multimodal CNN on a large dataset of nurses' biosignals, both labeled and unlabeled, optimizing for individual physiological differences [28]. Tanvir et al. show by leveraging self-supervised learning on wearable biosignal data, personalized multimodal stress prediction system outperforms traditional supervised models with minimal manual annotations, addressing the challenges of label scarcity and biosignal heterogeneity [29].

Table 1 provides a summary of the literature review.

Table 1. Summary of literature review.

Study	Focus	Opportunities
Hannun et al. [6]	ECG deep learning	Exploration of hybrid models combining ECG with other biosignals for improved stress prediction.
Spathis et al. [11]	Speech-enabled devices	Integration of voice-based feedback mechanisms to provide real-time stress relief interventions.
Zhu et al. [12]	EDA wearables	Development of compact and user-friendly wearable devices for mass adoption.
Ninh et al. [15]	Consumer EDA devices	Design of consumer-centric applications that utilize EDA data for wellness and mental health tracking.
Eren et al. [16]	Empatica E4 device	Incorporation of multi-sensor data for a holistic health-monitoring system.
Pakarinen et al. [17]	Mental states	Broadening the scope to include the detection of other mental states like anxiety or excitement.
Kalimeri et al. [18]	Multimodal framework	Development of adaptive systems for other differently abled individuals beyond the visually impaired.
SimCLR [19] and BOYL [20]	Contrastive learning	Application of contrastive learning techniques to other images.
Pöppelbaum et al. [22]	Time series analysis	Implementation in real-time systems for quick anomaly detection in biosignals.
Robert et al. [23]	EDA stress prediction	Exploration of non-invasive techniques for real-world applications.
CLOCS [24]	ECG learning	Expansion to include patient-specific health recommendations based on ECG patterns.
Sarkar et al. [26]	ECG emotion	Development of emotion-aware devices and applications for personalized user experiences.
Eldede et al. [26]	Time series learning	Application in industries like finance or meteorology where time series data are abundant.
Yang et al. [27]	TimeCLR	Incorporation of multivariate time series data for more-complex predictions.
Sunmin et al. [28]	Time series representation	Optimized personalized multimodal model
Tanvir et al. [29]	Less annotated data	Personalized multimodal machine learning model with least amount of labeled data

3. Methodology

We propose a two-step process for training mobile sensing models, which can predict subjective labels such as stress using only a few training examples per user: (1) personalized SSL for representation learning of temporal EDA dynamics per user and (2) fine-tuning the pre-trained model to the stress-prediction task. During SSL, the pretext task helps the model learn interim data representations without ground truth labels. The pretext task is designed to predict the missing segments of the input data given the remaining segments. After this representation is learned, the downstream task involves fine-tuning the weights from the pretext task towards training the neural network model to predict stress. The overall architecture is shown in Figure 1.

As depicted in Figure 1, the personalized SSL model was designed to accept the raw EDA signal for each subject. The raw EDA signal is divided into chunks of 7000-dimensional vectors, as described in Section 3.3, generating a large dataset of 7910 data points to pre-train the model. The pre-training phase involved the use of a 1D CNN model to predict 40 data points, as detailed in Section 3.3. The weights learned in the pre-training phase are transferred to another 1D CNN model, which is fine-tuned for the stress-prediction task.

In addition, a second 1D CNN model with the same architecture as the fine-tuned model was employed for stress prediction, but without any pre-training. This is our control model, which we used as a baseline to quantify the benefits of our SSL over personalization without SSL.

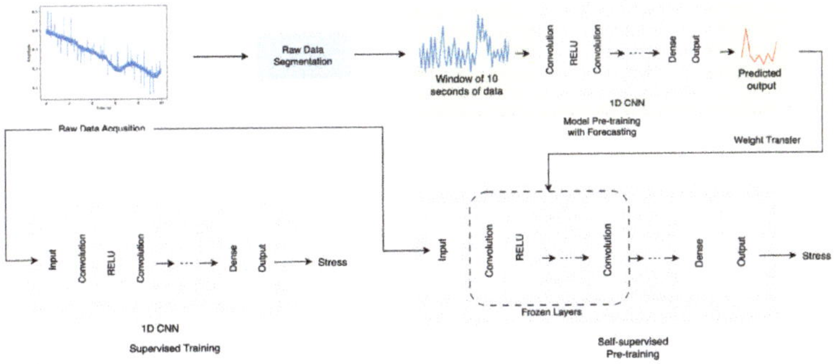

Figure 1. Overall process of our personalized stress-prediction framework. The raw signal is segmented into distinct, but overlapping data points. A forecasting model is used for self-supervised pre-training. These weights are fine-tuned to the stress-prediction task (**right model**). We compared this model against a supervised learning model without self-supervised pre-training (**left**).

We compared these two models using varying numbers of labeled data points, as described in Sections 4.2 and 4.3.

We performed a subject-dependent study by directly comparing the following two models trained and evaluated separately per subject:

- **Model A**: stress prediction via supervised learning;
- **Model B**: stress prediction with a model pre-trained with SSL and fine-tuned using the same supervised learning strategy as Model A.

3.1. Dataset

We used the WESAD [14] dataset to evaluate our methodology. The WESAD [14] dataset is a freely accessible multimodal physiological dataset containing ECG, EDA, EMG, respiration (RESP), core body temperature (TEMP), and three-axis acceleration (ACC). Biosignals were collected from 15 healthy adults (mean age 27.5; standard deviation (SD) = 2.4)) when they were subjected to one of three conditions: neutral, stress, or amusement, in a controlled laboratory setting. The researchers used the Trier Social Stress Test (TSST) to induce anxiety. Two devices: Empatica E4 and RespiBAN, were used to collect signals for this dataset. Using the RespiBAN device, the data were acquired from each participant for around 33 min at a sampling rate of 700 Hz. Multiple sensors, including ECG, EDA, EMG, RESP, TEMP, and ACC, are included in the RespiBAN device. The Empatica E4 records sensor data on BVP at 64 Hz, EDA at 4 Hz, TEMP at 4 Hz, and ACC at 32 Hz. Participants were asked six questions from the State-Trait Anxiety Inventory (STAI) to derive insight into their degree of anxiety. Each question was answered using a four-point Likert scale. The STAI questions are as follows:

- Question 1: I feel at ease.
- Question 2: I feel nervous.
- Question 3: I am jittery.
- Question 4: I am relaxed.
- Question 5: I am worried.
- Question 6: I feel pleasant.

In this study, we used stress data for the baseline condition only. Our models were trained using EDA signal data from the RespiBAN device with a sampling rate of 700 HZ.

3.2. Label Representation

We converted the categorical ordinal outcome variables (i.e., the Likert scale responses to the questionnaires) into a representation that maintained the categorical nature of the responses, as well as the ordinal nature. In the WESAD dataset, participants were given six questions from the STAI (see Section 3.1 for details). Participants were asked to rate this question on a four-point Likert scale. Therefore, each question was labeled between 1 and 4. To model the ordinal regression task, we converted the original labels of (1, 2, 3, 4) into the probabilities of (0.25, 0.5, 0.75, 1.0). Because the four-point Likert chart used in the original evaluation was equally spaced, these labels were quantified and distributed uniformly. These labels are subjective since the models use only within-subject data and participants are internally consistent in their labeling (i.e., we assumed that a rating of 3 consistently indicates higher severity than a rating of 2 on the same question within each participant's set of ratings).

3.3. Self-Supervised Pre-Training

The use of self-supervised pre-training, an unsupervised approach in which data are self-labeled and, subsequently, fine-tuned using supervised learning approaches to extract important feature representations, has proven to be more effective than supervised training alone in an increasing number of applications [19]. The self-supervised pre-training approach focuses on learning a high-level representation of data without using ground truth labels, which is also known as the pretext task. A pre-trained model enables efficient transfer to a target task since the representation it has learned is already suited (or readily transferable) for a given job. SSL in this manner is the same technology that powers large-scale language models like ChatGPT and natural language training tasks powered by BERT [30].

We pre-trained our model through forecasting, a similar technique used to pre-train OpenAI's GPT language model [31]. A separate model was pre-trained for each human subject using only the data from that subject. To pre-train our model, we employed a 1D CNN, a standard neural network architecture for signal prediction [32]. Prior research has demonstrated the robustness of the 1D CNN in 1D signal processing tasks, particularly in the domain of biosignals or 1D signals [6]. One of the key advantages of 1D CNNs is their ability to automatically learn relevant features from the input signal, eliminating the need for manual feature engineering. This can save time and effort while also improving the model's performance, as it can adaptively learn the most-discriminative features for a given task.

Moreover, 1D CNNs can capture information at different time scales due to the use of multiple neural layers and multiple independent learned kernels. This makes this family of architectures particularly helpful when dealing with signals with complicated hierarchical patterns or events that occur at different time scales. Additionally, 1D CNNs can handle input data with noise better than other machine learning algorithms, as the convolutional layers can learn to focus on the most-important features and ignore noise or irrelevant signals. Figure 2 illustrates the architecture that was used in this study for pre-training the model as a knowledge representation of the raw EDA signal. To maintain consistency, we used the same model architecture for both self-supervised pre-training and supervised training. We used the root-mean-squared error (RMSE) as our evaluation metric.

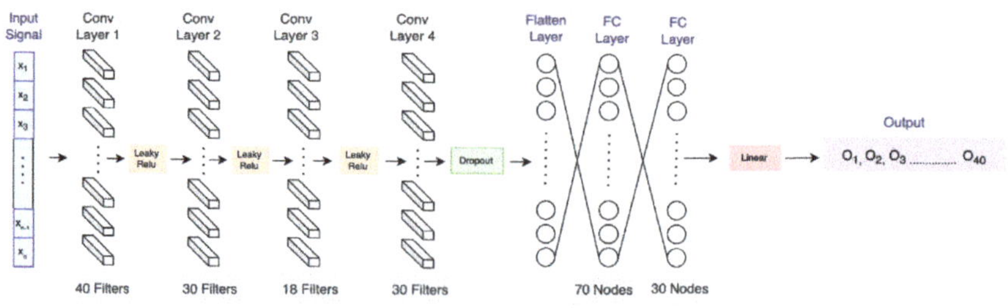

Figure 2. The 1D CNN architecture for the pretext task.

The pretext 1D CNN model was implemented with an input shape of (7000, 1), consisting of four 1D convolution layers, each utilizing a leaky ReLU activation function. The first convolution layer has 40 filters, followed by a layer with 30 filters, and then, a layer with 18 filters. The fourth convolution layer has 30 filters and uses a leaky ReLU activation function. Moreover, the model includes two dense layers, one with 70 nodes and the other with 30 nodes. The final layer is an output layer with a linear activation function. The convolution layers are responsible for extracting important features from the EDA signal, while the dense layers utilize these features to make a stress prediction.

The model was pre-trained on the entirety of the EDA signal for each participant. We divided the whole signal into fixed windows (each containing a 7000-dimensional vector) (Figure 3). Figure 3 illustrates an example of the data points in the training set with overlapping information. We represent the signal as $X_1 \cdots\cdots X_n$. Our method segments this signal into multiple fixed windows, each of length 7000 points. So, the first window captures the sequence $X_1, X_2 \cdots\cdots X_{7000}$. The purpose of this window is to predict the next 40 points, i.e., $X_{7001}, X_{7002} \cdots\cdots X_{7040}$.

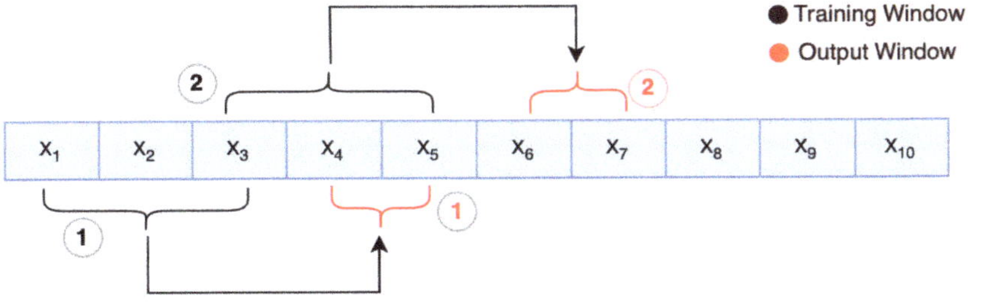

Figure 3. We used signal forecasting as our self-supervised pretext task. A sliding window was used to predict the following chunk of the EDA signal.

However, instead of progressing to a completely new window after this, we introduced overlap. The next window starts only 100 points after the beginning of the previous window, i.e., $X_{100}, X_{101} \cdots\cdots X_{7100}$. Similarly, this window aims to predict the sequence $X_{7101}, X_{7102} \cdots\cdots X_{7140}$.

By consistently overlapping windows by 100 points, we ensured that the model was exposed to various transitional patterns in the data. This overlapping approach continued until the end of the signal, resulting in a total of 7910 data samples for each participant. The motivation behind this strategy was twofold: it maximized the utility of available data and equipped the model to make stress predictions based on 10 s segments, offering a granular understanding of the participant's stress evolution.

3.4. Downstream Stress-Prediction Task

Self-supervised pre-training offers the benefit of optimizing data efficiency during the fine-tuning process for subsequent downstream activities. The difficulty in sourcing high-quality labels makes this a critical scenario for use in mobile sensing research. We conducted a thorough quantitative analysis of this added benefit by contrasting the efficiency of freshly trained, solely supervised models against that of those pre-trained using self-supervised representations.

In this stage, we used the same 1D CNN architecture that we used for model pre-training. However, in this architecture, the feature extractor layers were frozen, and the rest of the layers were fine-tuned to the stress-prediction task. For this downstream task, we modified the model with 3 new dense layers for the final prediction. The architecture for stress quantifying is shown in Figure 4. As illustrated in Figure 4, the fine-tuned model shares the same set of convolution layers and activation functions as the pretext 1D CNN model. However, it has three dense layers, the first one with 50 nodes, followed by a dense layer with 30 nodes, and the final dense layer with 10 nodes. The output layer has a linear activation function, and the predicted output is stress. When fine-tuning a pre-trained model, including extra fully connected (FC) layers has several benefits. Firstly, a pre-trained model often originates from a general or differing task. By integrating a new FC layer, the model acquires the capability to focus on patterns explicitly tailored for the new task, here stress prediction, facilitating superior feature extraction and representation for that particular task. Adding new FC layer ensures that the specific knowledge from the original pre-trained task does not dominate, offering the model a new layer to optimize and adapt to the unique features of the new task. This assures a more-harmonious transition and improved performance in the new task domain.

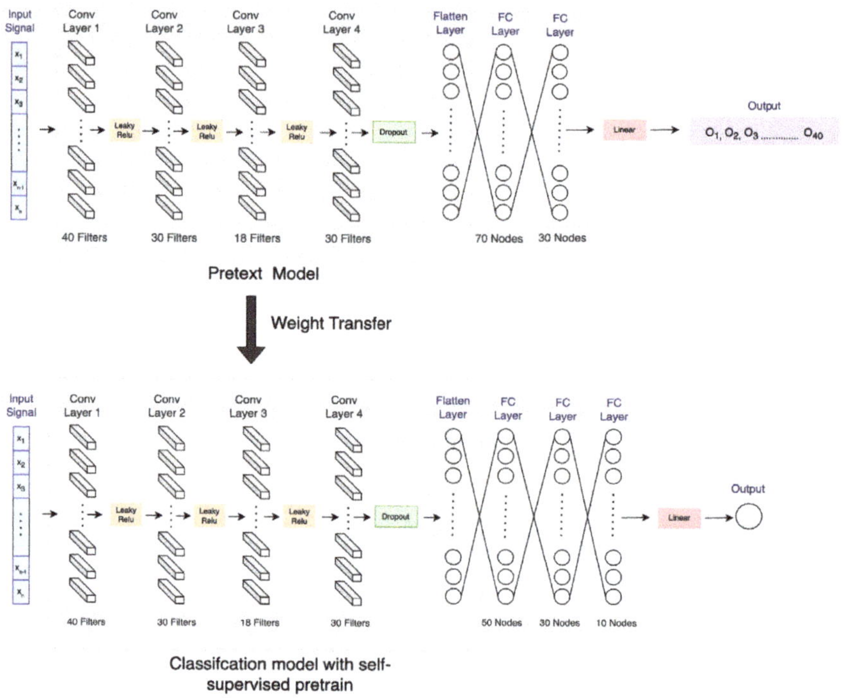

Figure 4. The 1D CNN architecture for fine-tuning the pre-trained network towards the downstream stress-prediction task.

In the case of purely supervised training, the same architecture as the fine-tuned model was utilized to facilitate a direct comparison between the methods.

3.5. Experimental Procedures

For our experiment, we selected a fixed number of random data points having a window size of 7000, which corresponds to 10 s of data to train our model in both SSL and solely supervised manners with exactly the same set of data points. In both cases, we utilized the same model architecture and the same sampled data points. To train using SSL, we transferred the weights from the pre-trained model to the downstream task (Section 3.4). The average RMSE of the trained model using 10 data points is shown in Section 4.2. In this experiment, all models were subjected to an identical test set.

4. Results

We used the RMSE to evaluate our models, as regression models commonly utilize the RMSE as a statistic for assessing model performance. For a given test set, a model's RMSE measures the average distance between the expected values and the actual values. It is measured as the square root of the average of the squared differences between the predicted and actual values. The RMSE is helpful because it penalizes large mistakes over smaller ones and quantifies far apart the mistakes in the original units of the dataset. A smaller RMSE indicates that the model performed with less error.

4.1. Pre-Trained Models

For pre-training purposes, all the models were trained using data coming from a single subject. Figure 5 demonstrates the RMSE of the pre-trained models of all 15 subjects. The RMSE score is a measure of how well a model performed in predicting values compared to the actual values. For example, Subject 2's pre-trained model achieved an RMSE score of 0.024, meaning that the model's predictions were, on average, 0.024 units away from the actual values. In other words, the model's predictions had an average error of 0.024 units. The lower the RMSE score, the better the model's performance is. A smaller RMSE value indicates that the model is making more-accurate predictions, while a higher RMSE value indicates that the model is making larger errors. The low RMSE values we achieved across subjects suggested that our pre-trained models were well-trained and learned the underlying dynamics of each subject's EDA signals.

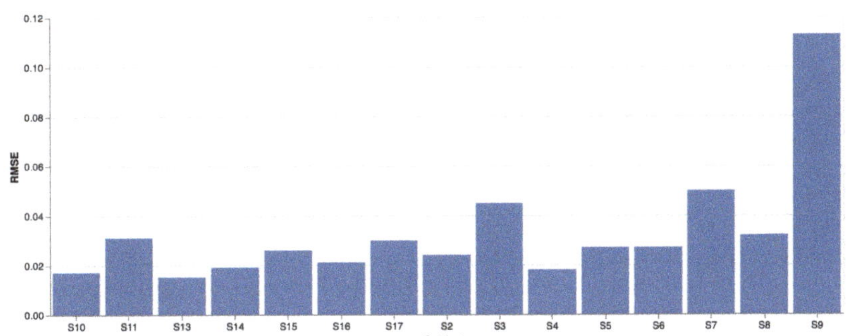

Figure 5. RMSE for the signal forecasting pre-training task for all subjects. The low RMSE indicates that the model learned the baseline dynamics of each user's EDA biosignal.

4.2. Evaluation Using Pre-Trained Models

Figure 6 displays the RMSE score of all participants for each question in the WESAD dataset while training on a randomly sampled subset of 10 data points in both SSL and supervised modes. We conducted bootstrapped sampling using five independent samples, and the same samples were used to compare the SSL pre-trained and purely supervised models. From Figure 6, we observe that, in most of the cases, the RMSE score was lower for the SSL-based models than purely supervised trained models. We observed that the SSL models outperformed the purely supervised models in approximately 90% of cases.

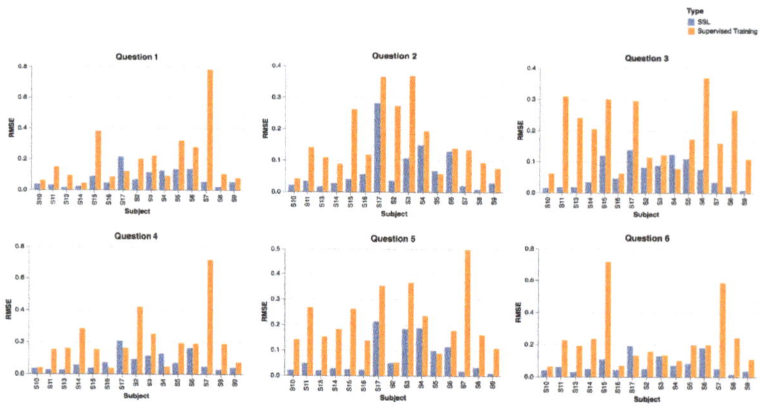

Figure 6. Comparison of the RMSE between a model fine-tuned after SSL vs. purely supervised training for all subjects and for all questions.

Across the six questions, the performance metrics are depicted using RMSE values, comparing self-supervised learning (SSL) against purely supervised training. For Question 1, SSL excelled particularly with Subject S8, demonstrating a significantly lower RMSE. For Question 2, SSL showed more-favorable results for a majority of the subjects, especially for S2 and S3. For Question 3, the most-commendable SSL performance was observed for S7. Moving to Question 4, S8's RMSE for SSL was notably efficient. For Question 5, both S3 and S8 stood out with SSL achieving lower RMSEs, while for Question 6, S7 was once again a highlight for SSL. Consistently, SSL demonstrated superior performance, with lower RMSE values being indicative of its effectiveness across subjects.

4.3. Results for a Demonstrative User

We compared purely supervised training and SSL, as shown in Figure 7. Our research indicated that the models employing SSL techniques required significantly less data to achieve comparable performance to those models that did not use SSL methods. We observed that the models that employed SSL techniques required less than 30% of the data needed by the models that did not use SSL techniques.

We saw that the models that only used fully supervised training methods needed more data to obtain the same RMSE as similar SSL models that were trained with the same number of labeled data points. This illustrates how SSL methods can speed up data-heavy applications by making them more efficient.

In addition to the benefits of preserving data, our findings demonstrated that SSL methods were stable across training runs. The RMSE of the purely supervised method varied drastically (had a high standard deviation) across bootstrapped samples, but the performance of the SSL models was more stable. The fluctuation of the purely supervised model indicated that its performance (as measured by the RMSE or other metrics) can vary significantly across different training runs or data samples. This variability can be problematic in real-world situations where there may be limited labeled data or data of varying quality. In contrast, SSL methods offer a more-stable way of learning, as the performance of the SSL models was less susceptible to fluctuations and remained more consistent across training runs or data samples. This stability is particularly useful in situations where data are limited or noisy, as it allows for more-efficient and -reliable model training. Therefore, the finding that SSL models are more stable than non-SSL models is an important contribution of this study, highlighting the potential benefits of using SSL methods in real-world applications.

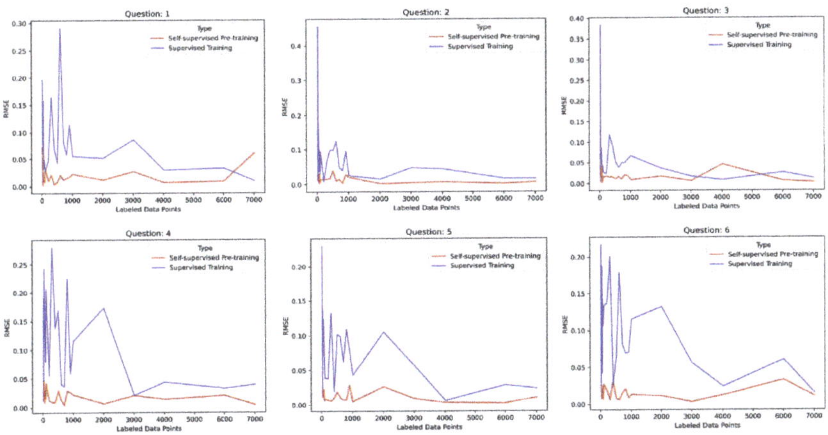

Figure 7. Comparison of the performance between SSL pre-training vs. purely supervised training for Subject 2 for all questions over different sets of labeled data points.

5. Discussion

5.1. Implications for Mobile Sensing Systems

Mobile sensing systems have traditionally been unable to detect psychiatric and mental health outcomes such as stress due to the inherent subjectivity of the labels and variability across users. SSL on biosignals, such as the methodology introduced and evaluated here, provides an opportunity for mobile sensing solutions that detect complex psychiatric events in a personalized manner. Personalization of models is one of the leading challenges and opportunities in machine learning for healthcare and digital psychiatry [33]. From a user interaction standpoint, users are only required to provide a few (on the order of ten) labeled examples of the adverse event of interest.

Through the use of a limited number of labeled examples for the targeted adverse event, this methodology effectively reduces the user labeling burden while simultaneously facilitating the development of more-tailored and -precise models. This approach not only improves the overall user experience, but also amplifies the probability of user engagement and adherence to digital therapies due to the improved user experience required to achieve a high-performing personalized mobile sensing model.

Personalization through SSL is likely to work in other domains as well. There are numerous digital healthcare research efforts that are attempting to build machine learning models for recurring conditions and events that are traditionally infeasible for machine learning due to the subjectivity of the classes. For example, some digital therapies for pediatric autism use computer vision models to predict facial expressions evoked by conversational partners [34]. Often, such digital therapeutic systems involve the curation of user-centric data [35]. Such systems provide a clear opportunity for self-supervised personalization, as described here. Personalizing the emotion-recognition model powering such digital therapies towards frequent conversational partners by the child is possible with the methods described here.

The interaction paradigm demonstrated here is similar to how Apple's Face ID works. Once the face recognition system is set up with only a few examples provided by the end users, it can be used repeatedly to unlock the device. Our primary goal is to demonstrate that this user interaction workflow can be adapted to mobile and wearable health settings.

In terms of implementation platforms, the HCI paradigm demonstrated here can be applied to a wide range of systems, such as smartphone apps, wearable devices, and laptops. For example, a smartphone app could use our technique to provide real-time stress monitoring and personalized tips for dealing with stress, while a wearable device could use the model to identify stress levels during physical activities or to monitor stress levels throughout the day.

The choice of platform depends on a number of factors, such as the specific use case, user preferences, and the desired amount of user activity. For example, a smartphone app might be preferred by individuals who want to actively track their stress levels and receive feedback, while a wearable device might be preferred by people who want to passively track their stress levels and have less contact.

5.2. Limitations and Future Work

While this work demonstrated promise for personalized learning for mobile sensing, our evaluation involved only a single dataset (WESAD) and a single modality (EDA). In future work, we would like to see our evaluation expanded to numerous biosignal datasets and health outcomes. Moving forward, an important direction for further investigation is to examine the integration of multiple signals within a single model, potentially enhancing its predictive capabilities and overall performance. Additionally, the importance of explainability in the medical informatics domain cannot be overstated. In future research, there is considerable potential to extend this study by exploring how different features influence our personalized model, thus enhancing its interpretability and applicability throughout the field. It is unclear whether the personalized SSL we presented will generalize to other health events that are not as strongly correlated as EDA and stress. If the method does generalize, then this work has the potential to become widely adopted in several HCI fields including wearable computing, affective computing, and mobile sensing.

There are inherent limitations to the WESAD dataset that we used for the evaluation. The WESAD dataset provides data from controlled experimental situations where realistic emotional engagement is a challenge. As the participants were required to assess their emotional state after each condition (i.e., baseline, amusement, stress, meditation), there is no continuous annotation of the participant's emotional state in this dataset. Therefore, there is the possibility of not obtaining the participant's actual affective state after each task. During data collection, some variables, such as a participant's proficiency in spoken English and familiarity with the provided subject under the stress condition, may introduce bias. Also, the participants' ages ranged from 25 to 30, which may have introduced bias into the findings.

In future work, we recommend testing the system using real-time, unimodal data obtained from participants in a more-comprehensive and -unconstrained experimental setup. This approach could potentially lead to a better understanding of the system's performance and generalizability in real-world scenarios, further strengthening the practical applicability of our findings. Nevertheless, the WESAD dataset is a frequently used dataset in the field of affective computing using wearable data [36].

6. Conclusions

We presented a novel method for personalizing deep learning models for the prediction of subjective outcomes such as stress using continuous biosignals. We demonstrated the low labeling requirement for fine-tuning the model after self-supervised pre-training. This method can enable high-performance personalized modeling with minimal manual annotation effort from end users. This technique enables deep learning models to be tailored to an individual's specific physiological reactions, resulting in more-precise and -personalized stress prediction. This has the potential to significantly increase the efficacy of stress management and preventive digital interventions while also reducing the load of the human annotation that is generally necessary for tailored models. Overall, our findings showed that self-supervised learning can enable increasingly individualized mobile sensing solutions.

Author Contributions: Conceptualization, P.W.; methodology, P.W.; software, T.I.; validation, P.W.; formal analysis, P.W., T.I.; investigation, P.W.; resources, P.W.; writing—original draft preparation, T.I.; writing—review and editing, P.W., T.I.; visualization, T.I.; supervision, P.W.; project administration, P.W.; funding acquisition, P.W. All authors have read and agreed to the published version of the manuscript.

Funding: This research was funded by National Institute of General Medical Sciences (NIGMS) grant number U54GM138062 and Medical Research Award fund of the Hawai'i Community Foundation grant number MedRes_2023_00002689.

Data Availability Statement: The dataset analyzed during the current study is available at https://ubicomp.eti.uni-siegen.de/home/datasets/icmi18/, accessed on 29 October 2023.

Acknowledgments: The project described was supported by grant number U54GM138062 from the National Institute of General Medical Sciences (NIGMS), a component of the National Institutes of Health (NIH), and its contents are solely the responsibility of the author and do not necessarily represent the official view of NIGMS or NIH. The project was also supported by a grant from the Medical Research Award fund of the Hawai'i Community Foundation, grant number MedRes_2023_00002689.

Conflicts of Interest: The authors declare no conflict of interest.

References

1. Cohen, S.; Janicki-Deverts, D.; Miller, G.E. Psychological stress and disease. *JAMA* **2007**, *298*, 1685–1687. [CrossRef] [PubMed]
2. Paredes, P.; Chan, M. CalmMeNow: Exploratory Research and Design of Stress Mitigating Mobile Interventions. In Proceedings of the CHI'11 Extended Abstracts on Human Factors in Computing Systems, Vancouver, BC, Canada, 7–12 May 2011. [CrossRef]
3. Giannakakis, G.; Grigoriadis, D.; Giannakaki, K.; Simantiraki, O.; Roniotis, A.; Tsiknakis, M. Review on psychological stress detection using biosignals. *IEEE Trans. Affect. Comput.* **2019**, *13*, 440–460. [CrossRef]
4. Healey, J.; Picard, R. Detecting stress during real-world driving tasks using physiological sensors. *IEEE Trans. Intell. Transp. Syst.* **2005**, *6*, 156–166. [CrossRef]
5. LeCun, Y.; Bengio, Y.; Hinton, G. Deep learning. *Nature* **2015**, *521*, 436–444. [CrossRef]
6. Hannun, A.Y.; Rajpurkar, P.; Haghpanahi, M.; Tison, G.H.; Bourn, C.; Turakhia, M.P.; Ng, A.Y. Cardiologist-level arrhythmia detection and classification in ambulatory electrocardiograms using a deep neural network. *Nat. Med.* **2019**, *25*, 65–69. [CrossRef]
7. Schmidt, P.; Reiss, A.; Duerichen, R.; Van Laerhoven, K. Wearable affect and stress recognition: A review. *arXiv* **2018**, arXiv:1811.08854.
8. Geiger, R.S.; Cope, D.; Ip, J.; Lotosh, M.; Shah, A.; Weng, J.; Tang, R. "Garbage in, Garbage out" Revisited: What Do Machine Learning Application Papers Report about Human-Labeled Training Data? *Quant. Sci. Stud.* **2021**, *2*, 795–827. Available online: https://direct.mit.edu/qss/article-pdf/2/3/795/1970760/qss_a_00144.pdf (accessed on 5 November 2021). [CrossRef]
9. Dharmawan, Z. Analysis of Computer Games Player Stress Level Using EEG Data. In Proceedings of the 11th International Conference on Computer Games: AI, Animation, Mobile, Educational and Serious Games, La Rochelle, France, 21–23 November 2007; The University of Wolverhampton: Wolverhampton, UK, 2007.
10. Wickramasuriya, D.S.; Qi, C.; Faghih, R.T. A state-space approach for detecting stress from electrodermal activity. In Proceedings of the 2018 40th Annual International Conference of the IEEE Engineering in Medicine and Biology Society (EMBC), Honolulu, HI, USA, 18–21 July 2018.
11. Spathis, D.; Perez-Pozuelo, I.; Brage, S.; Wareham, N.J.; Mascolo, C. Self-supervised transfer learning of physiological representations from free-living wearable data. In Proceedings of the Conference on Health, Inference, and Learning, Virtual, 8–10 April 2021.
12. Zhu, L.; Ng, P.C.; Yu, Y.; Wang, Y.; Spachos, P.; Hatzinakos, D.; Plataniotis, K.N. Feasibility study of stress detection with machine learning through eda from wearable devices. In Proceedings of the ICC 2022—IEEE International Conference on Communications, Seoul, Republic of Korea, 16–20 May 2022.
13. Yadav, M.; Sakib, M.N.; Nirjhar, E.H.; Feng, K.; Behzadan, A.; Chaspari, T. Exploring Individual Differences of Public Speaking Anxiety in Real-Life and Virtual Presentations. *IEEE Trans. Affect. Comput.* **2020**, *13*, 1168–1182. [CrossRef]
14. Schmidt, P.; Reiss, A.; Duerichen, R.; Marberger, C.; Van Laerhoven, K. Introducing wesad, a multimodal dataset for wearable stress and affect detection. In Proceedings of the ICMI '18: International Conference on Multimodal Interaction, Boulder, CO, USA, 16–20 October 2022.
15. Ninh, V.T.; Smyth, S.; Tran, M.T.; Gurrin, C. Analysing the performance of stress detection models on consumer-grade wearable devices. *arXiv* **2022**, arXiv:2203.09669.
16. Eren, E.; Navruz, T.S. Stress Detection with Deep Learning Using BVP and EDA Signals. In Proceedings of the 2022 International Congress on Human-Computer Interaction, Optimization and Robotic Applications (HORA), Ankara, Turkey, 9–11 June 2022.
17. Pakarinen, T.; Pietilä, J.; Nieminen, H. Prediction of Self-Perceived Stress and Arousal Based on Electrodermal Activity. In Proceedings of the 2019 41st Annual International Conference of the IEEE Engineering in Medicine and Biology Society (EMBC), Berlin, Germany, 23–27 July 2019. [CrossRef]
18. Kalimeri, K.; Saitis, C. Exploring multimodal biosignal features for stress detection during indoor mobility. In Proceedings of the 18th ACM International Conference on Multimodal Interaction, Tokyo, Japan, 12–16 November 2016.

19. Chen, T.; Kornblith, S.; Norouzi, M.; Hinton, G. A simple framework for contrastive learning of visual representations. In Proceedings of the 37th International Conference on Machine Learning, Vienna, Austria, 13–18 July 2020.
20. Grill, J.B.; Strub, F.; Altché, F.; Tallec, C.; Richemond, P.; Buchatskaya, E.; Doersch, C.; Avila Pires, B.; Guo, Z.; Gheshlaghi Azar, M.; et al. Bootstrap your own latent-a new approach to self-supervised learning. *Adv. Neural Inf. Process. Syst.* **2020**, *33*, 21271–21284.
21. Zhang, J.; Ma, K. Rethinking the augmentation module in contrastive learning: Learning hierarchical augmentation invariance with expanded views. In Proceedings of the 2022 IEEE/CVF Conference on Computer Vision and Pattern Recognition (CVPR), New Orleans, LA, USA, 18–24 June 2022.
22. Pöppelbaum, J.; Chadha, G.; Schwung, A. Contrastive learning based self-supervised time series analysis. *Appl. Soft Comput.* **2022**, *117*, 108397. [CrossRef]
23. Matton, K.; Lewis, R.A.; Guttag, J.; Picard, R. Contrastive Learning of Electrodermal Activity Representations for Stress Detection. In Proceedings of the Conference on Health, Inference, and Learning, Cambridge, MA, USA, 13 June 2023; pp. 410–426.
24. Kiyasseh, D.; Zhu, T.; Clifton, D.A. Clocs: Contrastive learning of cardiac signals across space, time, and patients. In Proceedings of the International Conference on Machine Learning, Virtual, 18–24 July 2021.
25. Sarkar, P.; Etemad, A. Self-supervised ECG representation learning for emotion recognition. *IEEE Trans. Affect. Comput.* **2020**, *13*, 1541–1554. [CrossRef]
26. Eldele, E.; Ragab, M.; Chen, Z.; Wu, M.; Kwoh, C.K.; Li, X.; Guan, C. Self-supervised contrastive representation learning for semi-supervised time series classification. *IEEE Trans. Pattern Anal. Mach. Intell.* **2023**, 1–15. [CrossRef] [PubMed]
27. Yang, X.; Zhang, Z.; Cui, R. TimeCLR: A self-supervised contrastive learning framework for univariate time series representation. *Knowl.-Based Syst.* **2022**, *245*, 108606. [CrossRef]
28. Sunmin, E.; Sunwoo, E.; Peter, W. SIM-CNN: Self-Supervised Individualized Multimodal Learning for Stress Prediction on Nurses Using Biosignals. *medRxiv* **2023**. [CrossRef]
29. Tanvir, I.; Peter, W. Personalized Prediction of Recurrent Stress Events Using Self-Supervised Learning on Multimodal Time-Series Data. In Proceedings of the AI & HCI Workshop at the 40th International Conference on Machine Learning (ICML), Honolulu, HI, USA, 23–29 July 2023.
30. Devlin, J.; Chang, M.W.; Lee, K.; Toutanova, K. Bert: Pre-training of deep bidirectional transformers for language understanding. *arXiv* **2018**, arXiv:1810.04805.
31. Radford, A.; Narasimhan, K.; Salimans, T.; Sutskever, I. Improving language understanding by generative pre-training. *OpenAI* **2018**.
32. Ancillon, L.; Elgendi, M.; Menon, C. Machine learning for anxiety detection using biosignals: A review. *Diagnostics* **2022**, *12*, 1794. [CrossRef]
33. Washington, P.; Mutlu, C.O.; Kline, A.; Paskov, K.; Stockham, N.T.; Chrisman, B.; Deveau, N.; Surhabi, M.; Haber, N.; Wall, D.P. Challenges and opportunities for machine learning classification of behavior and mental state from images. *arXiv* **2022**, arXiv:2201.11197.
34. Washington, P.; Voss, C.; Kline, A.; Haber, N.; Daniels, J.; Fazel, A.; De, T.; Feinstein, C.; Winograd, T.; Wall, D. SuperpowerGlass: a wearable aid for the at-home therapy of children with autism. *Proc. ACM Interact. Mob. Wearable Ubiquitous Technol.* **2017**, *1*, 1–22. [CrossRef]
35. Washington, P.; Kalantarian, H.; Kent, J.; Husic, A.; Kline, A.; Leblanc, E.; Hou, C.; Mutlu, C.; Dunlap, K.; Penev, Y.; et al. Training an emotion detection classifier using frames from a mobile therapeutic game for children with developmental disorders. *arXiv* **2020**, arXiv:2012.08678.
36. Liapis, A.; Faliagka, E.; Katsanos, C.; Antonopoulos, C.; Voros, N. Detection of Subtle Stress Episodes During UX Evaluation: Assessing the Performance of the WESAD Bio-Signals Dataset. In *Human-Computer Interaction—INTERACT 2021*; Ardito, C., Lanzilotti, R., Malizia, A., Petrie, H., Piccinno, A., Desolda, G., Inkpen, K., Eds.; Springer International Publishing: Cham, Switzerland, 2021; pp. 238–247.

applied sciences

MDPI

Article

Speech Emotion Recognition Using Deep Learning Transfer Models and Explainable Techniques

Tae-Wan Kim and Keun-Chang Kwak *

Department of Electronics Engineering, Interdisciplinary Program in IT-Bio Convergence System, Chosun University, Gwangju 61452, Republic of Korea; gyd03002@naver.com
* Correspondence: kwak@chosun.ac.kr; Tel.: +82-062-230-6086

Abstract: This study aims to establish a greater reliability compared to conventional speech emotion recognition (SER) studies. This is achieved through preprocessing techniques that reduce uncertainty elements, models that combine the structural features of each model, and the application of various explanatory techniques. The ability to interpret can be made more accurate by reducing uncertain learning data, applying data in different environments, and applying techniques that explain the reasoning behind the results. We designed a generalized model using three different datasets, and each speech was converted into a spectrogram image through STFT preprocessing. The spectrogram was divided into the time domain with overlapping to match the input size of the model. Each divided section is expressed as a Gaussian distribution, and the quality of the data is investigated by the correlation coefficient between distributions. As a result, the scale of the data is reduced, and uncertainty is minimized. VGGish and YAMNet are the most representative pretrained deep learning networks frequently used in conjunction with speech processing. In dealing with speech signal processing, it is frequently advantageous to use these pretrained models synergistically rather than exclusively, resulting in the construction of ensemble deep networks. And finally, various explainable models (Grad CAM, LIME, occlusion sensitivity) are used in analyzing classified results. The model exhibits adaptability to voices in various environments, yielding a classification accuracy of 87%, surpassing that of individual models. Additionally, output results are confirmed by an explainable model to extract essential emotional areas, converted into audio files for auditory analysis using Grad CAM in the time domain. Through this study, we enhance the uncertainty of activation areas that are generated by Grad CAM. We achieve this by applying the interpretable ability from previous studies, along with effective preprocessing and fusion models. We can analyze it from a more diverse perspective through other explainable techniques.

Keywords: speech emotion recognition; explainable model; deep learning; YAMNet; VGGish; audible feature

1. Introduction

In modern society, speech is used in various fields, including human–computer interaction, emotion analysis, and voice-based services. Speech is a representative way for users to express information, emotions, and thoughts. Therefore, it has become important to accurately receive and analyze speech data acquired from computers, smartphones, smartwatches [1], and smart homes to understand the emotions and thoughts of users. The information obtained from speech data is used to improve the quality of products and services. It is analyzed in various fields, such as mental state recognition, emotion classification, emotional analysis, the Internet of Things, and speech recognition systems [2]. It is also used for decision-making and health-status monitoring by understanding the emotional states of individuals or groups [3]. Unnecessary elements, such as environmental noise, breakage, and errors in speech classification add uncertainty to the inferred results. This leads to distrust in the model in terms of the correctness of the area focused on and the performed classification. Applying appropriate preprocessing can remove these unnecessary elements while increasing the quality of voice data [4].

Additionally, appropriate feature extraction methods are required for analyzing speech complexity and diversity [5]. A spectrogram shows the shape of the extracted features, which allows visual inspection of the frequency component changes over time. Moreover, it can be analyzed by viewing it as an image and then applying a computer vision technique [6]. In a spectrogram study, an explainable model can be applied to determine the relationship between the input and output data to identify which time–frequency domain influences the results of the classification model. When the results of a classification model are analyzed using an explainable model, the reliability of the former is increased, and its performance can be improved by additional research and analysis [7].

This study converted acquired speech signals into spectrogram images for analysis in the time–frequency domain. Unnecessary elements (such as noise, silence, and disconnection, etc.) that could lead to an incorrect decision-making process through the classification model were processed. Such elements are inevitably created in the process of acquiring speech. Instead of manual removal, an algorithm using Gaussian distribution and correlation coefficients was applied to exclude unnecessary divisions, which reduced the learning time and computational resource consumption. Three datasets were used for emotion classification to ensure that the classification model could be generalized. To improve classification performance, a visual geometry group-like audio classification model (VGGish) and yet another mobile network (YAMNet) model were combined to effectively extract emotion-related features from data acquired in diverse environments and lines. The combined model collected more information and extracted more features than the independent models. In the combined model, a late-fusion method was used to classify emotions by learning the same training data independently and then sharing information in the layer before classification. Additionally, by applying three explainable models to the classified results, the emotional feature section in the input time–frequency domain images was confirmed in various ways. The activation region extracted with gradient-weighted class activation mapping (Grad CAM) was analyzed in the time domain, and an algorithm was designed to convert it into a speech file. The converted voice section contained features related to each emotion in the recorded speech. These features can be directly checked by a user to increase the model's reliability and serve as data for further research.

The remainder of this paper is structured as follows: Section 2 presents the related research on spectrogram image analysis using deep learning and interpretable techniques. Section 3 describes the spectrogram transformation methods and Gaussian data selection (GDS) mechanism used in the data preprocessing in this study. Section 4 presents the features of VGGish and YAMNet and the structure and characteristics of the fusion model designed using these models. Section 5 describes the interpretable techniques (Grad CAM, LIME, and occlusion sensitivity) that were used for identifying the activation area. Section 6 explains the three datasets employed for designing a generalized model applicable to various environments and contexts. Section 7 discusses the analysis of the experimental setup and the results, and Section 8 concludes the study.

2. Related Work

2.1. Studies Applying Deep Learning to Spectrogram Images

This section presents studies conducted on spectrograms in which a one-dimensional (1D) signal was converted into two-dimensional (2D) data by applying deep learning to obtain more information and applications. Each study used preprocessing methods and network designs for speech research.

Xi [8] added specific values to insufficient areas to reduce confusion in training and classification when dividing speech data containing imbalanced time. This was achieved by using the IEMOCAP dataset. Padded data were trained and classified by a model that used a convolutional neural network (CNN) and long short-term memory (LSTM). The model was evaluated by weighted accuracy (WA), which assigns weights according to the number of samples when data are imbalanced. It was also evaluated using unweighted accuracy (UA), which reflects equally regardless of the number of samples. The evaluation of the accuracy of the emotion classification model by WA and UA showed that WA was evaluated at 71.45%, and UA was evaluated at 64.22% when specific values were padded. When the length of speech data was imbalanced, WA reached 68.86%, and UA was at 57.45%, showing slight variations. Badshah [9] constructed a model using a CNN and a fully connected layer. The model's performance was compared with that of the fine-tuned, pretrained AlexNet using seven-emotion data contained in the Berlin dataset for effective speech emotion recognition (SER). AlexNet showed an imbalance in that the accuracy was high in certain classes but low in others; therefore, the mean accuracy was 56.19%. The proposed model was confirmed to be even more effective than AlexNet, with a mean accuracy of 56.38%. Zhang [10] used speech data containing MUOC classroom atmosphere information to check and observe the atmospheric and environmental characteristics of a classroom containing many people. Filter bank, Mel-frequency Cepstral Coefficients (MFCC), and spectrogram features were collected to improve performance and reduce loss. Each feature was processed using an independently trained hybrid neural network combining CNN and LSTM models. The information collected from each feature map, independently processed by the network, was classified into six types of classroom atmospheres. When all the collected features were combined and classified, the lowest loss rate was 24.64%. Raja [11] conducted a study to confirm an effective data type when recognizing emotions using the Berlin dataset speech data. Speech data in 1D audio type was converted to a 2D image type by MFCC and used for training support vector machine (SVM), 1D-CNN, and 2D-CNN models. Each model classified seven emotions for each gender: SVM, using 1D audio-type data had the lowest performance, whereas the 2D-CNN model using 2D image-type data from the MFCC showed the highest performance, achieving 92.5% accuracy in all classes. Thus, transforming speech data into 2D image-type data is effective when classifying speech data. Zheng [12] proposed training NAO robots to respond according to a recognized user's emotion using CNN and random forest (RF) models with the CASIA emotion dataset from China. The data that the robots collected in everyday environments were mixed with noise and had lower purity than the data used for training. Therefore, to improve the generalization performance compared to those of existing methods, features of the speech data were extracted using the CNN model and the extracted feature map was classified using the RF classifier for six emotions. When classified through CNN, a performance of 81.43% was achieved, and when using RF together with CNN, the performance was increased to 84.68%, confirming that using CNN and RF together was effective in the learning process for NAO robots. Heng [13] converted speech data to spectrograms to extract time–frequency features from the IEMOCAP dataset and divided each spectrogram into certain sizes. Emotion-related features were extracted using a CNN, and temporal features were learned and extracted using an LSTM. The extracted features were classified into six classes and evaluated using the WA and UA methods. WA achieved 64%, while UA achieved 56%.

Classification studies applying deep learning to spectrogram images show high performance when the amount of data is small, but most studies using a lot of other data show low accuracy. It can be confirmed that emotional features were not properly extracted in a lot of data.

2.2. Studies Applying Deep Learning and Explainable Methods to Spectrograms

This section presents various studies in which deep learning was applied to 2D spectrogram images, using explainable models. The model's decision-making process was verified by applying explainable techniques to increase its reliability, and activation areas were also used as data.

Yuanyuan [14] converted speech data in the IEMOCAP dataset into spectrogram images and extracted feature maps using AlexNet. The feature maps processed attention using the tanh and softmax activation functions to highlight the essential feature channels in the attention layer. They identified that the model, applied by CNN and LSTM, achieved a WA of 68.8% and UA of 59.4%; however, the accuracy was effectively improved to a WA of 70.4% and a UA of 63.9% when attention was applied. The focus area of the model was visually confirmed using Grad CAM. Carofilis [15] proposed recognizing a speaker's place of local origin using the VCTK dataset. Speech data were converted into spectrogram images and trained using CNN models. The essential areas created using Grad CAM were combined with a spectrogram to create new feature vectors. These feature vectors were applied to various machine learning algorithms (MLAs) to classify a speaker's place of local origin. The model performances were evaluated using the unweighted average recall (UAR) and macro average accuracy (MAA) and compared with those of other methods, such as the speech wave input and other MLA methods. SVM was measured as 0.348 in MAA and 0.340 in UAR, GaussianNB was measured as 0.262 in MAA and 0.262 in UAR, and passive aggressive was measured as 0.351 in MAA and 0.356 in UAR. Bicer [16] conducted a study on acoustic scene classification, in which sound signals were analyzed to identify the environment and scene to manage and analyze the surroundings. This study used the dataset employed in the DCASE 2016 challenge. Spectrogram images converted into speech signals were trained using ResNet to classify three different environments and identify the areas that influenced the classification decision. The classification achieved an accuracy of 91.82% and the time–frequency area related to the classified class is highlighted using Grad CAM. This highlighted area is then converted into a sound signal for confirmation. Cesarelli [17] used PCG signal data from Kaggle to train phonocardiogram signals with various hyperparameter values and 2D-CNN models and to classify normal and abnormal sounds. That model was evaluated with an accuracy of 86%, and the decision of the model to classify normal and abnormal sounds in the time domain of the heartbeat was confirmed using Grad CAM for the results. Lee [18] conducted a study to predict the recovery of patients who underwent thyroid cancer surgery by converting their speech sounds before and after surgery into spectrograms. The training involved the use of EfficientNet and LSTM, with patients and vocal data provided by DIRAMS. The results showed that the trained model achieved an evaluation score of 0.822 by AUROC. Additionally, Grad CAM was used to confirm the area affected in the time-frequency domain corresponding to the classification.

In a study that applied deep learning and explanatory techniques to the spectrogram, the decision-making process of the model was mainly confirmed using only Grad CAM. However, since the information that can be obtained with a heat map is limited, it is advantageous to use more diverse models and aspects.

3. Materials and Methods

This section describes the method for treating unnecessary data by preprocessing speech data. It also introduces a constructed network that can accurately classify and apply speech data across various contexts. Subsequently, explainable techniques and the method for their use to analyze the output of a model from various aspects are discussed. Figure 1 shows the common architecture of various proposed analyses that apply explainable models for emotion recognition.

In this study, speech data were converted using short-time Fourier transform (STFT), used as input for a CNN-based network, and then divided in time based on the network input size. Data selection was performed for each segmented region using a Gaussian distribution and correlation coefficients to treat the unnecessary data. This process resulted in a reduction of data scale, training time, and memory consumption. The network design independently extracted various features from the selected data, synthesizing them for training and classification. Three explainable models were applied to analyze the classified results. Based on these analyses, the decision-making process was examined, and the activation time–frequency area corresponding to emotions was identified. Subsequently, the activation area identified through Grad CAM was applied to the speech data to directly identify linguistic and phonetic characteristics.

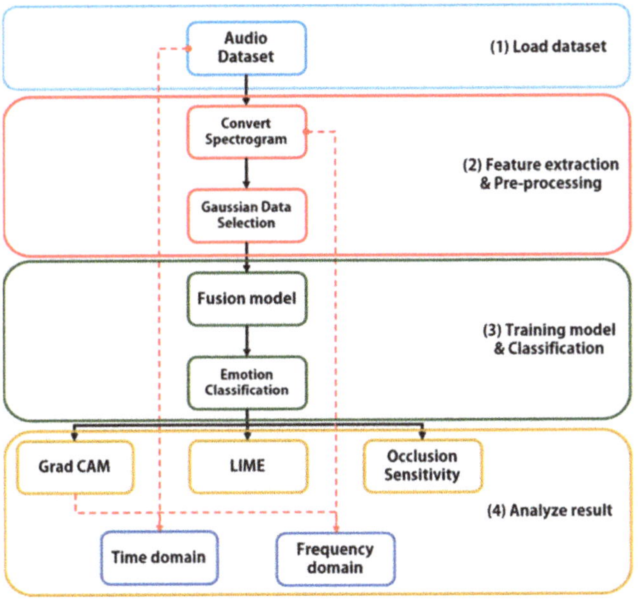

Figure 1. Diagram of speech emotion recognition and analysis using gradient-weighted class activation mapping (Grad CAM) and local interpretable model-agnostic explanations (LIME).

3.1. Convert Speech Data to Spectrogram Images

Speech contains a large amount of information in the time and frequency areas. Using raw speech data is inadequate for capturing all speech information. Therefore, this information can be converted to a spectrogram for study and analysis because it can confirm the change in the time–frequency area, allowing direct visualization. This study converted a speech signal to a spectrogram image using STFT, a frequently used method for conversion, using the parameters listed in Table 1. Figure 2 shows the progressing of STFT, a representative technology for converting speech signals into the time–frequency domain. It divides time into window sizes and applies a fast Fourier transform (FFT) to each section to obtain the frequency information. To obtain the desired frequency range, the filter parameters listed in Tables 2 and 3 were used when converting a spectrogram. The spectrogram was then divided according to the model input size, with an overlap of a certain size incorporated into the time domain.

Table 1. Summary of the related literature.

Author	Purpose	Dataset	Model	Performance
Xi	Speech emotion classification	IEMOCAP	CNN+LSTM	WA: 71.45, UA: 64.22
Badshah	Speech emotion recognition	Berlin	CNN, AlexNet	56.19%, 56.38%
Zhang	Classroom atmosphere classification	MUOC classroom atmosphere information	CNN+LSTM	Error rate: 24.64%
Raja	Speech emotion classification	Berlin dataset (EMO-DB)	SVM, 1D-CNN, 2D-CNN	92.5%
Zheng	Speech emotion classification	CASIA emotion dataset	CNN + random forest (RF)	75.57%
Heng	Speech emotion classification	IEMOCAP	CNN+LSTM	WA: 64, UA: 56
Yuanyuan	Speech emotion recognition	IEMOCAP	AlexNet, CNN+LSTM/Grad CAM	WA: 70.4, UA: 63.9

Table 1. Cont.

Author	Purpose	Dataset	Model	Performance
Carofilis	Speaker's place recognition	VCTK	CNN/Grad CAM	MAA: 0.351, UAR: 0.356
Bicer	Acoustic scene classification	DCASE 2016 challenge dataset	ResNet/Grad CAM	91.82%
Cesarelli	Heartbeat sound classification	Heart sound database in Kaggle	2D-CNN/Grad CAM	86%
Lee	Predict sound recovery	Patients and vocal data by DIRAMS	EfficientNet + LSTM/Grad CAM	AUROC: 0.822

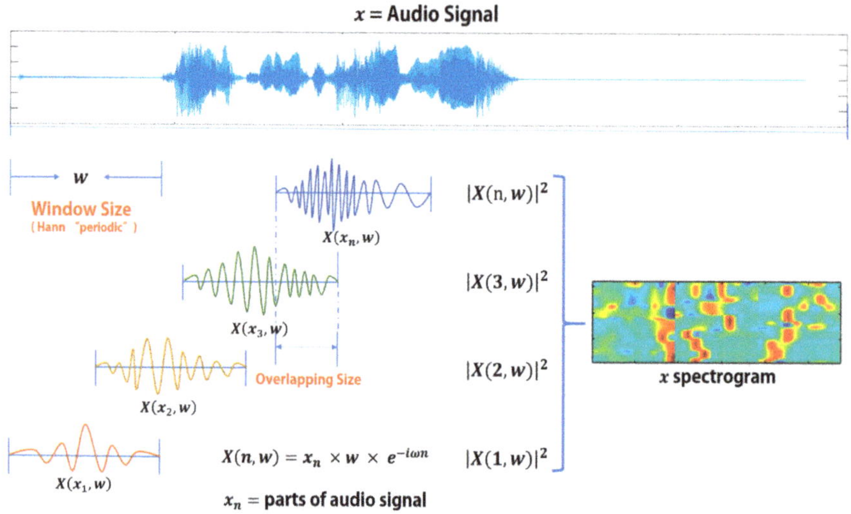

Figure 2. Speech-data-to-spectrogram conversion process.

Table 2. Short-time Fourier transform (STFT) parameters to convert log-Mel spectrogram.

	Window Size	Overlapping Size	Window Type	Range of Frequency
STFT parameter	1200	720	Hann "periodic"	One-way

Table 3. Audio filter parameters involving the fast Fourier transform (FFT).

	Number of Frequency Band	Sampling Rate	Frequency Scale	FFT Length
Audio filter	64 channels	48,000	Mel	1200

3.2. Gaussian Data Selection Mechanisms

When acquiring speech data, matching the length of the data is difficult, even if the same lines are used. The data length varies depending on the speaker's pronunciation speed, interruptions, and noise. The consumption of computing resources increases with the increase in the data scale, which leads to inclusion of unnecessary sections, unrelated to emotions. Various data preprocessing methods are being studied to select and exclude unnecessary sections.

Figure 3 illustrates the application of a Gaussian distribution and correlation coefficients to select unnecessary sections in the acquired data. The selection process excludes heterogeneous data based on the correlation coefficients in the divided data section rather than simply removing sections with low or high data values by Algorithm 1. After calculating the mean and variance of the divided section, expressed as a Gaussian distribution, the correlation coefficients between all distributions are calculated, normalized, and selected based on the set threshold. Using the above method, sections having a low correlation with the data containing emotional features (i.e., sections that are heterogeneous from the Gaussian distribution of the emotional feature section) are excluded from learning. Accordingly, the data scale and computing resource consumption are reduced while maintaining classification accuracy.

Algorithm 1. Pseudocode of Gaussian data selection algorithm.

Gaussian Data Selection Algorithm

$$Audiodata = \{x_1, x_2, \ldots, x_N\}, N = number\ of\ data$$
$$S_1 = STFT(x_1), S_N = \{S_1, S_2, \ldots, S_N\}$$
$$S_i = \{S_{i1}, S_{i2}, \ldots, S_{iD}\}, D = number\ of\ divided\ for\ each\ data$$
$$\mu_{ij} = mean\left(S_{ij}\right), \sigma_{ij} = std\left(S_{ij}\right)$$
$$G_{ij} = Gaussian\left(S_{ij}; \mu_{ij}, \sigma_{ij}\right)$$
$$C_i = Sum(Correlation\ Coefficient(G_{i1}, G_{i2}, \ldots, G_{iD}), Dim = 1)$$
$$C_i = [C_1, \ldots, C_D], Score_i = normalize(C_i)$$
$$Selected\ data = \left\{S_{ij} \middle| Score_{ij} > T\right\}, T = Threshold$$

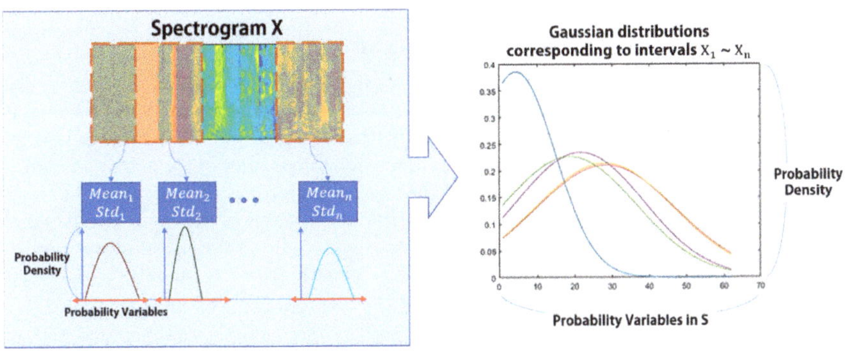

Figure 3. Applying Gaussian data selection to a speech spectrogram.

4. Late-Fusion Model Design with VGGish and YAMNet

4.1. Features of VGGish and YAMNet Models

Figure 4 shows the structure of the VGGish model developed by Google that is used for speech recognition and classification in this study. It is designed as a CNN by modifying an existing visual geometry group (VGG) network for image classification in speech data processing.

The model above, designed to extract features from 2D data rather than 1D data in the time domain, uses a convolutional layer that learns the spatial patterns and features of an input image through weights and batch normalization. An activation function layer, which allows learning highly complex patterns by applying nonlinear features, is used to output the spatial feature vectors of the audio images for analysis and classification. A global pooling layer is not applied to preserve the spatial feature information in the time–frequency domain of the input spectrogram. The number of channels in the fully connected layer is designed to be large enough to generate a feature map larger than the input data. The output information is synthesized and used for classification, utilizing the location characteristics of the time–frequency domain that can be obtained for each pooling layer.

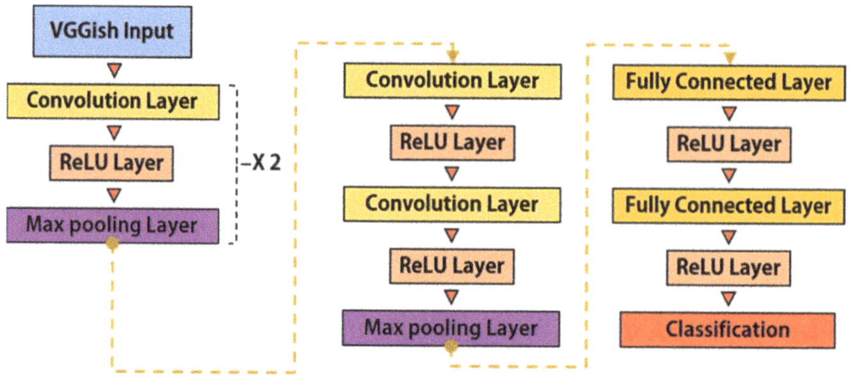

Figure 4. VGGish network structure for video game genre identification using spectrograms and headphones (VGGish), incorporating rectified linear unit (ReLU).

In VGGish, feature maps were extracted for each pooling layer, except for the first pooling layer. The size of the feature map extracted from the network is [24 × 16 × 128/12 × 8 × 256/6 × 4 × 512], respectively. Each feature map aggregates information that can be obtained from each layer by adjusting and fusing the number of channels.

Similar to VGGish, YAMNet, as shown in Figure 5, is an audio classification model developed by Google. It is a transfer learning model that learns from a large-scale dataset to perform 512 different speech recognition tasks, including animal sounds, cars, music, nature, and human conversations. This model is based on a CNN and consists of a convolution layer that can extract spatial patterns and features of multiple images. It also contains a pooling layer, which increases computational efficiency by reducing the spatial dimensions, as well as an activation function layer. Using a global pooling layer before the classification layer, the model focuses on the channel characteristics of the extracted feature map rather than the time–frequency positional characteristics of the feature map input from the previous layer. It is designed to identify the overall features of the input spectrogram image and does not rely on the positional features. Figure 6 shows the classification process of combining the feature maps obtained from each transfer learning model. Here, feature maps in VGGish were obtained by each pooling layer except for the first pooling layer.

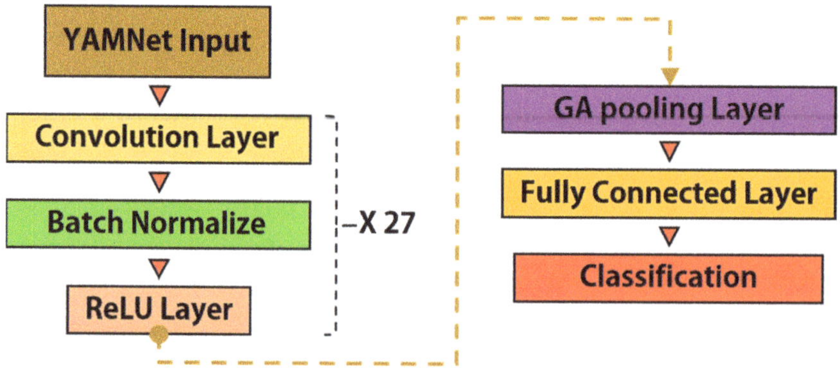

Figure 5. Diagram illustrating the network structure of YAMNet (yet another mobile network) and its integration with the genetic algorithm (GA).

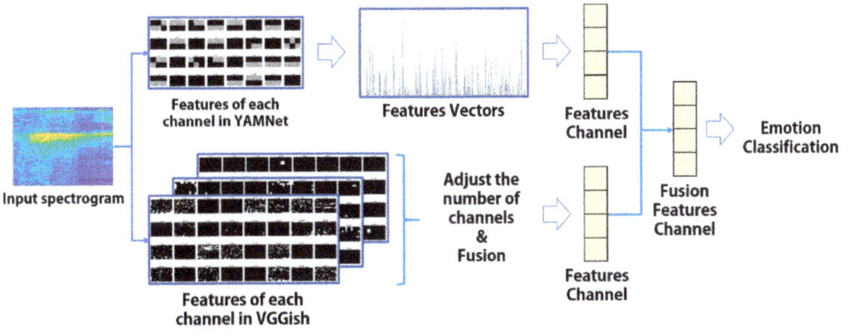

Figure 6. Feature extraction and combination in the fusion transfer learning model.

4.2. Introduction to the Late-Fusion Model

The fusion method combines the information extracted from different data sources or models to achieve a better performance than independent models. More cases can be learned by combining information from models with information from feature extraction methods, which are also used to integrate information from multiple sensor data.

This study selected a late-fusion method to input the same data into YAMNet and VGGish, learn in parallel, and appropriately combine the obtained information to improve the classification results. Figure 7 shows the area activated using Grad CAM in the layer before classification, when the same spectrogram image is input to each model. Owing to the structural differences between the models, VGGish achieves a high location resolution by extracting locational features in the time–frequency domain of the image. Conversely, YAMNet is designed to identify overall features of an image and does not rely on locational features to analyze information. Consequently, there is a difference in analyzing information.

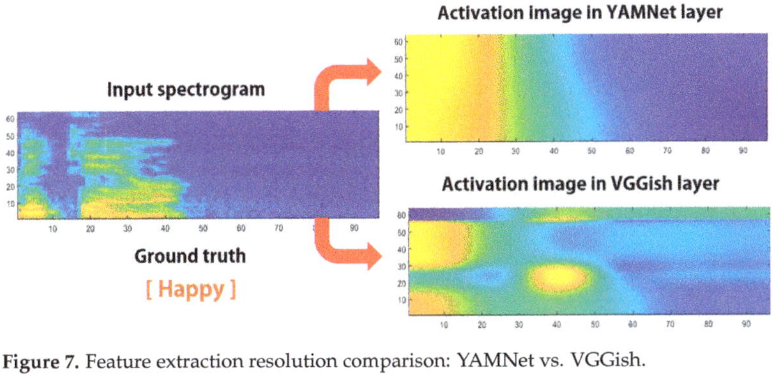

Figure 7. Feature extraction resolution comparison: YAMNet vs. VGGish.

Figure 8 shows the designed model that extracts patterns and features for emotion classification from preprocessed data and integrates information to classify the emotion classes. New feature information is generated by adding the information obtained from each layer of VGGish. Three types of data are synthesized, and a network that synthesizes the feature information and classifies the emotions in the final classification layer is designed. When combining features in a fusion model, the addition or multiplication method is mainly used. However, in the above network, to reduce the influence between the feature channels, a depth-combining method is used to combine the features extracted using the two models. This method not only maintains the information but also classifies it through the interaction of various information in the fully connected layer.

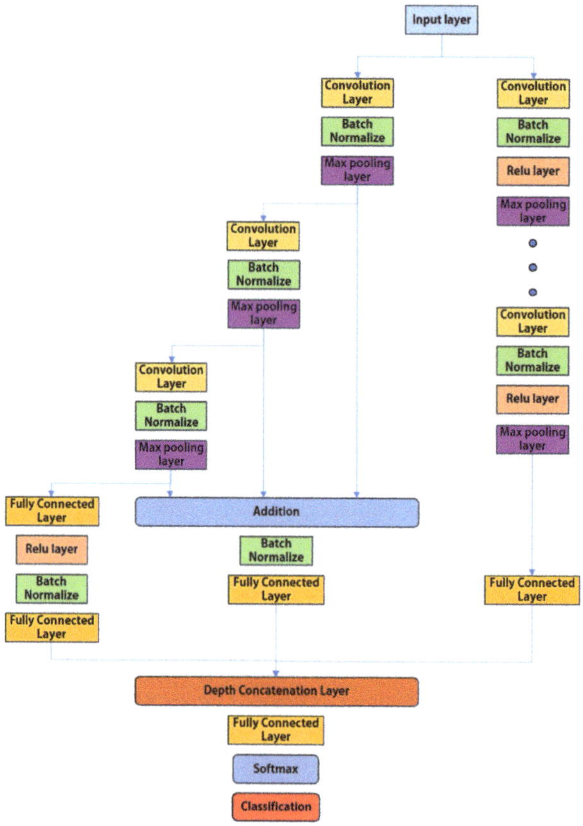

Figure 8. Late-fusion networks of YAMNet and VGGish.

5. Explainable Artificial Intelligence Model

For artificial intelligence (AI) to assist user judgment and be used in activities such as production, confirming the basis and validity of the results is necessary. Figure 9 shows an explainable model (explainable AI) that uses data and labels in conjunction with machine and deep learning models to understand and interpret the factors and areas that affect the input data. This technology can improve the performance of the machine and deep learning modules by confirming incorrect classifications and predictions. It also improves reliability by making it easier for users to understand. A decision tree or linear regression model is simple. Therefore, the decision-making process can be confirmed using the model itself. Other complex models require additional processing, such as Grad CAM, activation, occlusion sensitivity, and LIME.

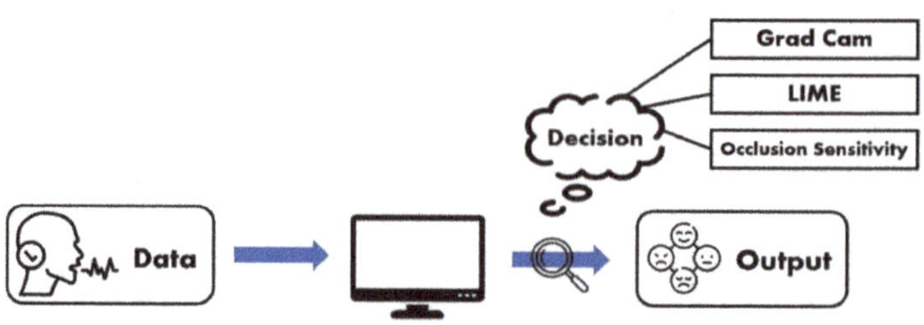

Figure 9. Explanation of explainable AI.

5.1. Grad CAM Technique

Grad CAM creates a focus area that uses the gradient of the classification class, which uses a backpropagation gradient to describe the class classification of a model [19]. An input image is passed through a CNN to generate a feature vector, and the class is classified using this feature vector. As the score of the classified class, the gradient collected for each channel in the previous layer is used as a weight to determine how much each channel influences the class score. The spatial area related to the class is obtained from the feature map, restored to the original size, and expressed visually. As can be seen in Figure 10, Grad CAM uses a spectrogram that is converted to examine the changes in both the time and frequency domains. Subsequently, the spectrogram passes through a CNN, and the results demonstrate which time and frequency section are essential for the classification class by restoring them to the size of the original.

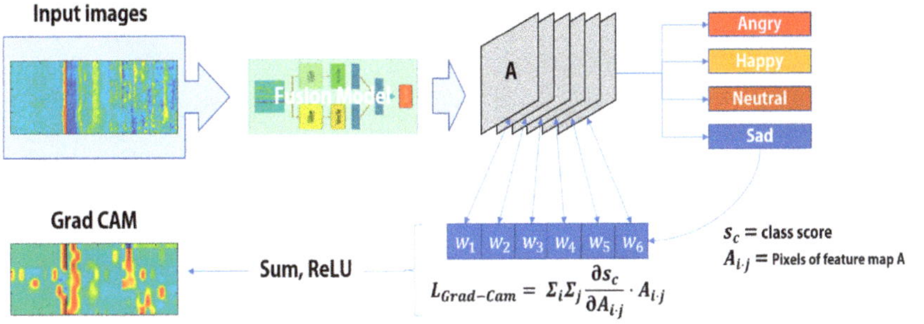

Figure 10. Creation process of Grad CAM.

5.2. LIME Technique

LIME is an explainable technique that determines how small areas, such as pixels of the input data, affect model classification [20]. As shown in Figure 11, the above method transforms a specific area of the input image by adding noise, inputs the transformed areas into the model, and measures the prediction results of the model. A vector is created from the measured feature values for each pixel or specific area, and training is performed using a simple model, such as linear regression, based on the prediction results of the images corresponding to the feature vector.

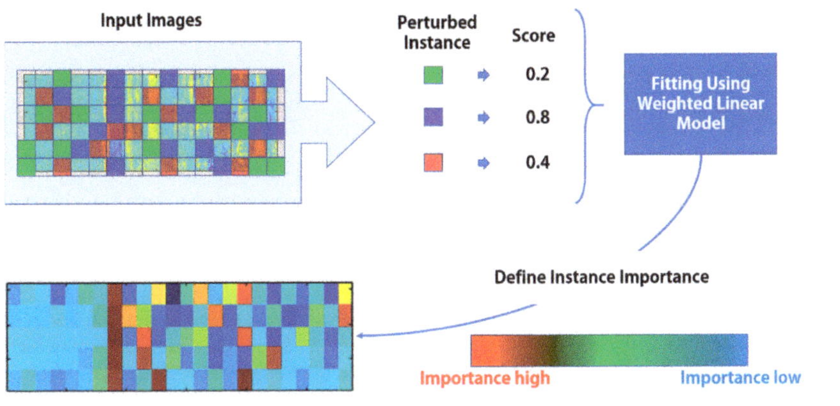

Figure 11. Creation process of LIME.

The trained model calculates the influence of each pixel or specific area of the original image in the image class classification and visualizes it as a heatmap. The predicted results are measured by transforming various time–frequency pixel areas in the spectrogram image, and the model learns to determine which areas influenced the classification.

5.3. Occlusion Sensitivity Technique

Figure 12 shows how occlusion sensitivity can be achieved by blocking a specific area of the image inputted into the model. The impacted areas were determined by checking the results based on occlusion sensitivity. Continuously altering the position of the blocked area visually illustrates the extent of influence of each position on the model predictions. The above method examines the influence of the area by repeatedly covering the image and a specific part of the voice or text, filling the area with random or average values, and entering them into the model to check for changes in accuracy.

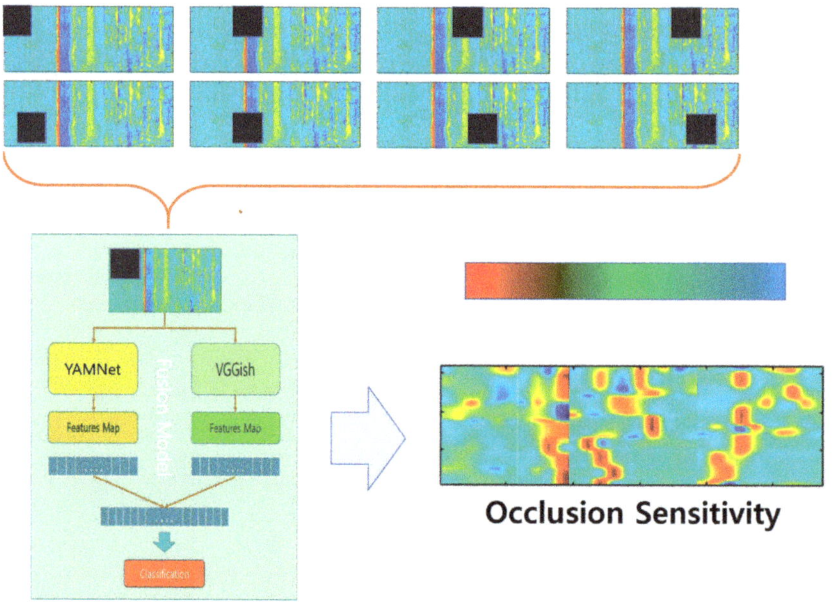

Figure 12. Occlusion sensitivity creation process.

6. Speech Emotion Datasets and Data Selection Method

To evaluate the performance of the proposed model, we use three datasets (CSU 2021, CSU2022, and AI-Hub), acquired from different environments. These datasets were constructed by Korean speech. The entire data from these datasets are combined and used for both training and validation.

6.1. CSU 2021 Speech Emotion Dataset

The above dataset was obtained from 100 people in 2021 at Chosun University, comprising the general public, theater actors, and AI characters. A total of 40 lines, with 10 lines related to each of the four distinct emotions from dramas or movies, were collected. As shown in Figure 13, the speeches were recorded by the participants in a quiet space to mitigate noise, using a Sony stereo lavalier microphone (ECM-LV1). This microphone is used to record ten voices for each of the four emotions from both theater actors and the general public, resulting in 40 voices. The AI character uses Typecast, an AI voice actor service, and the Prosody program to create ten basic voices and ten voices with adjusted speed and tone. All AI voices are produced by a single AI character in the same environment. Consequently, 80 voice data points, 20 for each emotion, were generated. The voices were recorded through a microphone and configured, as shown in Figure 14. Data samples are as shown in Figure 15.

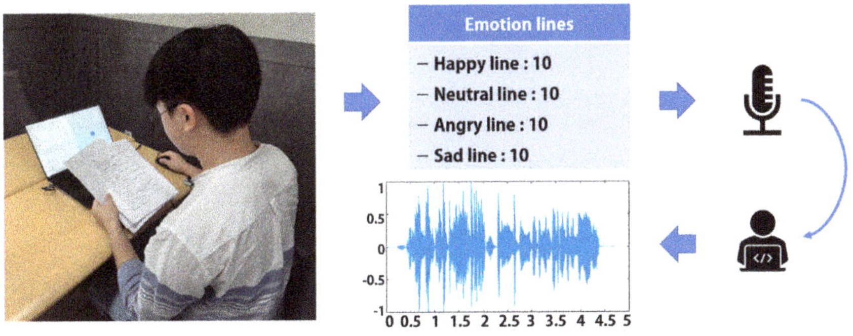

Figure 13. Data acquisition process.

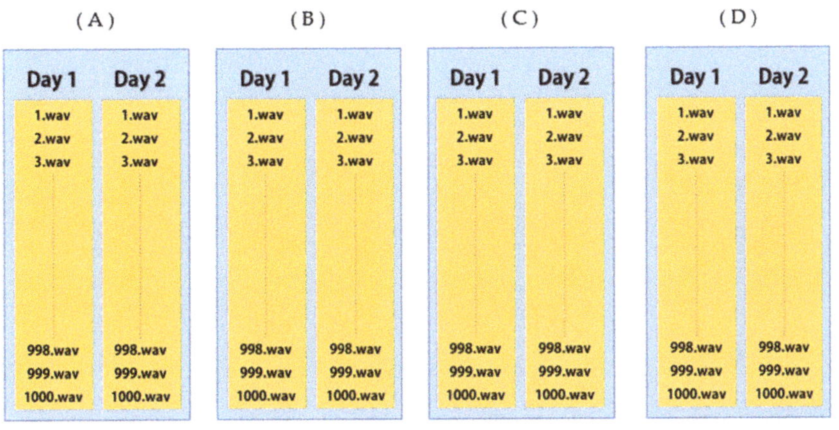

Figure 14. CSU 2021 speech emotion dataset—general public: (**A**) angry, (**B**) happy, (**C**) neutral, and (**D**) sad.

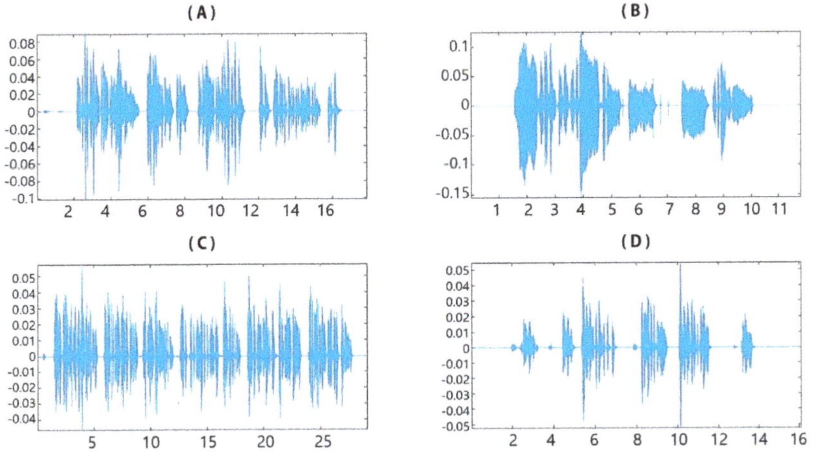

Figure 15. CSU 2021 data samples: (**A**) angry, (**B**) happy, (**C**) neutral, and (**D**) sad.

6.2. CSU 2022 Speech Emotion Dataset

The dataset above, created by Chosun University in 2022, comprises data from 200 members of the general public. It was acquired for classification into eight emotional states: happy, neutral, angry, sad, chagrin, disgust, fear, and surprise. For each emotion, ten situations and ten short lines suitable for it were selected to prompt participants to act with the intended emotions. A Sony stereo lavalier microphone (ECM-LV1) was used as the acquisition equipment to record signals at 48 kHz. They were recorded alone in a quiet space to minimize noise as much as possible. The data were organized in the WAV format, with each participant contributing ten files per emotion, a total of 80 files per person. The overall dataset, consisting of 16,000 files, was configured as shown in Figure 16. Data samples are as shown in Figure 17.

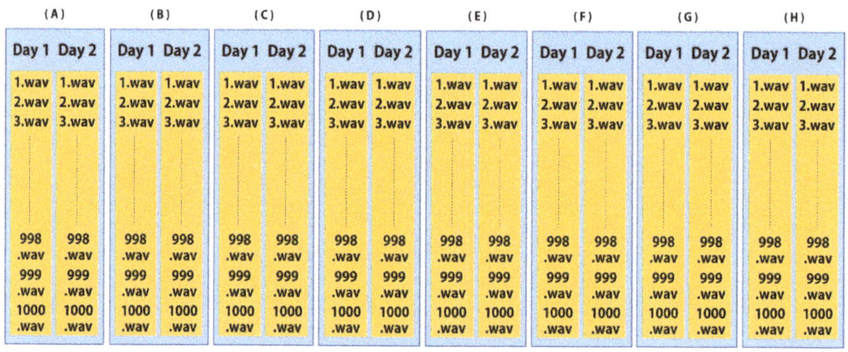

Figure 16. CSU 2022 speech emotion dataset—general public: (**A**) happy, (**B**) neutral, (**C**) angry, (**D**) sad, (**E**) chagrin, (**F**) disgust, (**G**) fear, and (**H**) surprised.

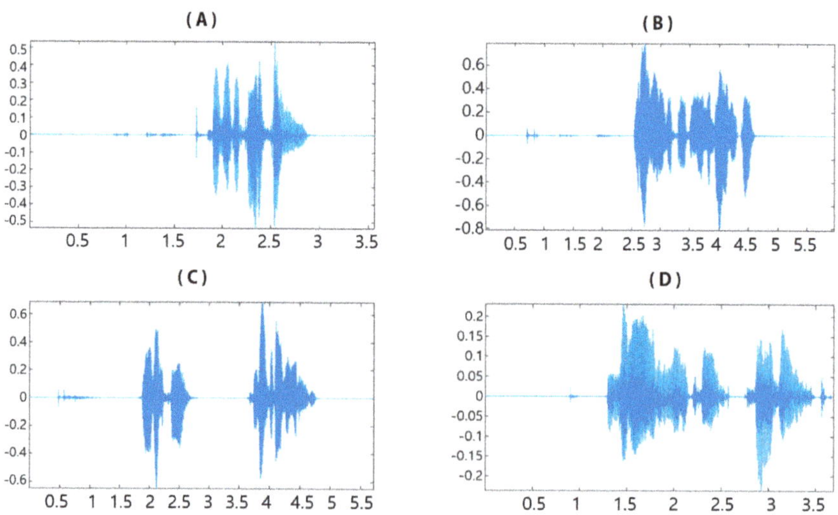

Figure 17. CSU 2022 data samples: (**A**) angry, (**B**) happy, (**C**) neutral, and (**D**) sad.

6.3. AI-Hub Dataset for Emotion Classification

The above data are from the AI-Hub's public data [21]. AI-Hub is an AI-integrated platform that anyone can utilize and participate in by supporting the AI infrastructure (AI data, AI SW API, computing resources) necessary for developing AI technology, products, and services. Among the existing public data, FER 2013 shows a large difference in the amount of data for each emotion, and the facial emotion data are acquired in low quality. The SFEW data were high-quality data but small in size, with approximately 2000 cases. In the case of CMU-MOSI, the speech domain was limited to movie reviews and the emotion classification was limited to positive and negative; thus, AI-Hub's public data were compiled. The dataset was gathered from among 100 aspiring actors and acting experts, acquiring seven emotional classes: happy, surprised, neutral, fearful, disgusted, angry, and sad. A total of 10,351 videos and voices were included by performing speech and acting, 100 times per emotion. The speech files were configured as shown in Figure 18. Data samples are as shown in Figure 19.

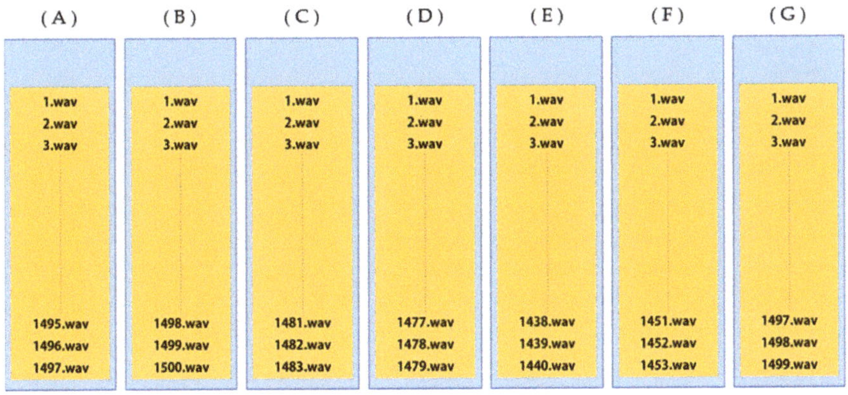

Figure 18. AI-Hub dataset for emotion classification: (**A**) happy, (**B**) neutral, (**C**) angry, (**D**) sad, (**E**) disgust, (**F**) fear, and (**G**) surprised.

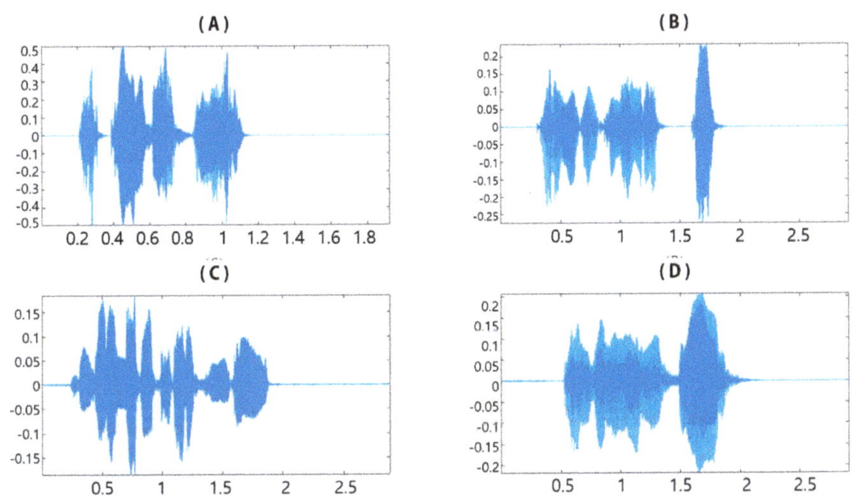

Figure 19. AI-Hub emotion classification dataset samples: (**A**) angry, (**B**) happy, (**C**) neutral, and (**D**) sad.

6.4. Gaussian Data Selection

When speech is divided into time domains according to the model input size, unnecessary sections unrelated to the features to be classified and predicted are generated. To effectively select and exclude this section, GDS preprocessing using a Gaussian distribution and correlation coefficients was performed. Figure 20 shows the number of sequence segmentations for each file in the training data before applying the GDS and the number of sequence segmentations for each file in the training data after the application. The data before application are divided, consisting of 165,240 data points. After the application, unnecessary sections are reduced to 140,885, a total of 24,385 data points are excluded, and the data are reduced by 15%. These results confirm that the learning time and the time consumed computing resources can be saved.

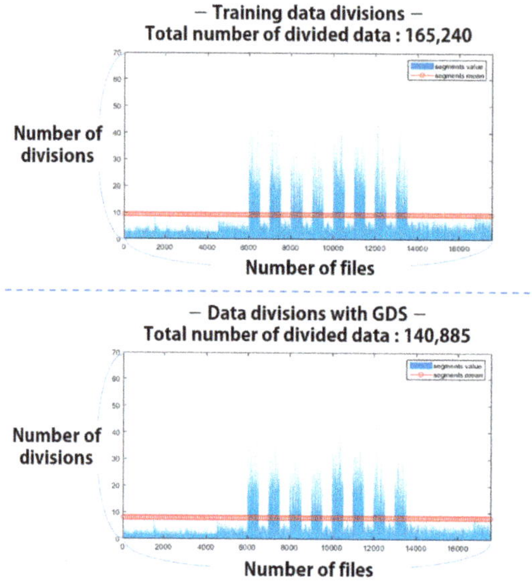

Figure 20. Change in the number of sequence segmentations after Gaussian data selection (GDS).

7. Experimental Findings and Results

7.1. Training Environment and Parameters

The hardware used for the experiments was NVIDIA GeForce GTX TITAN X, 32G RAM, and Intel(R) Xeon(R) CPU E5-1650 v3. The parameters of the audio filter and STFT for conversion to a log-Mel spectrogram were adjusted considering the hardware performance and experimental time. Table 4 lists the hyperparameters used to learn the designed network after data preprocessing. The optimization function uses adaptive moment estimation (Adam), which is frequently implemented in deep learning.

Table 4. Training hyper-parameter.

	Solver	Training Rate	Epoch	Batch Size
Training hyper-parameter	Adam	0.01	20	128

7.2. Accuracy Analysis per Class

Classification was performed on the sequence segmentation sections using the above model. The accuracy values of the sections corresponding to the original data were synthesized, and the average value was used to define the class. Learning and validation data were conducted by mixing data from the entire dataset and dividing it into 85:15 ratios. Figure 21 shows the accuracy of the developed fusion model, demonstrating high accuracy in classifying the four core emotions. As shown in Figure 22, the GDS is applied to remove data that do not affect learning. Its accuracy was analyzed using test data in which the same data selection was applied. The total number of data points was not affected, and as the number of sequence segmentation sections corresponding to each data point decreased by 15%, the learning time decreased, while the accuracy remained similar.

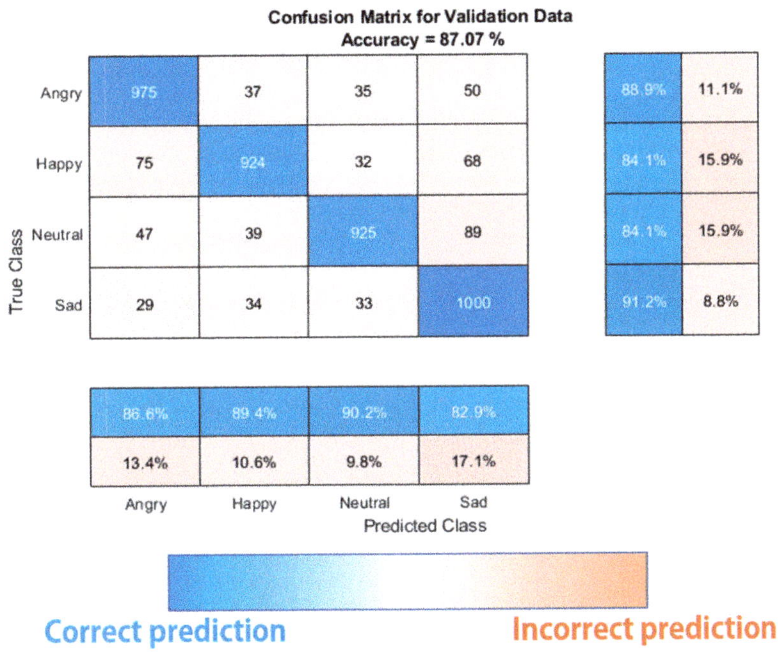

Figure 21. Custom YAMNet–VGGish late-fusion network—classification accuracy.

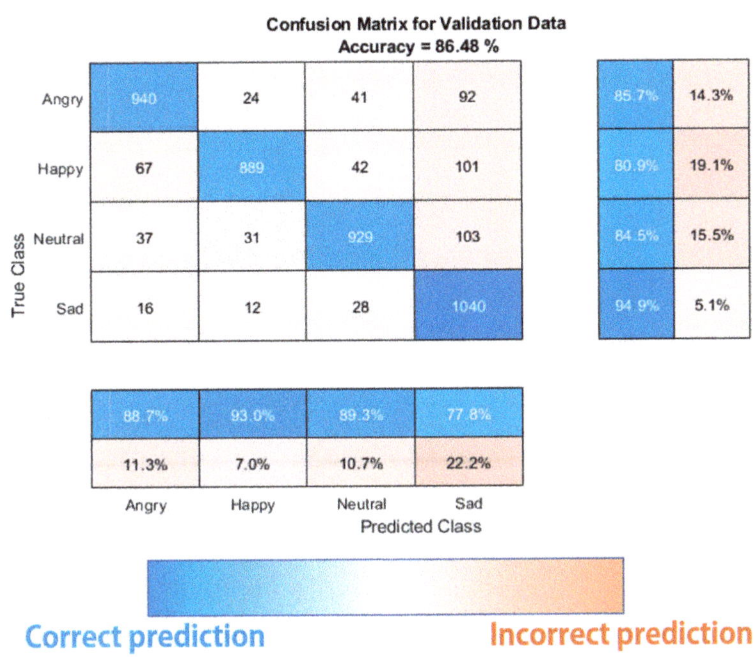

Figure 22. Classification accuracy with Gaussian data selection.

Table 5 shows the evaluation of the classification performance before and after applying the GDS. The results indicate a similar classification accuracy with and without GDS. However, the training time demonstrates a reduction from approximately 90 min to 70 min, resulting in a 22% decrease in time and memory consumption. Following the classification, various explainable models were applied to the network to analyze the focused areas. This analysis aimed to identify the sections used for correct classification and those leading to incorrect classifications. Such insights allow model users to understand the model behavior and facilitate efforts to improve its performance in the future.

Table 5. Comparison of performance before and after Gaussian data selection (GDS).

	Accuracy	Recall	F1 Score	Training Time
Before GDS Results	86.54%	0.8681	0.8653	89.87 (min)
After GDS Results	85.82%	0.8614	0.8583	70.62 (min)

Figure 23 compares the performances before and after applying the GDS to the designed fusion model and existing transfer learning models, VGGish and YAMNet, in terms of accuracy, recall, and F1 score. Recall is an evaluation indicator representing the ratio of what the model predicts as positive to actual positives. The F1 score is the harmonic average of the model precision and recall and is an indicator of the evaluation by considering the two. YAMNet shows the lowest performance, and VGGish outperforms YAMNet. The designed model shows improved performance in terms of all evaluation indicators compared to the existing transfer learning model. There is only a small difference before and after applying the GDS.

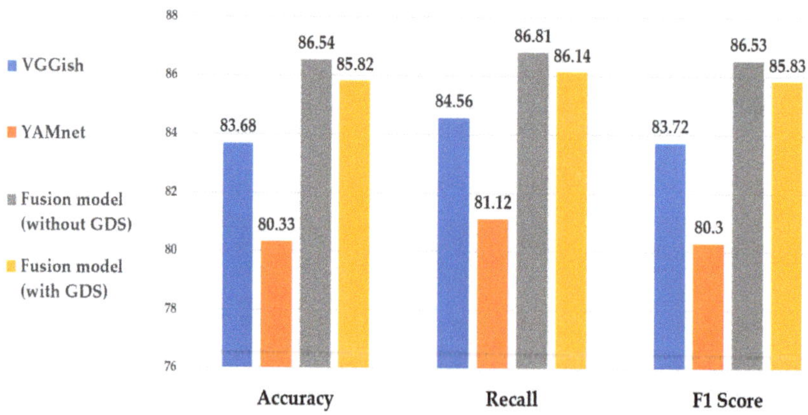

Figure 23. Performance comparison with existing models (accuracy, recall, and F1 score).

7.3. Focus Area Analysis with Explainable Model

Various preprocessing and training were performed to train the time–frequency characteristics related to emotion in the input data. Explainable techniques were subsequently used to confirm the features' components used for classifying the emotions in the model. Figure 24 shows the characteristics of the frequency domain. The activation for each emotion can be determined based on the statistics of the entire dataset. In the case of anger and happiness, relatively high-frequency regions are commonly activated, whereas in the case of neutrals and sadness, lower-frequency regions are activated.

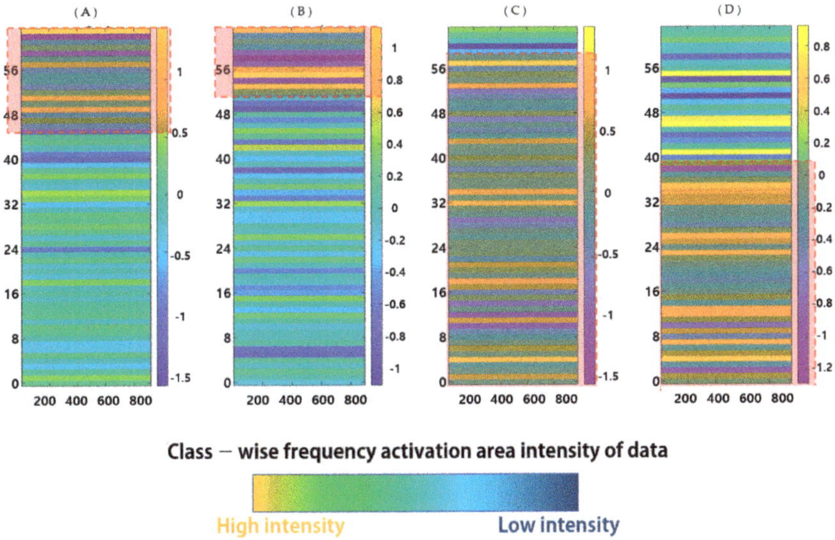

Figure 24. Emotional activation frequency region: (**A**) angry, (**B**) happy, (**C**) neutral, and (**D**) sad.

Figure 25 shows the activated area when the speech obtained using lines related to anger is converted into a spectrogram. The focused area is analyzed using the trained model and Grad CAM. The above method can be seen in the red area, where the time–frequency region influences the decision-making of the model. It is confirmed that the model focuses on areas with large values and combines areas with various values to classify emotions.

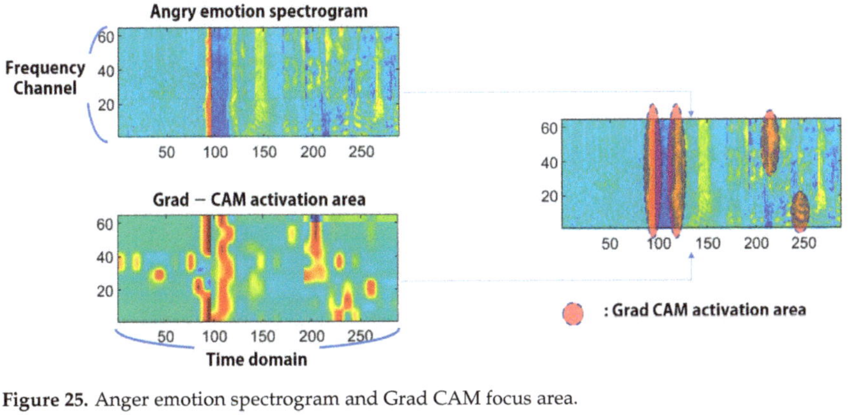

Figure 25. Anger emotion spectrogram and Grad CAM focus area.

Figures 26–29 show images that verify the model's decision-making process by applying Grad CAM, LIME, and occlusion sensitivity to the speech spectrograms. In images in which the explainable technique is applied, areas of the input spectrogram that influence the model's decision-making can be identified. Grad CAM uses gradient information through class scores in the model. Therefore, it has a high level of interpretation regarding which areas are important. In the case of LIME and occlusion sensitivity, by checking the extent to which a certain area influences the model classification, the areas that affect classification differently from Grad CAM can be determined.

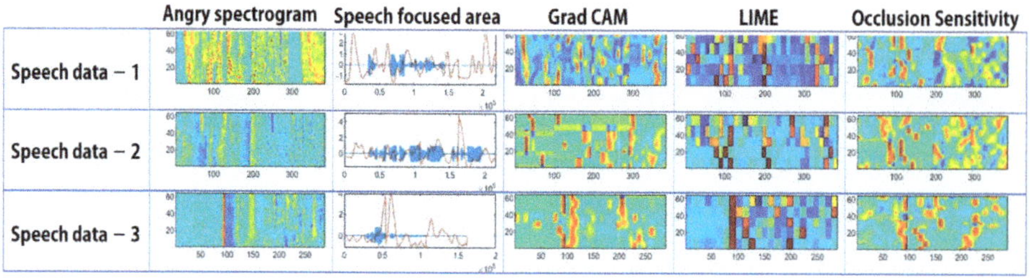

Figure 26. Anger emotion spectrogram (raw signal, Grad CAM, LIME, and occlusion sensitivity).

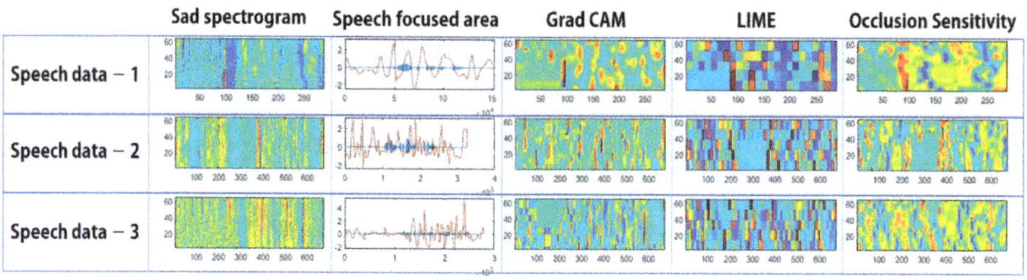

Figure 27. Sad emotion spectrogram (raw signal, Grad CAM, LIME, and occlusion sensitivity).

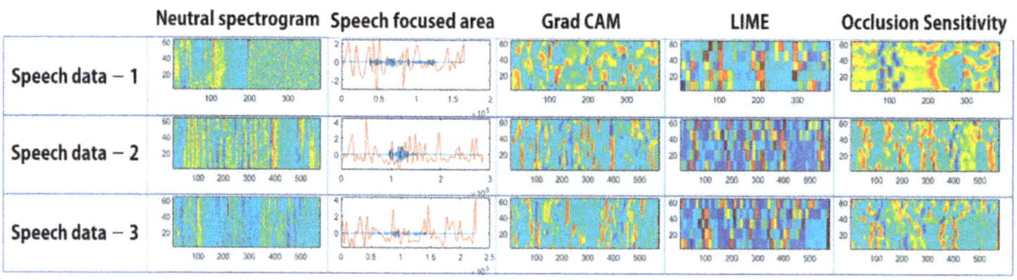

Figure 28. Neutral emotion spectrogram (raw signal, Grad CAM, LIME, and occlusion sensitivity).

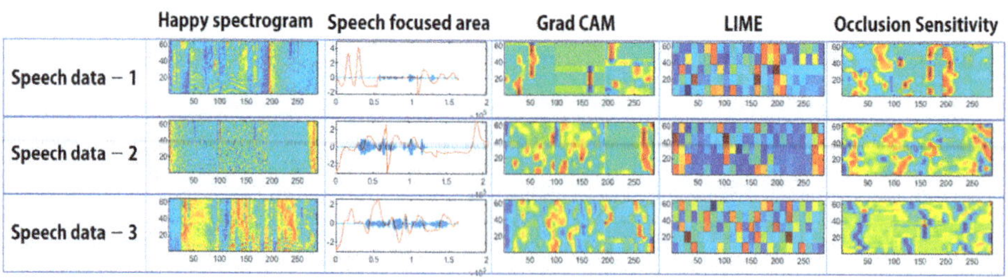

Figure 29. Happy emotion spectrogram (raw signal, Grad CAM, LIME, and occlusion sensitivity).

7.4. Applying the Focus Areas of the Explainable Models to Audio

Figure 30 shows that the influence of the frequency, obtained from Grad CAM, is added to the time domain to examine time features rather than frequency features in the input image. Many frequency areas are considered to be concentrated in specific periods, indicating that words or intonation during these times play an important role in classification. When the parameters used for spectrogram conversion are reversed to restore the size of the original speech signal, it becomes difficult to perceive it audibly due to noise. Therefore, convolution with a filter value of one is applied to a rapidly vibrating part and postprocessed to stabilize it, ensuring it sounds natural when heard. Speech from areas with positive activation values are then extracted to determine which words, phrases, and intonations influence the classification decision.

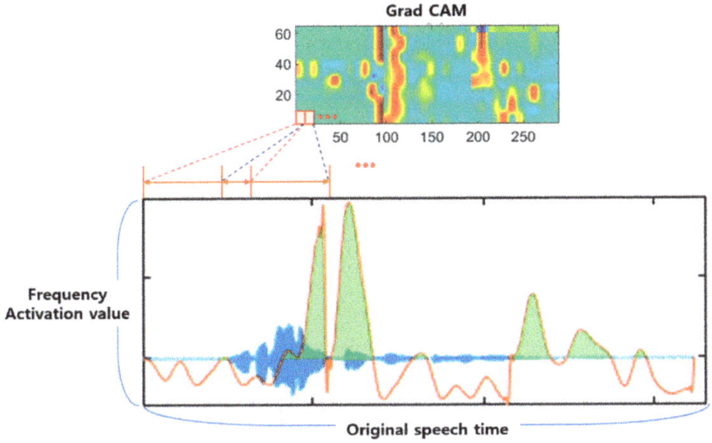

Figure 30. Restoration of audio signal using Grad CAM with a focus on specific areas in the image.

Figure 31 shows, among the happy emotion lines, the line "Call for sure, I love skiing so much." The line is analyzed by restoring the audio resolution to the area that the model focused on when classifying the emotion. When analyzing the visually expressed activation area by applying it to speech, the model focuses on the sections "for sure" and "so much". Therefore, it is confirmed that the focus is on the emotional characteristics that appear in each emotion's intonation or word elements during speech. In the case of a neutral emotion, we identified the focus on uniform distribution throughout the dialogue.

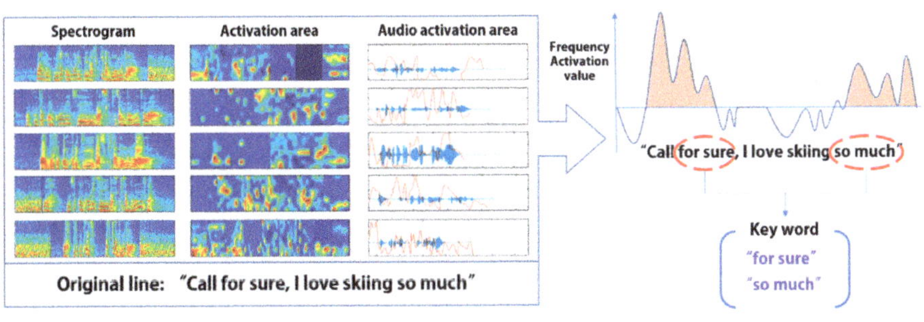

Figure 31. Applying the happy emotion Grad CAM focus area to speech data.

8. Conclusions

In this study, we conducted a study to learn the emotion classification model through various Korean-based data and to increase the reliability of the classification results. In order to enhance the accuracy of model decision-making, uncertain factors must be minimized during the learning process, and generalization capabilities must be achieved by extracting a lot of information from input data. To do this, we created refined data through a Gaussian data selection algorithm that selects the data needed as a correlation coefficient by representing data from three datasets converted into spectrograms with STFTs as Gaussian distributions for each segmented interval. Through this algorithm, unnecessary elements were reduced to make learning clearer, and the required learning time and computing resources could be reduced. In order to learn accurate features from the refined data, YAMNet and VGGish were combined, resulting in the generation of structural features for each model. This confirmed that combining each model in the proposed manner has higher performance than using it individually. The trained model confirmed the decision-making process in many aspects by applying various explanatory techniques. By analyzing the two-dimensional activation area in both time and frequency domains, respectively, the frequency domain activated for each emotion was identified, and the model's concentration area was converted into an audio file to directly check the process. In this study, the activation area of the model was converted into an audio file so that it could be confirmed. However, there is a limitation wherein people may not understand the output if the model does not focus on word features. In future studies, it is expected that this research will contribute to the classification of voice emotions by assessing whether high performance is maintained in data from other languages and by further investigating whether the activation area can be correctly identified.

Author Contributions: Conceptualization, T.-W.K. and K.-C.K.; methodology, T.-W.K. and K.-C.K.; software, T.-W.K. and K.-C.K.; validation, T.-W.K. and K.-C.K.; formal analysis, T.-W.K. and K.-C.K.; investigation, T.-W.K.; resources, K.-C.K.; data curation, K.-C.K.; writing—original draft preparation, T.-W.K.; writing—review and editing, K.-C.K.; visualization, T.-W.K. and K.-C.K.; supervision, K.-C.K.; project administration, K.-C.K.; funding acquisition, K.-C.K. All authors have read and agreed to the published version of the manuscript.

Funding: This study was supported by a research fund from Chosun University, 2023.

Institutional Review Board Statement: Not applicable.

Informed Consent Statement: Not applicable.

Data Availability Statement: Not applicable.

Conflicts of Interest: The authors declare no conflict of interest.

Abbreviations

SER	Speech emotion recognition	IEMOCAP	Interactive emotional dyadic motion capture database
STFT	Short-time Fourier transform	MUOC	Massive open online course
Grad CAM	Gradient-weighted class activation mapping	EMO	Emotional speech database
LIME	Local interpretable model-agnostic explanations	CASIA	Chinese Academy of Sciences Institute of Automation
VGGish	Visual geometry group-like audio classification model	VCTK	Voice cloning toolkit
YAMNet	Yet another mobile network	DCASE	Detection and classification of acoustic scenes and events
GDS	Gaussian data selection	DIRAMS	Dongnam Institute of Radiological & Medical Sciences
CNN	Convolutional neural network	AI	Artificial intelligence
LSTM	Long short-term memory	CSU	Chosun University
UA	Unweighted accuracy	RF	Random forest
WA	Weighted accuracy	MLAs	Machine learning algorithms
MFCC	Mel-frequency cepstral coefficients	UAR	Unweighted average recall
SVM	Support vector machine	MAA	Macro average accuracy

References

1. Mekruksavanich, S.; Jitpattanakul, A. Sensor-based Complex Human Activity Recognition from Smartwatch Data Using Hybrid Deep Learning Network. In Proceedings of the 36th International Technical Conference on Circuits/Systems, Computers and Communications (ITC-CSCC), Jeju, Republic of Korea, 27–30 June 2021; pp. 1–4.
2. Nassif, A.B.; Shahin, I.; Attili, I.; Azzeh, M.; Shaalan, K. Speech recognition using deep neural networks: A systematic review. *IEEE Access* **2019**, *7*, 19143–19165. [CrossRef]
3. Latif, S.; Qadir, J.; Qayyum, A.; Usama, M.; Younis, S. Speech technology for healthcare: Opportunities, challenges, and state of the art. *IEEE Rev. Biomed. Eng.* **2020**, *14*, 342–356. [CrossRef] [PubMed]
4. Cho, J.; Kim, B. Performance analysis of speech recognition model based on neuromorphic architecture of speech data preprocessing technique. *J. Inst. Internet Broadcast Commun.* **2022**, *22*, 69–74.

5. Lee, S.; Park, H. Deep-learning-based Gender Recognition Using Various Voice Features. In Proceedings of the Symposium of the Korean Institute of Communications and Information Sciences, Seoul, Republic of Korea, 17–19 November 2021; pp. 18–19.
6. Fonseca, A.H.; Santana, G.M.; Bosque Ortiz, G.M.; Bampi, S.; Dietrich, M.O. Analysis of ultrasonic vocalizations from mice using computer vision and machine learning. *Elife* **2021**, *10*, e59161. [CrossRef] [PubMed]
7. Lee, Y.; Lim, S.; Kwak, I.Y. CNN-based acoustic scene classification system. *Electronics* **2021**, *10*, 371. [CrossRef]
8. Ma, X.; Wu, Z.; Jia, J.; Xu, M.; Meng, H.; Cai, L. Emotion recognition from variable-length speech segments using deep learning on spectrograms. *Proc. Interspeech* **2018**, *2018*, 3683–3687.
9. Badshah, A.M.; Ahmad, J.; Rahim, N.; Baik, S.W. Speech Emotion Recognition from Spectrograms with Deep Convolutional Neural Network. In Proceedings of the 2017 International Conference on Platform Technology and Service (PlatCon), Busan, Republic of Korea, 13–15 February 2017; pp. 1–5.
10. Zhang, S.; Li, C. Research on feature fusion speech emotion recognition technology for smart teaching. *Mob. Inf. Syst.* **2022**, *2022*, 7785929. [CrossRef]
11. Subramanian, R.R.; Sireesha, Y.; Reddy, Y.S.P.K.; Bindamrutha, T.; Harika, M.; Sudharsan, R.R. Audio Emotion Recognition by Deep Neural Networks and Machine Learning Algorithms. In Proceedings of the 2021 International Conference on Advancements in Electrical, Electronics, Communication, Computing and Automation (ICAECA), Virtual Conference, 8–9 October 2021; pp. 1–6.
12. Zheng, L.; Li, Q.; Ban, H.; Liu, S. Speech Emotion Recognition Based on Convolution Neural Network Combined with Random Forest. In Proceedings of the 2018 Chinese Control and Decision Conference (CCDC), Shenyang, China, 9–11 June 2018; pp. 4143–4147.
13. Li, H.; Zhang, X.; Wang, M.J. Research on speech Emotion Recognition Based on Deep Neural Network. In Proceedings of the 2021 IEEE 6th International Conference on Signal and Image Processing (ICSIP), Nanjing, China, 22–24 October 2021; pp. 795–799.
14. Zhang, Y.; Du, J.; Wang, Z.; Zhang, J.; Tu, Y. Attention-based Fully Convolutional Network for Speech Emotion Recognition. In Proceedings of the 2018 Asia-Pacific Signal and Information Processing Association Annual Summit and Conference (APSIPA ASC), Honolulu, HI, USA, 12–15 November 2018; pp. 1771–1775.
15. Carofilis, A.; Alegre, E.; Fidalgo, E.; Fernández-Robles, L. Improvement of accent classification models through grad-transfer from spectrograms and gradient-weighted class activation mapping. *IEEE/ACM Trans. Audio Speech Lang. Process.* **2023**, *31*, 2859–2871. [CrossRef]
16. Bicer, H.N.; Götz, P.; Tuna, C.; Habets, E.A. Explainable Acoustic Scene Classification: Making Decisions Audible. In Proceedings of the 2022 International Workshop on Acoustic Signal Enhancement (IWAENC), Bamberg, Germany, 5–8 September 2022; pp. 1–5.
17. Cesarelli, M.; Di Giammarco, M.; Iadarola, G.; Martinelli, F.; Mercaldo, F.; Santone, A. Deep Learning for Heartbeat Phonocardiogram Signals Explainable Classification. In Proceedings of the 2022 IEEE 22nd International Conference on Bioinformatics and Bioengineering (BIBE), Taichung, Taiwan, 7–9 November 2022; pp. 75–78.
18. Lee, J.H.; Lee, C.Y.; Eom, J.S.; Pak, M.; Jeong, H.S.; Son, H.Y. Predictions for three-month postoperative vocal recovery after thyroid surgery from spectrograms with deep neural network. *Sensors* **2022**, *22*, 6387. [CrossRef] [PubMed]
19. Selvaraju, R.R.; Cogswell, M.; Das, A.; Vedantam, R.; Parikh, D.; Batra, D. Grad-cam: Visual explanations from deep networks via gradient-based localization. In Proceedings of the IEEE International Conference on Computer Vision 2017, Venice, Italy, 22–29 October 2017; pp. 618–626.
20. Ribeiro, M.T.; Singh, S.; Guestrin, C. "Why should I trust you?" Explaining the predictions of any classifier. In Proceedings of the 22nd ACM SIGKDD International Conference on Knowledge Discovery and Data Mining, San Francisco, CA, USA, 13–17 August 2016; pp. 1135–1144.
21. Available online: http://www.aihub.or.kr/aihubdata/data/view.do?currMenu=120&topMenu=100&dataSetSn=259&aihubDataSe=extrldata (accessed on 13 October 2023).

applied sciences

MDPI

Article

The Quantification of Myocardial Fibrosis on Human Histopathology Images by a Semi-Automatic Algorithm

Diana Gonciar [1,2], Alexandru-George Berciu [3,*], Alex Ede Danku [3], Noemi Lorenzovici [3], Eva-Henrietta Dulf [3,*], Teodora Mocan [4,5], Sorina-Melinda Nicula [6] and Lucia Agoston-Coldea [1]

1 2nd Department of Internal Medicine, Iuliu Hațieganu University of Medicine and Pharmacy, 400012 Cluj-Napoca, Romania; dianagonciar@gmail.com (D.G.); luciacoldea@yahoo.com (L.A.-C.)
2 Department of Pathology, Iuliu Hațieganu University of Medicine and Pharmacy, 400012 Cluj-Napoca, Romania
3 Automation Department, Faculty of Automation and Computer Science, Energy Transition Research Center, Technical University of Cluj-Napoca, 400114 Cluj-Napoca, Romania; alex.danku@aut.utcluj.ro (A.E.D.); noemi.lorenzovici@gmail.com (N.L.)
4 Physiology Department, Iuliu Hațieganu University of Medicine and Pharmacy, 400012 Cluj-Napoca, Romania; teodora_mocan@yahoo.com
5 Department of Nanomedicine, Regional Institute of Gastroenterology and Hepatology, 400158 Cluj-Napoca, Romania
6 Department of Pathology, Săcele Municipal Hospital, 505600 Săcele, Romania; nsorina.melinda@gmail.com
* Correspondence: alexandru.berciu@campus.utcluj.ro (A.-G.B.); eva.dulf@aut.utcluj.ro (E.-H.D.)

Abstract: (1) Background: Considering the increasing workload of pathologists, computer-assisted methods have the potential to come to their aid. Considering the prognostic role of myocardial fibrosis, its precise quantification is essential. Currently, the evaluation is performed semi-quantitatively by the pathologist, a method exposed to the issues of subjectivity. The present research proposes validating a semi-automatic algorithm that aims to quantify myocardial fibrosis on microscopic images. (2) Methods: Forty digital images were selected from the slide collection of The Iowa Virtual Slidebox, from which the collagen volume fraction (CVF) was calculated using two semi-automatic methods: CIELAB-MATLAB® and CIELAB-Python. These involve the use of color difference analysis, using Delta E, in a rectangular region for CIELAB-Python and a region with a random geometric shape, determined by the user's cursor movement, for CIELAB-MATLAB®. The comparison was made between the stereological evaluation and ImageJ. (3) Results: A total of 36 images were included in the study ($n = 36$), demonstrating a high, statistically significant correlation between stereology and ImageJ on the one hand, and the proposed methods on the other ($p < 0.001$). The mean CVF determined by the two methods shows a mean bias of 1.5% compared with stereology and 0.9% compared with ImageJ. Conclusions: The combined algorithm has a superior performance compared to the proposed methods, considered individually. Despite the relatively small mean bias, the limits of agreement are quite wide, reflecting the variability of the images included in the study.

Keywords: machine learning; myocardial fibrosis; semi-automatic quantification

1. Introduction

Heart failure is a condition with a strong negative impact on the survival of patients, as well as having a high financial burden due to its increased incidence, with a lifetime risk of occurrence of 20% [1]. The mechanism behind it is the cardiac remodeling process, which includes cardiomyocyte injury (hypertrophy, apoptosis and necrosis) and fibrosis [2]. In myocardial fibrosis, type I collagen predominantly accumulates (to the detriment of type III collagen), which is more stable and rigid; the consequences of this are increased myocardial stiffness, decreased contractility, diastolic dysfunction, decreased myocardial perfusion, and increased risk of arrhythmia [3]. Considering the prognostic role of fibrosis, its identification is essential [4]. Current assessment options include serum markers, magnetic resonance imaging, and endomyocardial biopsy [5]. The histological evaluation of fibrosis is still the gold standard, with the significant disadvantage that it may miss a focal process due to spatial heterogeneity and the fact that extensive sampling is not feasible [5].

In both endomyocardial biopsies and autopsy specimens, the assessment of fibrosis is part of the pathologist's routine activities. Myocardial fibrosis is of two types: diffuse and replacement [6]. Replacement fibrosis involves the necrosis of cardiomyocytes and their replacement with scar tissue, thus leading to thick collagen fibers that form confluent areas of more than 2 mm, uninterrupted by the interposition of cardiomyocytes [7]. Diffuse fibrosis includes interstitial and perivascular fibrosis, resulting in the accumulation of fine collagen fibers (of approximately 10–500 μm) surrounding groups of cardiomyocytes or individual cells, without forming confluent areas [7]. Diffuse fibrosis comprises three patterns, which most often coexist: microscars (small areas of replacement fibrosis arising in the context of isolated cardiomyocyte death), perivascular deposits (around arterioles and intramyocardial vascular branches), and deposits around the perimysium and endomysium [8].

The extent of fibrosis can be quantified by measuring the collagen volume fraction (CVF), which represents the ratio of the proportion of collagen and the totality of the examined myocardial tissue, being reported to have a prognostic role in patients with hypertrophic cardiomyopathy [9]. The assessment can also be performed semi-quantitatively, although the threshold values for defining severe fibrosis are highly variable from one study to another [5], without a consensus at the moment. Although special stains for collagen fibers are used to evaluate fibrosis, the hematoxylin–eosin (H&E) stain is routinely performed in laboratories, being inexpensive and rapid. It allows fibrosis visualization, although it provides low contrast compared to other stains [10].

As a result of digitization, numerous computational methods have been developed to assist physicians and, at the same time, to encourage standardization [11–14]. Several methods to quantify fibrosis on microscopic images have been reported, but most are focused on the liver [15,16] and kidney [17]. Additionally, the technical details available in the literature are few, and the validation is frequently performed via semi-quantitative comparison performed by the pathologist, which is influenced by subjectivity and brings an additional volume of work [18]. As a result of the significant development of omic technologies, the quantitative information generated based on the analyzed biological processes requires the integration and modeling of the data, an area where machine learning strategies can have an impact [19,20]. In cardiovascular pathology, a computational sequencing method was applied for the spatial transcriptomics of the aorta dissection, succeeding in the spatial localization of different cell subpopulations [21]. Employing a technique based on graph contrastive learning and multi-task learning can enhance spatial localization in transcriptomics [22]. Single-cell RNA sequencing is the preferred method for highlighting distinct, unknown cells and might also be performed to evaluate intercellular communication and the mechanisms of fibrogenesis in the heart [23]. Still, the performance of studies in this field is limited by the missing values arising from biological considerations [24]. Machine learning methods [25] or deep learning models are proposed to tackle this challenge [26].

The present paper proposes the validation of a machine learning algorithm developed on digital images, which aims to quantify collagen deposition in the myocardium using the usual H&E staining. This will facilitate the work of the pathologist by providing a fast, easy-to-use tool that creates the premises of reproducibility in the quantification of fibrosis. The method is based on the CIELAB color space color variation analysis algorithm implemented in MATLAB® version R2024a and Python version 3.11.7. The implementation in MATLAB® started from results available in [27] and has been improved to work efficiently on histopathologic images, while the implementation in Python belongs to the authors of this paper. The proposed method will be tested by stereology; the preferred method will be used when it is desired to obtain quantitative data from microscopic sections [28], and the quantification will be performed by ImageJ, the most widely used software in this field [29].

2. Materials and Methods

2.1. Database Creation and Image Analysis

Forty digital images of myocardial fibrosis were extracted from the histopathology collection of the digital slide collection of The Iowa Virtual Slidebox [30] using Biolucida Cloud Viewer (version 2024.2.0; MBF Bioscience-MicroBrightField, Inc., Williston, VT, USA). Those considered relevant were selected by the pathologist, excluding the subendocardial and subepicardial areas, or the region close to the heart valves. For the qualitative evaluation of the performance of the algorithm, the images obtained immediately after the application of the algorithm were also acquired, later being visually compared by the pathologist with the original ones. Two pathologists manually outlined the areas of myocardial fibrosis to serve as a model for the selection of the region of interest by the researchers who developed and implemented the algorithm.

2.2. Stereology Analysis

Regarding Stereology Analyzer (version 4.3.4; ADCIS, Saint Contest, France), the software superimposes a grid over the image to be analyzed, whose pattern and spacing can be changed. For the present work, we used a sampling interval of 30 pixels and a pattern size of 7 pixels, resulting in a minimum of 599 test points for the evaluated images. Each test point was manually evaluated by the pathologist and classified as having fibrosis or not. In the end, the program automatically generates stereology volume fraction (%), in this case CVF, which was calculated as the ratio between the number of test points with fibrosis and the total number of control points.

2.3. ImageJ Analysis

CVF determination by ImageJ, version 1.54g (Wayne Rasband and contributors, National Institutes of Health, Bethesda, MD, USA; http://imagej.org (accessed on 1 August 2024)) was performed manually as follows: after opening the image, converting to grayscale and adjusting contrast and brightness, thresholding values were set to select only areas with fibrosis. Thresholding was performed manually for each image, selecting the "Default" option from the ImageJ menu. The threshold adjustment was performed visually, so the region of interest could be properly highlighted.

For segmentation and measurements, the binary conversion of the image was performed, and through the "Analyze Particles" option, the CVF value was obtained.

Stereology and ImageJ evaluation were performed by the same pathologist 3 months apart, blinded to the results obtained by the other methods.

2.4. Algorithm Description

The developed algorithm is based on the implementation in two programming languages, Python and MATLAB®, of the color analysis method based on the CIELAB spectrum [31]. The multi-language implementation, together with the differentiation of the fibrosis mini-region selection mode, ensures robustness in terms of testing the capabilities of the CIELAB color spectrum in semi-automated fibrosis detection from histopathology images.

In both cases, the first step is to select a histopathological image that the user wishes to analyze. The next step appeals to the user's knowledge of histopathologic analysis and involves the manual selection of a small part of the histopathologic image that contains fibrosis based on the user's knowledge. In the MATLAB® implementation, the region has an irregular geometric shape and is determined by the cursor movement, while in Python, the region will always have a rectangular shape.

The next step is performed automatically and involves the color analysis of the region selected by the user. Starting from this color, the developed algorithm analyzes the whole histopathologic image at the pixel level and marks as fibrosis any pixel that has the specific color of the region selected by the user, taking into account the Delta E metric in the CIELAB color space. If the user does not have the necessary skills and selects a mini-region that does not contain fibrosis tissue, the algorithm will generate inappropriate results, detecting tissues in the whole image with a chromaticity similar to the one selected by the user.

The final result is represented as a new image in which the fibrosis tissue is marked using a different color from the original histopathological image. In addition, the performance metrics related to the number of fibrotic pixels, the original image size and the percentage of fibrotic tissue in the entire image are returned to the user in numerical form.

The flow diagram of the system is presented in Figure 1.

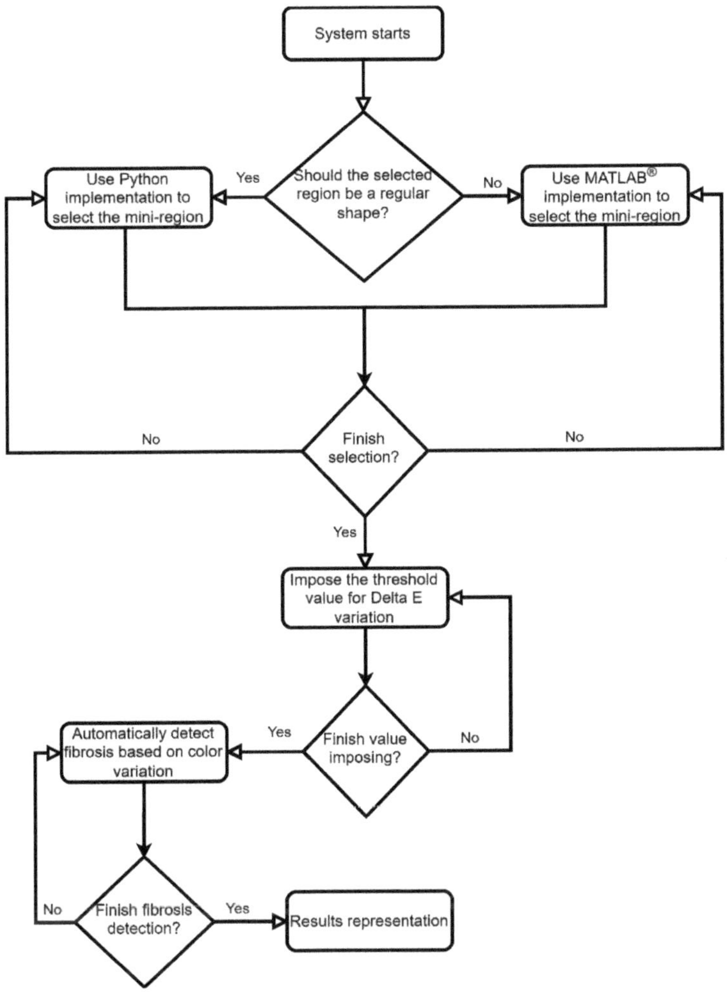

Figure 1. The flow diagram of the system.

2.5. Statistical Analysis

Data were analyzed with the Kolmogorov–Smirnov test to assess the distribution of the variables. Normally distributed results are presented as mean ± standard deviation (SD) or as 95% confidence interval (CI), or as median (25–75% interquartile range [IQR]) if non-normally distributed. The Pearson coefficient (r) was performed to evaluate the correlation between groups, being interpreted as follows: >0.7, very high correlation; 0.5–0.7, high correlation; 0.3–0.5, moderate correlation; 0.1–0.3, weak correlation; and <0.1, no correlation. Differences between groups were measured using the *t*-test for paired samples. For multiple comparisons, the Analysis of Variance (ANOVA) was used followed by the Bonferroni post hoc test to assess differences between each pair.

The Bland–Altman analysis was performed to test the concordance between methods. $p < 0.05$ was considered statistically significant. Online Statistics Calculator (DATAtab e.U. Graz, Austria. URL https://datatab.net (accessed on 1 August 2024)) and MedCalc Statistical Software version 22.032 (MedCalc Software Ltd., Ostend, Belgium; https://www.medcalc.org (accessed on 1 August 2024)) were used for the statistical analysis.

3. Results

Of the 40 images manually extracted from The Iowa Virtual Slidebox [30] with myocardial fibrosis, 1 was excluded because the stereological evaluation was difficult (pale colors, imprecise demarcation between cardiomyocytes and collagen fibers), and another 3 were excluded because the evaluation in ImageJ raised difficulties (poor contrast between fibrosis area and normal cardiomyocytes), resulting in a database of 36 images (n = 36). The means and SDs of CVF obtained by the four methods are shown in Table 1. All data were normally distributed.

Table 1. Descriptive parameters of the percentages of fibrosis assessed by different methods.

	ImageJ (%)	Stereology (%)	CIELAB-Python (%)	CIELAB-MATLAB® (%)
n	36	36	36	36
Mean ± SD	29.76 ± 7.25	30.33 ± 10.56	36.46 ± 8.11	21.29 ± 5.01

SD standard deviation.

When comparing CVF determined using ImageJ with that determined by stereology, a mean difference of 0.57% (95% CI: 1.26–2.4) was observed, with no significant difference between the two groups ($p = 0.532$). The Pearson correlation coefficient showed that there is a very high, statistically significant correlation between the two ($r = 0.88$, $p < 0.001$).

3.1. Performance Evaluation of the Algorithm Implemented in CIELAB-Python

CVF determined by running CIELAB-Python shows a high, positive, and statistically significant correlation, both with stereology ($r = 0.51$, $p = 0.001$) and ImageJ ($r = 0.56$, $p < 0.001$). Statistically significant differences were observed between CVF, determined on the one hand by CIELAB-Python, and on the other by stereology ($p < 0.001$) and ImageJ ($p < 0.001$). The mean differences were 6.13% (95% CI: 2.98–9.34) and 6.7% (95% CI: 4.24–9.17). In Figure 2, the images processed by ImageJ (A) and CIELAB-Python (B) are presented.

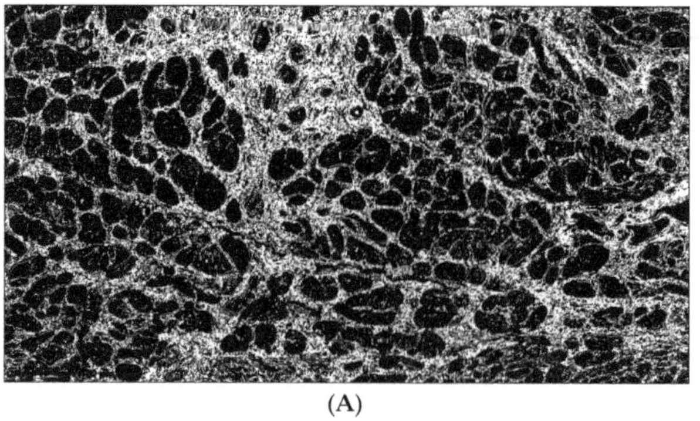

(A)

Figure 2. *Cont.*

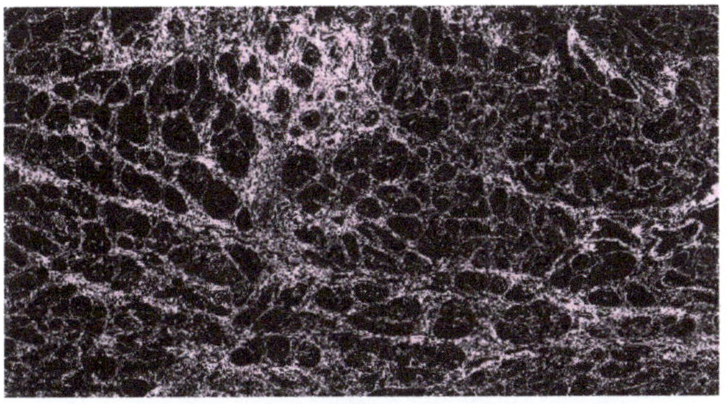

(B)

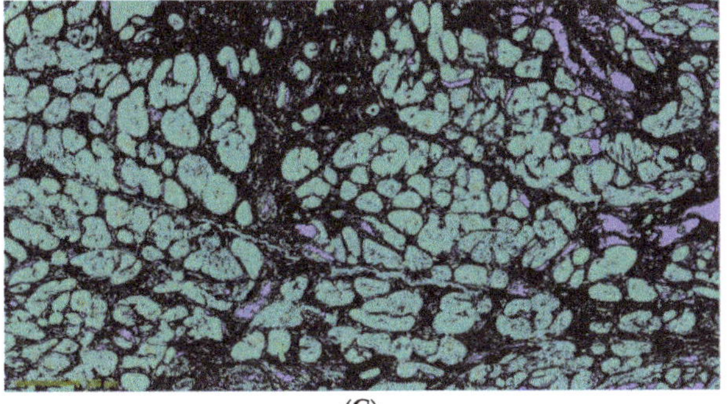

(C)

Figure 2. (**A**) Binary image after processing in ImageJ (fibrosis is represented in white). (**B**) CIELAB-MATLAB® (fibrosis is represented in pink). (**C**) CIELAB-Python (fibrosis is represented in black). Original image: The Iowa Virtual Slidebox [30].

3.2. Performance Evaluation of the Algorithm Implemented in CIELAB-MATLAB®

CVF determined by running CIELAB-MATLAB® showed a high, positive, and statistically significant correlation with both stereology (r = 0.64, $p < 0.001$) and ImageJ (r = 0.6, $p < 0.001$). Statistically significant differences were observed between CVF, determined on the one hand by CIELAB-MATLAB®, and on the other by stereology ($p < 0.001$) and ImageJ ($p < 0.001$). The mean differences were 9.04 (95% CI: 6.22–11.86) and 8.47% (95% CI: 6.49–10.49). Figure 2B highlights the generated layout. The pixels colored in black were those quantified by the algorithm.

3.3. Performance Evaluation of the Combined Algorithm

For further evaluations, the mean CVF between CIELAB-MATLAB® and CIELAB-Python (mean MATLAB®-Python) was calculated for each image.

The differences between the percentages determined by ImageJ, stereology and mean MATLAB®-Python were evaluated with the ANOVA test, which revealed no statistically significant difference between groups ($p = 0.45$). The results of Bonferroni post hoc tests are shown in Table 2.

The Pearson correlation coefficient showed that there is a high, positive, and statistically significant correlation between mean MATLAB®-Python and ImageJ and stereology (r = 0.59, $p < 0.001$ and r = 0.58, $p < 0.001$, respectively), with no significant differences between the two groups ($p = 0.39$). The results of the Bland–Altman analysis are shown in Table 3 and Figure 3A.

The Pearson correlation coefficient showed that there is a high, positive, and statistically significant correlation between stereology and mean MATLAB®-Python (r = 0.58, $p <$

0.001), with no significant differences between the two groups (p = 0.318). The results of the Bland–Altman analysis are shown in Figure 3B and Table 4.

Table 2. Bonferroni post hoc tests.

		Mean Diff.	Std. Error	t	p	95% CI Lower Limit	95% CI Upper Limit
Stereology (%)	ImageJ (%)	0.57	0.901	0.631	1	−1.26	2.4
Stereology (%)	Mean MATLAB®-Python	1.45	1.434	1.013	0.954	−1.46	4.37
ImageJ (%)	Mean MATLAB®-Python	0.88	1.031	0.858	1	−1.21	2.98

CI confidence interval.

Table 3. Summary of Bland–Altman analysis of the percentages of fibrosis returned by the mean MATLAB®-Python and ImageJ.

Summary of Bland–Altman	
Arithmetic mean	0.8847
95% Confidence interval	−1.2087 to 2.9782
P (H_0: Mean = 0)	0.3968
Lower limit	−11.2423
95% Confidence interval	−14.8535 to −7.6310
Upper limit	13.0117
95% Confidence interval	9.4005 to 16.6230

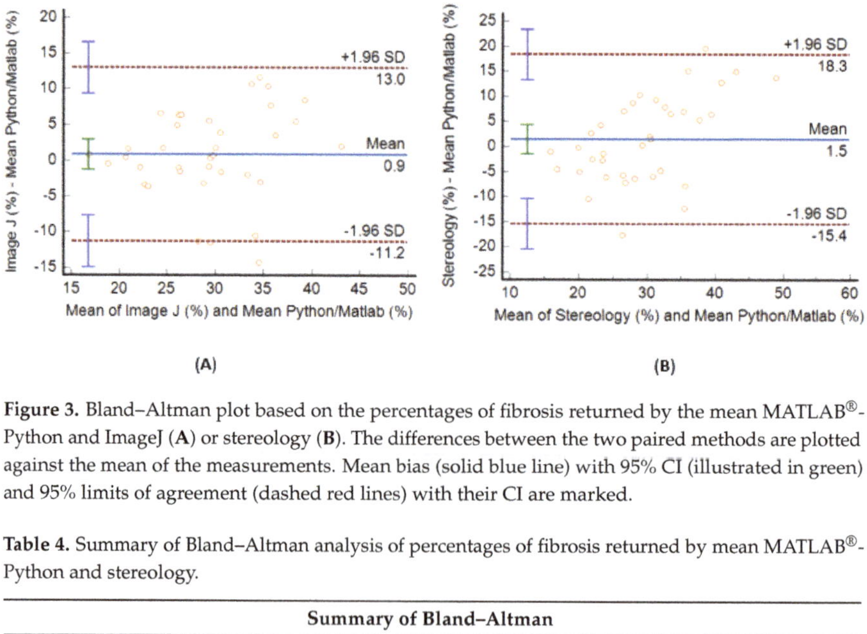

Figure 3. Bland–Altman plot based on the percentages of fibrosis returned by the mean MATLAB®-Python and ImageJ (**A**) or stereology (**B**). The differences between the two paired methods are plotted against the mean of the measurements. Mean bias (solid blue line) with 95% CI (illustrated in green) and 95% limits of agreement (dashed red lines) with their CI are marked.

Table 4. Summary of Bland–Altman analysis of percentages of fibrosis returned by mean MATLAB®-Python and stereology.

Summary of Bland–Altman	
Arithmetic mean	1.4531
95% Confidence interval	−1.4582 to 4.3643
P (H_0: Mean = 0)	0.3179
Lower limit	−15.4111
95% Confidence interval	−20.4330 to −10.3892
Upper limit	18.3172
95% Confidence interval	23.3391

4. Discussion

Remarkable advances have been made in the field of medical imaging in recent years thanks to the use of digitalized methods and, more recently, artificial intelligence [32,33].

The problem of validating the existing models is that comparisons are made with the visual assessment performed by the pathologist, which is subject to variability [18]. Stereology allows for the three-dimensional quantitative evaluation of two-dimensional microscopic sections, based on a mathematical principle derived from stochastic geometry [34]. Although a time-consuming method requiring manual analysis of each test point, it remains the gold standard for obtaining quantitative data [28]. Although it was observed that the CVF determined by stereology shows a high correlation with the CVF determined by CIELAB-MATLAB® and with that determined by CIELAB-Python, statistically significant differences were observed between the groups, which is why the performance of the combined algorithm was further tested. The CVF, calculated as the average of the values generated by the two algorithms, was not significantly different from the CVF calculated by stereology. Considering that any quantitative assessment involves error, the Bland–Altman analysis aims to establish the degree of agreement between two quantitative methods, allowing comparability [35]. Besides the quantification of mean bias, the method involves the expression of the limits of agreement (LoA), an interval in which 95% of the measured differences are included [35]. The Bland–Altman analysis revealed a relatively small mean of the differences between the two methods (1.5%), which was not significant, considering that the line of equality was included in the 95% CI of the mean difference. However, the LoA were relatively large (95% LoA—15.4–18.3).

Many image analysis programs have been developed over time, but ImageJ remains the most widely used [36], which is the reason why it was chosen as a second method for the validation of the results. A disadvantage of ImageJ is that low-contrast tissues can be difficult to assess [29], therefore three of the images were excluded from the study. A high correlation was also observed between the CVF determined by ImageJ and CIELAB-MATLAB® and CIELAB-Python, respectively, but still with significant differences between groups. The combined algorithm, however, showed a superior performance, with a mean bias of 0.9%, which was not significant (95% CI—1.2–2.9), and a narrower LoA than in the case of the comparison with stereology (95% LoA—11.2–13). Although the two proposed methods (MATLAB®, Python) quantify the same parameter, they offer different results because they are based on different approaches. The fibrosis mini-region is manually selected by the user, which induces randomness based on expertise. Furthermore, in MATLAB®, the selected region can have any shape, while in Python the selected region will always be a rectangle. In addition to the different working principles of the evaluated methods, the significant differences observed between the groups can also be caused by the management of the artifacts. In stereology, each test point is approached individually by the pathologist, while the algorithms implemented in Python or MATLAB® decide if a pixel represents fibrosis or not, depending on the color analysis.

Computer-assisted quantification of myocardial fibrosis is not a new idea, but it is an under-investigated field. A semi-automatic method implemented in ImageJ, also based on the CIELAB system reported by Hadi AM et al. [37], shows a very high correlation with stereology. The method was tested on post-mortem myocardial tissue stained with picrosirius red. The researchers reported a significant reduction in the time needed for evaluation (22% of the time needed for stereology). Stereology was also used as a reference in the study performed by Daunoravicius D et al. [18], which tested the assessment of fibrosis on endomyocardial biopsies. The authors proposed two different algorithms, based on colocalization and pattern recognition, both with high correlation with stereology, but with a minimal underestimation of the second one. The mean bias reported was close to zero, with the LoA was around $\pm$10%. In the study by Vasiljević JD et al. [38], the commercially available software tested, which identifies fibrosis based on color analysis, overestimated CVF by 3 $\pm$ 6.7%, with LoA of up to 16.3%. The LoA identified in the present study for the combined method, compared to stereology, is in line with those mentioned in the previous studies. Another method proposed by Zimmermann E et al. [39] for the quantification of myocardial fibrosis assumed infrared spectroscopic imaging combined with machine learning algorithms, and was able to generate virtual images stained with picrosirius red. Multiphoton microscopy has also proven its valuable contribution in this field, being able to visualize the microscopic structure of the myocardium on unstained sections [40].

The aim of this study was to validate a facile, semi-automatic method to quantify myocardial fibrosis and to compare it with stereological and ImageJ evaluation. In the case of this paper, the manual identification of fibrosis using histopathologic images was performed by two pathologists, and the user of the software application selected the mini-region, taking into account the manual markings. Moderate performances were observed for the proposed methods; however, performance was superior in the case of the combined method. Another limitation was caused by the examination of digital images, and not of the slide as a whole, which is why the calculated percentages cannot refer to the entire tissue fragment [41]. In a real-world scenario, there is a possibility of over- or underestimation of fibrosis [42,43]. The semi-automatic character of the algorithm is also subjected to intra- and inter-observer variability, as the ROI must be selected by an expert in the field that can distinguish between normality and abnormality. Thereby, the algorithm can be an aid to the pathologist, not a substitute. In a real-world scenario, the pathologist will only need to identify a mini-region with fibrosis in a histopathological image, and the algorithm will automatically identify fibrosis in the whole image, calculate the percentage of fibrosis tissue in the whole image and represent this fibrosis tissue with a different color. All these features reduce the time needed for pathologists to manually evaluate histopathological images to detect fibrosis in real life.

The differences observed between the methods can also be caused by the fact that a special stain for collagen was not used, a fact that predisposes results to poor contrast [37]. Among the variety of staining methods for collagen emphasis, it appears that the most suitable is picrosirius red, combined with subsequent examination in polarized light [44]. It also has an affinity for the fine collagen type III fibers, unlike Van Gieson or Masson trichrome stainings [44]. Therefore, the results presented may be underestimated. Regardless of the stain chosen, color variation is a problem in digital pathology methods, being attributed to the staining (different staining conditions, different reagents) and scanning slides of under different conditions [45]. Significant qualitative differences have been reported, even among slides stained in the same laboratory [16]. An advantage of the methods analyzed in the present study is that they showed a strong correlation with ImageJ quantification and stereology, although the database included diverse images in terms of color variability, contrast and artifacts encountered. New deep learning methods can generate virtual images with certain special stains, starting from H&E [10], with the potential to generate more comparable images. It is also important to consider the thickness of the sections because the area of collagen deposition is proportional to it [42].

The very high correlation observed between CVF determined by stereology and that assessed by ImageJ shows us that, in the conditions of exposed variability, judicious examination by the pathologist is the one that receives and provides reproducible results, an observation that was also reported by Astbury et al. [16]. In the present paper, the thresholding in ImageJ was performed manually because it was reported to be more accurate compared to automatic or semi-automatic segmentation, even though is more time-consuming [46]. Even so, considering the manual nature of this stage, it is a source of error due to subjectivity [47]. Multiple automatic methods have been reported, but choosing one is still a personal decision [48].

The authors of the present paper are, however, aware of this study's limitations. The presented data represent a preliminary pilot study on the accuracy of CIELAB-Python and CIELAB-MATLAB®. In order to achieve a power of 80% and a level of significance of 5% (two-sided), for detecting a true difference in means between the test and the standard reference group, the authors calculated a required sample size of 97 images.

5. Conclusions

The combination of the two proposed methods (CIELAB-Python and CIELAB-MATLAB®) has the potential to provide pathologists with a semi-automated method for quantifying myocardial fibrosis on H&E-stained slides. The algorithm was compared with Stereology and ImageJ, being superior due to its ability to reduce the time dedicated to analysis. Although the differences between the methods were small, the limits of agreement were relatively large, reflecting the variability of the images included in the database. Even though the obtained results are encouraging, a retest of the method should be taken into consideration to eliminate variable factors, especially those caused by the stain, on a larger data set, including the algorithm's performance across multiple users or with different stains. Moreover, regarding future directions, considering the generality of the proposed method in this paper for color analysis and marking pixels having a color close to a selected mini-region, the algorithm may be tested on images with fibrosis with a different localization (liver, kidney) or even on different lesions involving chromaticity differences (calcifications, amyloid deposits), requiring only the change of the region selected by the user.

Author Contributions: Conceptualization, L.A.-C., E.-H.D. and T.M.; methodology, D.G., S.-M.N. and A.-G.B.; software, A.-G.B., A.E.D. and N.L.; validation, D.G. and A.-G.B.; writing—original draft preparation, D.G.; writing—review and editing, A.-G.B., A.E.D., N.L., S.-M.N., T.M., E.-H.D. and L.A.-C.; supervision L.A.-C. and E.-H.D. All authors have read and agreed to the published version of the manuscript.

Funding: This work was partially supported by a grant of the Ministry of Research, Innovation and Digitization, CNCS-UEFISCDI, project number PN-III-P4-PCE-2021-0750, within PNCDI III. Alexandru G. Berciu acknowledges project 38 PFE in the frame of the program PDI-PFE-CDI 2021.

Institutional Review Board Statement: Not applicable.

Informed Consent Statement: Patient consent was waived due to using only images extracted from the open access database (The Iowa Virtual Slidebox).

Data Availability Statement: The original contributions presented in the study are included in the article, further inquiries can be directed to the corresponding authors.

Acknowledgments: We acknowledge the contribution of the Iowa Virtual Slidebox, an open-access database, through which the microscopic images from the present study could be obtained.

Conflicts of Interest: The authors declare no conflicts of interest.

References

1. Yancy, C.W.; Jessup, M.; Bozkurt, B.; Butler, J.; Casey, D.E.; Drazner, M.H.; Fonarow, G.C.; Geraci, S.A.; Horwich, T.; Januzzi, J.L.; et al. 2013 ACCF/AHA Guideline for the Management of Heart Failure: Executive Summary. *Circulation* **2013**, *128*, 1810–1852. [CrossRef] [PubMed]
2. Schirone, L.; Forte, M.; Palmerio, S.; Yee, D.; Nocella, C.; Angelini, F.; Pagano, F.; Schiavon, S.; Bordin, A.; Carrizzo, A.; et al. A Review of the Molecular Mechanisms Underlying the Development and Progression of Cardiac Remodeling. *Oxid. Med. Cell Longev.* **2017**, *2017*, 3920195. [CrossRef]
3. Azevedo, P.S.; Polegato, B.F.; Minicucci, M.F.; Paiva, S.A.R.; Zornoff, L.A.M. Cardiac Remodeling: Concepts, Clinical Impact, Pathophysiological Mechanisms and Pharmacologic Treatment. *Arq. Bras. Cardiol.* **2016**, *106*, 62–69. [CrossRef]
4. Nauffal, V.; Di Achille, P.; Klarqvist, M.D.R.; Cunningham, J.W.; Hill, M.C.; Pirruccello, J.P.; Weng, L.-C.; Morrill, V.N.; Choi, S.H.; Khurshid, S.; et al. Genetics of Myocardial Interstitial Fibrosis in the Human Heart and Association with Disease. *Nat. Genet.* **2023**, *55*, 777–786. [CrossRef]
5. Liu, T.; Song, D.; Dong, J.; Zhu, P.; Liu, J.; Liu, W.; Ma, X.; Zhao, L.; Ling, S. Current Understanding of the Pathophysiology of Myocardial Fibrosis and Its Quantitative Assessment in Heart Failure. *Front. Physiol.* **2017**, *8*, 238. [CrossRef]
6. Bengel, F.M.; Diekmann, J.; Hess, A.; Jerosch-Herold, M. Myocardial Fibrosis: Emerging Target for Cardiac Molecular Imaging and Opportunity for Image-Guided Therapy. *J. Nucl. Med.* **2023**, *64*, S49–S58. [CrossRef]
7. Galati, G.; Leone, O.; Pasquale, F.; Olivotto, I.; Biagini, E.; Grigioni, F.; Pilato, E.; Lorenzini, M.; Corti, B.; Foà, A.; et al. Histological and Histometric Characterization of Myocardial Fibrosis in End-Stage Hypertrophic Cardiomyopathy. *Circ. Heart Fail.* **2016**, *9*, e003090. [CrossRef]

8. López, B.; Ravassa, S.; Moreno, M.U.; José, G.S.; Beaumont, J.; González, A.; Díez, J. Diffuse Myocardial Fibrosis: Mechanisms Diagnosis and Therapeutic Approaches. *Nat. Rev. Cardiol.* **2021**, 18, 479–498. [CrossRef] [PubMed]
9. Arteaga, E.; de Araújo, A.Q.; Bernstein, M.; Ramires, F.J.A.; Ianni, B.M.; Fernandes, F.; Mady, C. Prognostic Value of the Collage Volume Fraction in Hypertrophic Cardiomyopathy. *Arq. Bras. Cardiol.* **2009**, 92, 210–214, 216–220. [CrossRef]
10. Naglah, A.; Khalifa, F.; El-Baz, A.; Gondim, D. Conditional GANs Based System for Fibrosis Detection and Quantification in Hematoxylin and Eosin Whole Slide Images. *Med. Image Anal.* **2022**, 81, 102537. [CrossRef]
11. Farris, A.B.; Vizcarra, J.; Amgad, M.; Donald Cooper, L.A.; Gutman, D.; Hogan, J. Image Analysis Pipeline for Renal Allograf Evaluation and Fibrosis Quantification. *Kidney Int. Rep.* **2021**, 6, 1878–1887. [CrossRef] [PubMed]
12. Bera, K.; Schalper, K.A.; Rimm, D.L.; Velcheti, V.; Madabhushi, A. Artificial Intelligence in Digital Pathology—New Tools fo Diagnosis and Precision Oncology. *Nat. Rev. Clin. Oncol.* **2019**, 16, 703–715. [CrossRef] [PubMed]
13. Dulf, E.-H.; Bledea, M.; Mocan, T.; Mocan, L. Automatic Detection of Colorectal Polyps Using Transfer Learning. *Sensors* **2021** 21, 5704. [CrossRef]
14. Stoleru, C.-A.; Dulf, E.H.; Ciobanu, L. Automated Detection of Celiac Disease Using Machine Learning Algorithms. *Sci. Rep* **2022**, 12, 4071. [CrossRef] [PubMed]
15. Masseroli, M.; Caballero, T.; O'Valle, F.; Del Moral, R.M.; Pérez-Milena, A.; Del Moral, R.G. Automatic Quantification of Live Fibrosis: Design and Validation of a New Image Analysis Method: Comparison with Semi-Quantitative Indexes of Fibrosis *J. Hepatol.* **2000**, 32, 453–464. [CrossRef]
16. Astbury, S.; Grove, J.I.; Dorward, D.A.; Guha, I.N.; Fallowfield, J.A.; Kendall, T.J. Reliable Computational Quantification of Live Fibrosis Is Compromised by Inherent Staining Variation. *J. Pathol. Clin. Res.* **2021**, 7, 471–481. [CrossRef] [PubMed]
17. Sánchez-Jaramillo, E.A.; Gasca-Lozano, L.E.; Vera-Cruz, J.M.; Hernández-Ortega, L.D.; Salazar-Montes, A.M. Automatec Computer-Assisted Image Analysis for the Fast Quantification of Kidney Fibrosis. *Biology* **2022**, 11, 1227. [CrossRef]
18. Daunoravicius, D.; Besusparis, J.; Zurauskas, E.; Laurinaviciene, A.; Bironaite, D.; Pankuweit, S.; Plancoulaine, B.; Herlin, P Bogomolovas, J.; Grabauskiene, V.; et al. Quantification of Myocardial Fibrosis by Digital Image Analysis and Interactive Stereology. *Diagn. Pathol.* **2014**, 9, 114. [CrossRef]
19. Wang, T.; Rentería, M.E.; Peng, J. Editorial: Data Mining and Statistical Methods for Knowledge Discovery in Diseases Based on Multimodal Omics. *Front. Genet.* **2022**, 13, 895796. [CrossRef]
20. Reel, P.S.; Reel, S.; Pearson, E.; Trucco, E.; Jefferson, E. Using Machine Learning Approaches for Multi-Omics Data Analysis: A Review. *Biotechnol. Adv.* **2021**, 49, 107739. [CrossRef]
21. Li, Y.-H.; Cao, Y.; Liu, F.; Zhao, Q.; Adi, D.; Huo, Q.; Liu, Z.; Luo, J.-Y.; Fang, B.-B.; Tian, T.; et al. Visualization and Analysis o Gene Expression in Stanford Type A Aortic Dissection Tissue Section by Spatial Transcriptomics. *Front. Genet.* **2021**, 12, 698124 [CrossRef]
22. Wang, T.; Shu, H.; Hu, J.; Wang, Y.; Chen, J.; Peng, J.; Shang, X. Accurately Deciphering Spatial Domains for Spatially Resolvec Transcriptomics with stCluster. *Brief. Bioinform.* **2024**, 25, bbae329. [CrossRef]
23. Li, W.; Lou, X.; Zha, Y.; Qin, Y.; Zha, J.; Hong, L.; Xie, Z.; Yang, S.; Wang, C.; An, J.; et al. Single-Cell RNA-Seq of Heart Reveals Intercellular Communication Drivers of Myocardial Fibrosis in Diabetic Cardiomyopathy. *Elife* **2023**, 12, e80479. [CrossRef [PubMed]
24. Long, X.; Yuan, X.; Du, J. Single-Cell and Spatial Transcriptomics: Advances in Heart Development and Disease Applications *Comput. Struct. Biotechnol. J.* **2023**, 21, 2717–2731. [CrossRef]
25. Yang, M.Q.; Weissman, S.M.; Yang, W.; Zhang, J.; Canaann, A.; Guan, R. MISC: Missing Imputation for Single-Cell RNA Sequencing Data. *BMC Syst. Biol.* **2018**, 12, 114. [CrossRef] [PubMed]
26. Wang, T.; Zhao, H.; Xu, Y.; Wang, Y.; Shang, X.; Peng, J.; Xiao, B. scMultiGAN: Cell-Specific Imputation for Single-Cel Transcriptomes with Multiple Deep Generative Adversarial Networks. *Brief. Bioinform.* **2023**, 24, bbad384. [CrossRef]
27. Color Segmentation by Delta E Color Difference. Available online: https://www.mathworks.com/matlabcentral/fileexchange/31118-color-segmentation-by-delta-e-color-difference (accessed on 22 August 2024).
28. Mühlfeld, C.; Schipke, J. Methodological Progress of Stereology in Cardiac Research and Its Application to Normal and Pathological Heart Development. *Cells* **2022**, 11, 2032. [CrossRef]
29. Gratz, D.; Winkle, A.J.; Dalic, A.; Unudurthi, S.D.; Hund, T.J. Computational Tools for Automated Histological Image Analysis and Quantification in Cardiac Tissue. *Methods X* **2020**, 7, 100755. [CrossRef]
30. Dee, F.R.; Leaven, T. *Iowa Virtual Slidebox*; University of Iowa Healthcare: Iowa City, IA, USA, 1999; Available online: https://biolucida.net/viewer/?page=viewer (accessed on 27 August 2024).
31. Cristoforetti, A.; Masè, M.; Ravelli, F. Model-Based Approach for the Semi-Automatic Analysis of Collagen Birefringence in Polarized Light Microscopy. *Appl. Sci.* **2023**, 13, 2916. [CrossRef]
32. Schüffler, P.; Steiger, K.; Weichert, W. How to Use AI in Pathology. *Genes. Chromosomes Cancer* **2023**, 62, 564–567. [CrossRef]
33. Danku, A.E.; Dulf, E.H.; Banut, R.P.; Silaghi, H.; Silaghi, C.A. Cancer Diagnosis with the Aid of Artificial Intelligence Modeling Tools. *IEEE Access* **2022**, 10, 20816–20831. [CrossRef]
34. Knudsen, L.; Brandenberger, C.; Ochs, M. Stereology as the 3D Tool to Quantitate Lung Architecture. *Histochem. Cell Biol.* **2021** 155, 163–181. [CrossRef]
35. Giavarina, D. Understanding Bland Altman Analysis. *Biochem. Med.* **2015**, 25, 141–151. [CrossRef]

36. Schneider, C.A.; Rasband, W.S.; Eliceiri, K.W. NIH Image to ImageJ: 25 Years of Image Analysis. *Nat. Methods* **2012**, *9*, 671–675. [CrossRef] [PubMed]
37. Hadi, A.M.; Mouchaers, K.T.B.; Schalij, I.; Grunberg, K.; Meijer, G.A.; Vonk-Noordegraaf, A.; van der Laarse, W.J.; Beliën, J.A.M. Rapid Quantification of Myocardial Fibrosis: A New Macro-Based Automated Analysis. *Anal. Cell. Pathol.* **2010**, *33*, 257–269. [CrossRef]
38. Vasiljević, J.D.; Popović, Z.B.; Otasević, P.; Popović, Z.V.; Vidaković, R.; Mirić, M.; Nesković, A.N. Myocardial Fibrosis Assessment by Semiquantitative, Point-Counting and Computer-Based Methods in Patients with Heart Muscle Disease: A Comparative Study. *Histopathology* **2001**, *38*, 338–343. [CrossRef] [PubMed]
39. Zimmermann, E.; Mukherjee, S.S.; Falahkheirkhah, K.; Gryka, M.C.; Kajdacsy-Balla, A.; Hasan, W.; Giraud, G.; Tibayan, F.; Raman, J.; Bhargava, R. Detection and Quantification of Myocardial Fibrosis Using Stain-Free Infrared Spectroscopic Imaging. *Arch. Pathol. Lab. Med.* **2021**, *145*, 1526–1535. [CrossRef] [PubMed]
40. Yang, Y.; Zheng, L.; Li, Z.; Chen, J.; Wu, X.; Ren, G.; Xiao, Z.; Li, X.; Luo, W.; Wu, Z.; et al. Multiphoton Microscopy Providing Pathological-Level Quantification of Myocardial Fibrosis in Transplanted Human Heart. *Lasers Med. Sci.* **2022**, *37*, 2889–2898. [CrossRef]
41. Hsia, C.C.W.; Hyde, D.M.; Ochs, M.; Weibel, E.R. ATS/ERS Joint Task Force on Quantitative Assessment of Lung Structure An Official Research Policy Statement of the American Thoracic Society/European Respiratory Society: Standards for Quantitative Assessment of Lung Structure. *Am. J. Respir. Crit. Care Med.* **2010**, *181*, 394–418. [CrossRef]
42. Schipke, J.; Brandenberger, C.; Rajces, A.; Manninger, M.; Alogna, A.; Post, H.; Mühlfeld, C. Assessment of Cardiac Fibrosis: A Morphometric Method Comparison for Collagen Quantification. *J. Appl. Physiol.* **2017**, *122*, 1019–1030. [CrossRef]
43. Testa, L.C.; Jule, Y.; Lundh, L.; Bertotti, K.; Merideth, M.A.; O'Brien, K.J.; Nathan, S.D.; Venuto, D.C.; El-Chemaly, S.; Malicdan, M.C.V.; et al. Automated Digital Quantification of Pulmonary Fibrosis in Human Histopathology Specimens. *Front. Med.* **2021**, *8*, 607720. [CrossRef] [PubMed]
44. López De Padilla, C.M.; Coenen, M.J.; Tovar, A.; De la Vega, R.E.; Evans, C.H.; Müller, S.A. Picrosirius Red Staining: Revisiting Its Application to the Qualitative and Quantitative Assessment of Collagen Type I and Type III in Tendon. *J. Histochem. Cytochem.* **2021**, *69*, 633–643. [CrossRef] [PubMed]
45. Murakami, Y.; Abe, T.; Hashiguchi, A.; Yamaguchi, M.; Saito, A.; Sakamoto, M. Color Correction for Automatic Fibrosis Quantification in Liver Biopsy Specimens. *J. Pathol. Inform.* **2013**, *4*, 36. [CrossRef] [PubMed]
46. Hore, S.; Chakraborty, S.; Chatterjee, S.; Dey, N.; Ashour, A.S.; Chung, L.V.; Le, D.-N. An Integrated Interactive Technique for Image Segmentation Using Stack Based Seeded Region Growing and Thresholding. *IJECE* **2016**, *6*, 2773. [CrossRef]
47. Moreira, A.C.; Appoloni, C.R.; Mantovani, I.F.; Fernandes, J.S.; Marques, L.C.; Nagata, R.; Fernandes, C.P. Effects of Manual Threshold Setting on Image Analysis Results of a Sandstone Sample Structural Characterization by X-Ray Microtomography. *Appl. Radiat. Isot.* **2012**, *70*, 937–941. [CrossRef]
48. Tadrous, P.J. On the Concept of Objectivity in Digital Image Analysis in Pathology. *Pathology* **2010**, *42*, 207–211. [CrossRef]

applied sciences

MDPI

Article

Towards Metric-Driven Difference Detection between Receptive and Nonreceptive Endometrial Samples Using Automatic Histology Image Analysis

Vidas Raudonis [1,*], Ruta Bartasiene [2], Ave Minajeva [3], Merli Saare [4,5], Egle Drejeriene [2], Agne Kozlovskaja-Gumbriene [2] and Andres Salumets [4,5]

1 Automation Department, Kaunas University of Technology, LT-44249 Kaunas, Lithuania
2 Department of Obstetrics and Gynecology, Lithuanian University of Health Sciences, LT-44307 Kaunas, Lithuania; ruta.bartasiene@lsmu.lt (R.B.); egle.drejeriene@lsmu.lt (E.D.); agne.gumbriene@lsmuni.lt (A.K.-G.)
3 Institute of Biomedicine and Translational Medicine, Tartu University, 51003 Tartu, Estonia; ave.minajeva@ut.ee
4 Institute of Clinical Medicine, Department of Obstetrics and Gynecology, Tartu University, 50406 Tartu, Estonia; merli.saare@ut.ee (M.S.); andres.salumets@ccht.ee (A.S.)
5 Competence Centre on Health Technologies, 50411 Tartu, Estonia
* Correspondence: vidas.raudonis@ktu.lt

Abstract: This paper presents a technique that can potentially help to determine the receptivity stage of the endometrium from histology images by automatically measuring the stromal nuclear changes. The presented technique is composed of an image segmentation model and the statistical evolution of segmented areas in hematoxylin and eosin (HE)-stained histology images. Three different endometrium receptivity stages, namely pre-receptive, post-receptive, and receptive, were compared. An ensemble-based AI model was proposed for histology image segmentation, which is based on individual UNet++, UNet, and ResNet34-UNet segmentation models. The performance of the ensemble-based technique was assessed using the Dice score and intersection over unit (IoU) values. In comparison to alternative segmentation architectures that were applied singly, the current ensemble-based method obtained higher Dice score (0.95) and IoU (0.90) values. The statistical comparison highlighted a noticeable difference in the number of nuclei and the size of the stroma tissue. The proposed technique demonstrated the positive potential for practical implementation for automatic endometrial tissue analysis.

Keywords: image segmentation; endometrial biopsy; histology image

1. Introduction

Infertility is the inability of a mature organism to produce offspring. The inability to become pregnant after 12 months or more of frequent, unprotected sexual activity defines this condition of the male or female reproductive system [1]. It is estimated that millions of people and couples worldwide struggle with infertility. According to estimates, one in six persons who are of reproductive age are impacted [1]. The prevalence of infertility accounts for 17.5% of the worldwide population [2]. Medically assisted reproduction (MAR), or in vitro fertilization (IVF), was developed to overcome the problem of infertility and was introduced into clinical practice more than 40 years ago. MAR technologies enable the fertilization of human oocytes and the creation of human embryos in vitro. Viable embryos can then be transferred into the woman's uterus, and the development of intrauterine pregnancy begins upon successful implantation. Since the beginning of successfully applying IVF in humans, these treatments have resulted in the birth of over 10 million children already. Several countries now see more than 3% of all births as a result of MAR [3]. However, the success of MAR remains limited despite the rapid development of related technologies [4–6].

Changes in the cellular or molecular composition of the innermost lining of the uterus, known as the endometrium, are critical for IVF success; its unique structure and receptivity allow the embryo to be implanted [7,8]. The highest receptivity of the endometrial tissue occurs during the so-called "window of implantation" (WOI) when optimal conditions for embryo implantation are established. Prior to the WOI or past this time, the chance of embryo implantation is scarce. Therefore, an endometrial receptivity assessment has proven to be advantageous for the success of IVF. Transcriptomic biomarkers are most commonly used to assess endometrial receptivity, as the expression levels of these biomarkers depend upon the receptivity status of the uterine tissue [9,10]. Hence, endometrial tissue transcriptome testing allows an optimal time for the personalized embryo transfer to be chosen [11,12]. In parallel, endometrial microbiota changes have also been shown to affect embryo implantation, which can be evaluated by tissue profiling during IVF [13,14]. However, the most common and widely used endometrial tissue evaluation is performed according to the Noyes dating criteria for histological sections [15]. These criteria are valid to date and are used in clinical pathology: when assessing the endometrial phase, both the glandular and stromal parameters must be evaluated [16,17]. Evaluating stromal cell changes, such as the extent of edema, is subjective, and very small-sized stromal cell nuclei cause further difficulties in their evaluation under standard light microscopy.

The clinical value of histological endometrial dating, which defines the individual WOI, has recently been shown to benefit patients with recurrent pregnancy loss [18]. Nevertheless, implementation of the latest technical breakthroughs in deep learning to establish AI-powered technologies to optimize histopathology assessments of endometrial tissue for IVF is still clearly lacking. Therefore, AI-driven clinical decision support tools for endometrial tissue assessments may offer efficient, metric-driven, objective, and accurate diagnoses for endometrial receptivity evaluation. The main aim of this research is to propose a computer-aided system for the evaluation of endometrial tissues from endometrial histological slides, which can be used as an automatic algorithm for endometrial receptivity assessments and predictions. This research paper is organized into seven main sections. The state-of-the-art in the current research topic is provided in the second section. Information about the research object, the proposed AI model, and its validation are given in the third, fourth, and fifth sections accordingly. The experimental setup and results are shown in the seventh section. The discussion, conclusions, and references are provided at the end of the research paper.

2. State-of-the-Art Review

Endometrial histologic dating criteria, such as thickness, glandular density, and maturation, are important in IVF, being crucial for the successful implantation of an embryo. These criteria are important predictors of the pregnancy outcome in IVF cycles. The endometrium is the innermost layer of the uterus and is the site of implantation of the fertilized egg during pregnancy. For the development of automated segmentation techniques for histologic images, several approaches merging computer vision and machine learning technologies have been put forth over the years. The automatic evaluation of histology images mainly depends on the target objects that have to be evaluated, such as cells, nuclei, glands, or tissue type. An automated segmentation algorithm based on morphology is first applied to light microscopy images stained with Hematoxylin and Eosin [19].

Image segmentation is the process of locating certain objects in an image or splitting it into several areas, each of which represents a different object or portion of the image. For the purpose of segmenting or dividing up images, deep learning techniques such as autoencoders like UNet are utilized. Segmentation is based on the transformation of a high-dimensional space to a lower-dimensional space [20]. Usually, two-dimensional data are down-sampled to a one-dimensional vector and again decoded to its original appearance. Researchers proposed several types of autoencoders, which are applied for image segmentation tasks, including plain fully convolutional autoencoders, multi-loss autoencoders, fully convolutional variational autoencoders, and repeated fully convolutional autoencoders. Different autoencoders distinguish themselves with their own strengths and weaknesses. Therefore, the selection of a specific structure of the segmentation model depends on the task and image characteristics. Gondim, with a group of researchers, proposed an assisting analysis tool that is used to examine the vascular network of bone histologic images. The proposed automatic method is based on a convolutional neural network (CNN) and random forest classifier (RFC) [21]. Novel segmentation methods are applied in the detection of individual nuclei in stained breast histopathology images [22] and segment whole biopsy slides [23]. The latter method employs a U-Net-like neural structure that was trained on a large annotated dataset. Ali et al. proposed a multiscale attention learning network (MSAL-Net) to segment individual nuclei in histopathology images [24]. The proposed methods include mathematical morphology, convolutional neural networks, random forest classifiers, and multiscale attention learning networks. These methods have shown promising results in the automatic segmentation of histology images. Several variants of U-Net have been proposed, each with its own strengths and weaknesses. Many limitations can be overcome by combining different variants of U-Net models and their strengths.

Our research investigates the potential of applying automatic histology image analysis for differentiating between receptive and nonreceptive endometrial samples using a metric-driven approach. Traditional assessment methods rely on a subjective evaluation by pathologists, introducing potential inconsistencies. Automatic image analysis offers an objective and quantitative alternative. This approach involves extracting the relevant metrics from histological images, which can then be used to distinguish between receptive and nonreceptive samples. This work explores the feasibility of this approach and paves the way for developing a reliable and automated system for endometrial receptivity assessment.

3. Research Object and Dataset

In this work, custom datasets of endometrial biopsy (these were stained with HE (Hematoxylin and Eosin)) histologic pictures in color were used. This dataset was produced as part of the ReadUteru initiative, an international effort that includes medical facilities in Lithuania and Estonia. The dataset included 150 whole-slide photos in color of endometrial biopsies (see example in Figure 1), together with manually segmented images (ground truth annotations). The endometrial samples from women receiving IVF therapy were divided into pre-receptive, receptive, and post-receptive groups using molecular profiling with the commercial beREADY test. Additionally, the majority of these biopsies were taken during the hormonal replacement treatment (HRT) IVF cycles.

Segmentation models are employed in order to divide the histological images into three different areas, such as endometrial glands, stroma, and other parts of the endometrial sample. The latter one is segmented based on the color, which is usually almost completely white. Areas with endometrial glands are detected using an AI model, and everything that is not glands or background is segmented as stroma. The endometrial glands' locations are indicated by the dark (grayish) regions (Figure 1 right). A team of pathologists from two countries created ground truth images (annotated photos). At various magnification settings, experts examined and annotated each whole-slide image. The original color whole-slide pictures are the same size as the ground truth segmentation maps. When using a 20× magnification, the size of a gland is typically not greater than 350 pixels. This region is much smaller than the total image—more than 100 times smaller.

The whole-slide images of endometrial biopsy cannot be used as training inputs because of the limited computational resources. The appropriate image size is 576 × 576 pixels when taking into account the available computing power and segmentation accuracy. The choice of image size is influenced by the computational resources that are available for image processing. Smaller image sizes can be processed quicker and require less memory, making them more suitable for resource-constrained environments. Additionally, the selection of such size is influenced by the desired balance between the image resolution and the processing speed. Larger image sizes can provide higher resolution inputs but at the cost of increased processing time and computational resources. The image parts that correlate with the gland position are also reduced up to 30 times due to the direct size reduction of the original whole-slide image to 576 × 576 pixels. It is challenging to segment such a small area because textural and structural information about the glands will be lost. We suggest using cropped regions of interest (RoI) of the whole-slide image instead of shrinking it, with each RoI being selected using an overlapping sliding window of size (576 × 576 pixels).

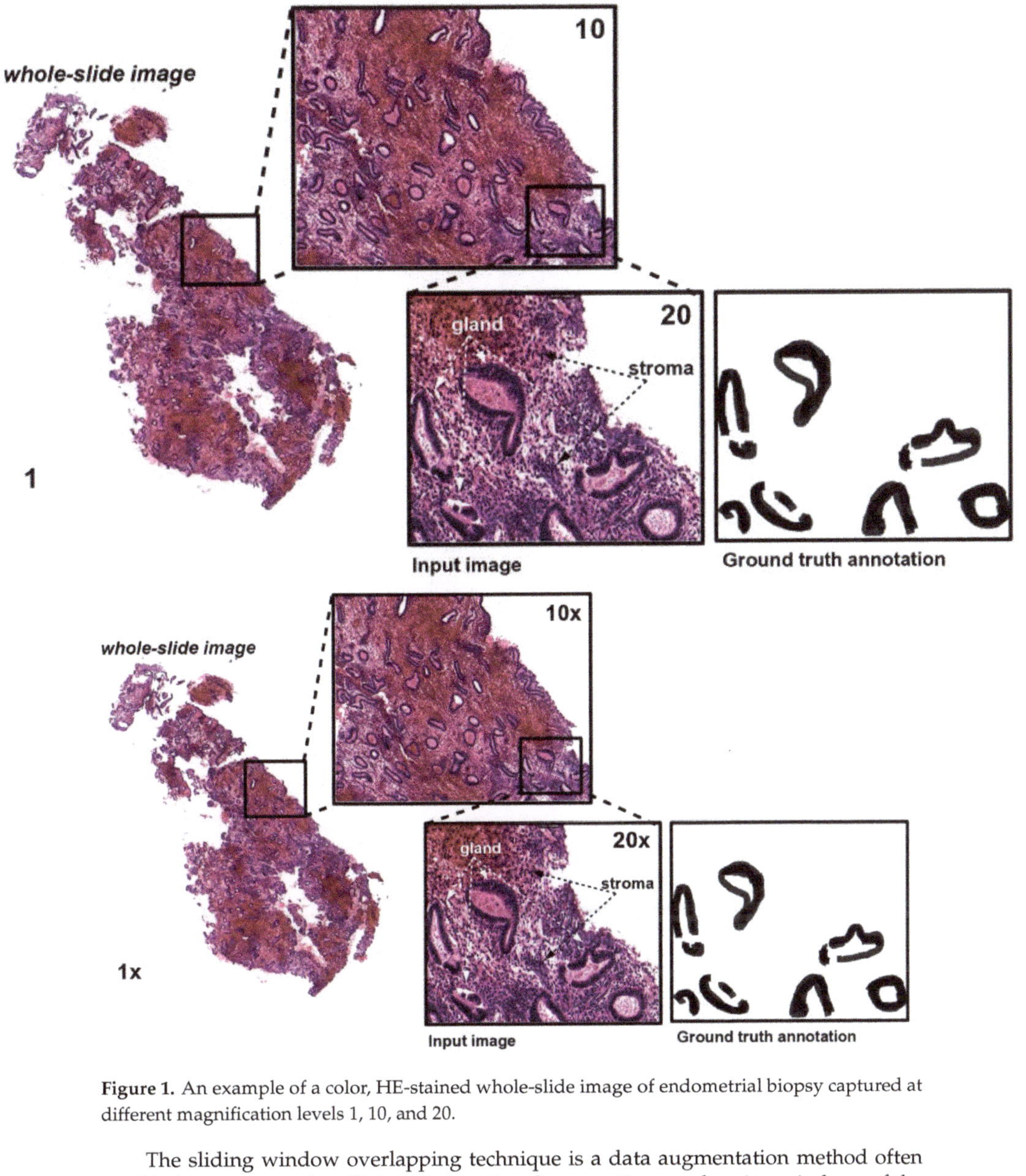

Figure 1. An example of a color, HE-stained whole-slide image of endometrial biopsy captured at different magnification levels 1, 10, and 20.

The sliding window overlapping technique is a data augmentation method often used in image processing. This technique involves creating overlapping windows of the original data to generate additional training samples for machine learning models. The overlapping windows help to capture more diverse patterns and variations in the data, thereby enhancing the model's ability to generate accurate segmentation predictions and partly solve overfitting problems. The sliding window with the overlap data augmentation technique involves using a fixed window length to extract samples from the original histology image with a certain degree of overlap with the consecutive window. We defined the 30% overlap between RoIs in our study. There are various benefits of using RoIs rather than whole-slide histology pictures. First, up to 15,000 pictures (RoIs with only black pixels are eliminated) are generated for training and testing, which is a 100 times increase compared to the required number of samples (from 150 whole-slide images). Second, there is a decrease in the demand for computing resources. Third, the endometrial glands retain their original size and shape. Overall, this technique contributes to improving the robustness and performance of machine learning models by enriching the training dataset with diverse samples.

The evaluation of the endometrium tissue is accomplished by estimating the size and density of the nuclei displacement. Firstly, we estimate the density of the nuclei next to the detected endometrium glands and, secondly, in the whole endometrium tissue (see Figure 2). Detection is conducted using an ensemble-based segmentation model that aggregates the outputs of three individual models (more info in Section 4). The resulting output is a segmentation map where the endometrium glands and all other tissues are segmented.

Metric-driven analysis is performed based on a segmentation map, which highlights the positions of the endometrium glands. The nucleus density is calculated using two grids of different densities, such as 30 and 50 μm (see Figure 3). Nuclei in the endometrium image are HE stained; therefore, they appear as blueish areas in the image, therefore, we estimate the size of a nucleus as a detected bluish area in the histologic image.

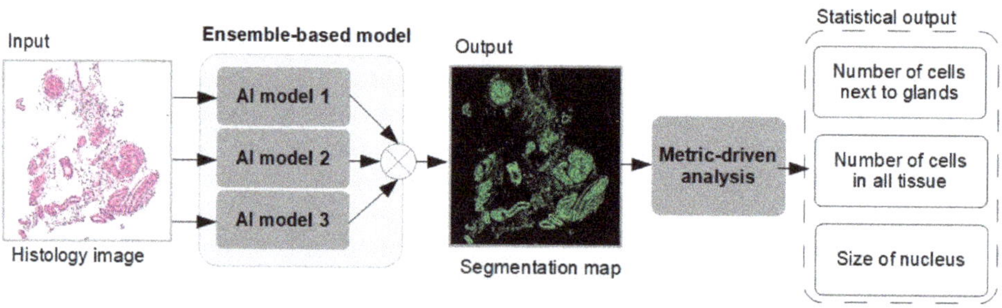

Figure 2. The block diagram of proposed evaluation method of endometrium tissue.

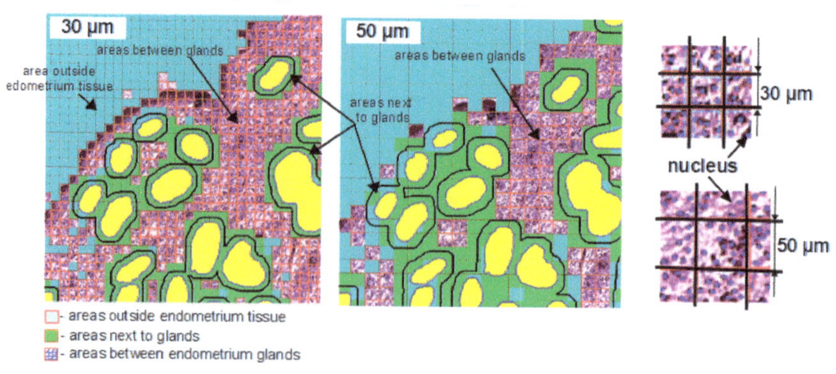

Figure 3. Grid-based estimation of nuclei density in the endometrial image.

4. Endometrial Tissue Segmentation Model

In the following section, the proposed gland detection method is described. The application of deep encoder–decoder CNN architectures of different depths and complexity was inspired by the complex appearance of the target object. The uterus endometrium has glands that highly vary in size, shape, and structure. These glands are tubular in shape and have ciliated columnar epithelium lining them. Due to the estrogen release and depending on the menstrual cycle, the appearance of the glands is changing. In this study, the ensemble-based detection model is investigated and built using segmentation model variants such as U-Net, U-Net++, and Residual U-Net. These models are selected due to their ability to capture intricate features and patterns within medical images, making them suitable for segmentation tasks. When used on various histology images, each segmentation model has a certain level of accuracy that it can achieve. These restrictions may manifest as slices of endometrial biopsies that are not of the same thickness, are not evenly lit, have varied image noise that may obscure key imaging findings or are simply taken at different times of the menstrual cycle. To increase accuracy and produce results that are reliable, all models that were trained on the same dataset are combined into one ensemble. The risk of complex model overfitting is managed through the size of the training dataset and the employment of regularization techniques. To mitigate overfitting, techniques such as dropout, batch normalization, and data augmentation were used. The resulting output, i.e., the predicted segmentation map of endometrial glands, is acquired using a weighted sum of all three individual segmentation maps. The weights are calculated by minimizing the criterion using the pseudo code given in Figure 4. The inverse of the intersection over unit (IoU) value is used as an optimization criterion in our work (1-IoU). The optimization starts from generating α and β values in the range from 0 to 1. The gamma (γ) weight is estimated as the difference between 1 and the sum of the α and β values. The weighted model output or prediction P is calculated in step 4, where P_{UNet++} is the prediction map given by the UNet++ model, $P_{Resnet34\text{-}UNet}$ is the prediction map given by the residual model, and P_{UNet} is the predictions of the UNet segmentation model. The intersection over unit value is estimated between manually annotated mask M and weighted prediction P. Optimized weights are estimated when the criterion meets the condition given in step 5. Final weights α^*, β^*, and γ^* are given in step 6. The final prediction map is calculated using the given weights: $\alpha = 0.346$, $\beta = 0.250$, and $\gamma = 0.404$.

```
1. Generate weights in range from 0 to 1: α = [0..1], β = [0..1]
2. For i, j in range(α, β)
3.     γ_{i,j} = 1 − (α_{i,j} + β_{i,j})
4.     P_{i,j} = P_{UNet++} · α_{i,j} + P_{Resnet34−UNet} · β_{i,j} + P_{UNet} · γ_{i,j}
5.     If Λ > min_{i,j}(1 − IoU(M, P_{i,j})) Then
6.             Λ = min_{i,j}(1 − IoU(M, P_{i,j})), α* = α_{i,j}, β* = β_{i,j}, γ* = γ_{i,j}
```

Figure 4. Pseudo code for calculating impact weights of each segmentation model in ensemble-based approach.

Figure 5 displays the proposed ensemble's functional diagram. The ensemble comprises the three deep neural network models ResNet34-UNet, UNet, and UNet++. The segmentation model processes the input image, and as a result, an output segmented image of the same as the input size is produced [25], called a segmentation map. The deep neural network encodes input data (color image) through the down-sampling path, decodes a segmentation map through the up-sampling path, and skips connections. A max-pooling layer and a sequence of convolutional layers with decreased size are used to build the down-sampling route. The down-sampling route effectively reduces the high-resolution image to low-resolution. The contextual information is extracted in the left part of the network (down-sampling path), and the spatial information is reconstructed in the right part of the network (up-sampling path). The output map, or segmentation map of the endometrial glands, is produced using the U-Net network's up-sampling route and is the same size as the input picture. A high-resolution picture was created in the up-sampling step by decoding the low-resolution image (or features). The color images of size 576 × 576 pixels are used as inputs. The size of the input images is gradually reduced; depth is gradually increased until the size of the features reaches 18 × 18 × 512 pixels. The middle convolutional layer is used as a bottleneck, and it is positioned between the encoder and decoder paths. The "bottleneck" consists of convolutional and batch-normalization layers. Through the concatenation of feature maps from the down-sampling side to the up-sampling side, skip connections are employed to transmit local features. The final output layer consists of a convolutional layer with a softmax activation function and a convolutional filter size of 1 × 1. The resulting output segmentation map consists of grayish blobs on a white background, which correspond to the area of the endometrial glands in a colored, HE-stained histology image. Adam optimizer and binary cross-entropy (BCE) loss function were used to train a U-Net network with 7.7 trainable parameters.

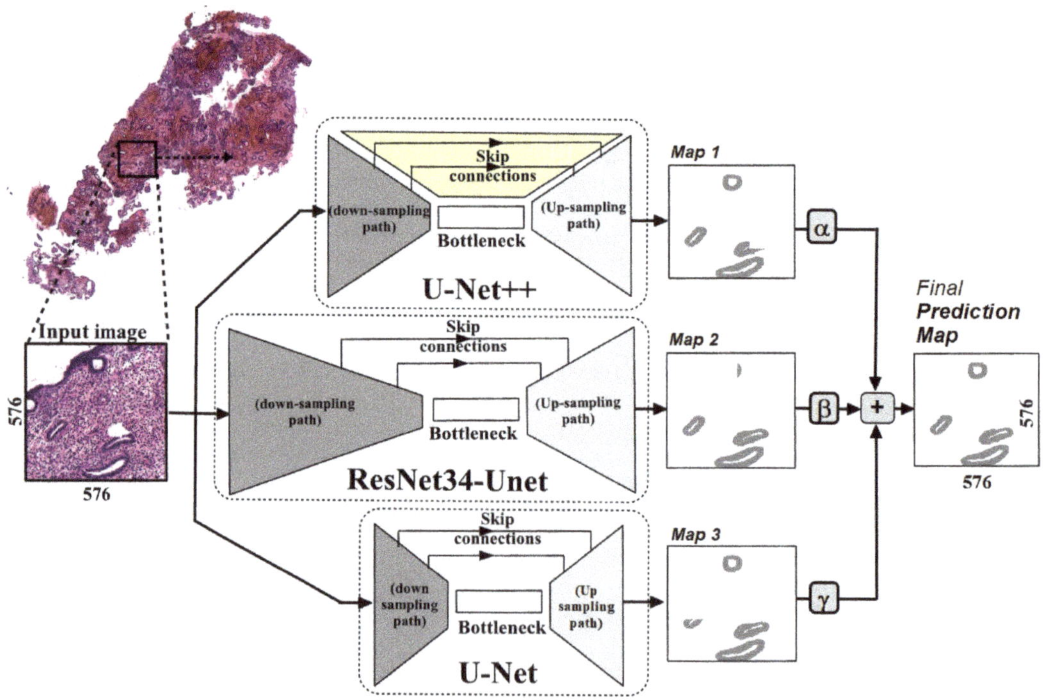

Figure 5. An illustration of the proposed ensemble-based segmentation model's functionality.

A U-Net++ type network serves as the second deep neural network in the ensemble of models. Nested and thick linkages serve as the model's foundation. It has skip connections that incorporate convolutional layers for passing semantic information from the encoder (down-sampling) to the decoder (up-sampling) paths. The dense skip connections are used to improve the gradient flow, i.e., training [26]. The U-Net++ model is efficient at collecting the fine features of 2D pictures used to define endometrial glands. The number of convolutional blocks is controlled by deep supervision. It prunes and adjusts the complexity of the network, keeping high performance (segmentation accuracy) and inference time. A segmentation map with a resolution of 576 × 576 pixels is the output of the U-Net++ model. This model was trained using the Adam optimizer with the loss function BCE and has around 9.1 million trainable parameters. The third pretrained ResNet34-Unet network is used as a part of the ensemble-based method. The ResNet34-based network is used as the semantic features encoding part of the segmentation model (the down-sampling path). A residual network is built from serially connected residual blocks that have skip connections. The enhanced attention module and a decoder block (the up-sampling route) make up the network's decoding section. There are two connections from the input for each residual block. Convolutional layers, batch normalization, and linear functions are applied to the initial input. The second input omits the further addition of the convolutions and functions. In order to preserve segmentation accuracy and resilience, residual networks assist in resolving the vanishing gradient problem that is typical in big and complicated networks. The residual U-Net model's up-sampling path resembles that of U-Net from the preceding description. Through skip connections, the up-sampling component receives the local data and concatenating features. This model was trained using the Adam optimizer with the loss function BCE and has around 21.6 million trainable parameters.

All mentioned models and ensemble-based segmentation methods segment only a small portion of the whole biopsy image. In order to reconstruct all the segmentation maps that correspond to the whole biopsy image, several processing steps have to be undertaken. There are three basic processes in this reconstruction flow: Each patch is stitched back onto the canvas in the same way that it was cropped from the original picture, and average prediction values are generated in the areas where patches overlap. The predictions are obtained from each image patch using the proposed segmentation model. Finally, a threshold value is used to determine the segmentation map of the expected glands. For purposes of paper representation, white was used to designate the pixels for which predictions were higher than 0.5; otherwise, white was used to mark the pixels.

5. Validation Metrics of Tissue Segmentation Model

The proposed segmentation model is evaluated using intersection over union (IoU) and Dice coefficient criteria. IoU is a performance metric often used in object detection and image segmentation applications to measure the accuracy of predicted bounding boxes. IoU estimates the intersection rate between predicted areas (segmentation maps produced by neural networks) and ground truth (provided by manual labeling). The range of intersection over union values is 0 to 1, with 0 denoting no overlap and 1 denoting a perfect overlap. In the case when comparative pixel-by-pixel analysis is performed, IoU is the first metric in the list, and it is defined using Formula (1).

$$IoU = \frac{TP}{(TP + FP + FN)}, \tag{1}$$

where *TP* is a true positive, *FP* is a false positive, and *FN* is a false negative (see Table 1 for a deeper explanation). The *TP*, *FP*, and *FN* terms are used to evaluate the object detection results because these values correspond to image areas (or the number of pixels).

Table 1. Model performance metrics.

True Positive (TP)	$TP = GT \wedge S$	It is a region of intersection between the manually labeled ground truth picture (GT) and the predicted segmentation map (S), which is the model output.
False Positive (FP)	$FP = (GT \vee S) - GT$	False positive refers to the anticipated area in the final segmentation map that is outside of the experts' provided ground truth areas.
False Negative (FN)	$FN = (GT \vee S) - S$	False negative refers to the quantity of pixels in the segmentation model's unpredicted area of the ground truth.

The Dice coefficient (DC) is a metric used in image segmentation and object detection tasks that measure the similarity between predicted and ground truth maps (the output of the models). The DC value ranges between 0 and 1, where 0 indicates the overlap between GT and S, and 1 indicates a perfect overlap (100% similarity). The Dice scores can be expressed through definitions of precision and recall (see Table 2).

Table 2. Description precision and recall terms.

precision	$\frac{TP}{TP+FP}$	Precision in object detection is the fraction of true positive detection among all positive detections.
recall	$\frac{TP}{TP+FN}$	Recall refers to the fraction of relevant instances that were successfully retrieved by the object detection system.

A high degree of accuracy means that the detection model produces fewer false positive detections than real positive detections. Recall gauges how well the endometrial glands were all properly identified in the histology picture using the glands identification model. Using Formula (2), the Dice coefficient is calculated. As recall and accuracy are averaged, *DC* reveals the model's overall performance or its capacity to identify and accurately categorize items in an image.

$$DC = \frac{2}{1/_{recall} + 1/_{precision}} \quad (2)$$

6. Experimental Setup and Results

In total, 15,000 annotated image sections were created by cropping whole-slide images with fixed-size sliding windows (see Section 4). All image samples of whole-slide histology images were taken from different menstrual cycle phases. The prepared training dataset is used to train the model to segment endometrial glands, irrespective of the menstrual cycle. The whole-slide picture parts from the custom dataset were split into the following groups at random: 70% of the data were provided for model training, 10% for model validation, and the remaining 20% were utilized for model testing. An Intel i7 CPU and an Nvidia RTX4090 GPU graphics card were used in a desktop PC for all computing, training, and testing. The segmentation results of the endometrial glands are shown in Figure 6. Several random image regions are shown that are taken from the test dataset. Additionally, from left to right, color image regions of a real histology image, ground truth annotation, and the model outputs are given (the U-Net, ResNet34-UNet, U-Net++, and ensemble-based methods) accordingly. In the given figure, endometrial glands are highlighted with dark-color pixels and the surrounding tissues with white-color pixels.

6.1. Histology Image Segmentation Results

The experimental findings show that various segmentation models provide various prediction outcomes or anticipated segmentation maps. In some instances, endometrial glands are appropriately and reliably segmented; however, in other instances, studied models were unable to detect fuzzy endometrial gland borders. On the other hand, combining the weighted predictions from three independent models produces outcomes that are superior to those of the individual models (see Figure 6).

The average IoU was 0.90 according to the ensemble-based technique. Among the three segmentation networks, this result is the best. When all three separate models are unable to reliably identify the endometrial glands from surrounding tissues, the IoU value of the ensemble-based model plummets dramatically. A Dice score of 0.95 on average was shown by the ensemble-based model. Comparing the ensemble-based approach to the other three deep neural networks, the given Dice score of the ensemble-based technique is the best (Table 3). When none of the three models successfully separate endometrial glands from their surroundings, such as other tissues, the Dice score of the ensemble-based technique suffers significantly. Table 3's bolded text highlights the examined approaches' best segmentation performance. The suggested ensemble-based strategy produced the best segmentation results, with IoU and Dice scores of 0.90 and 0.95, respectively. On the customized dataset, the U-Net deep neural network had the lowest accuracy, with IoU = 0.77 and Dice = 0.85 as a result.

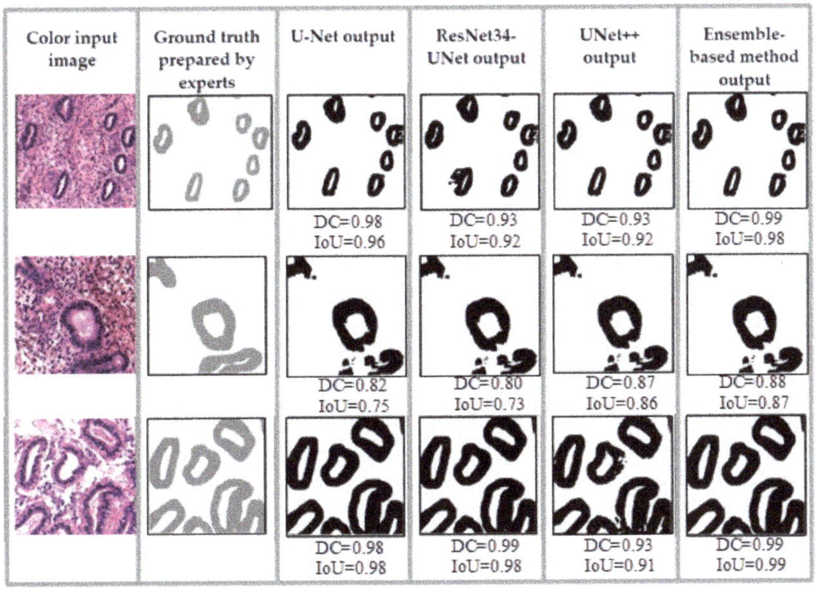

Figure 6. (From left to right): Original image section, corresponding ground truth annotation, endometrial glands segmentation results using the U-Net model, endometrial glands segmentation results using the residual U-Net model, endometrial glands segmentation results using the U-Net++ model, and endometrial glands results using the ensemble-based method.

Table 3. The ensemble-based model and its average output from three neural networks.

Performance Metric	U-Net	RestNet34-UNet	U-Net++	Ensemble
IoU	0.77	0.79	0.85	0.90
Dice Score	0.85	0.88	0.89	0.95

Figure 7 shows the detected positions of endometrial glands on whole-slide images obtained using the ensemble-based technique (the histology image is zoomed in for clarity). Above a colored, HE-stained histology picture, blue contour color patches indicate the probable sites of the endometrial glands.

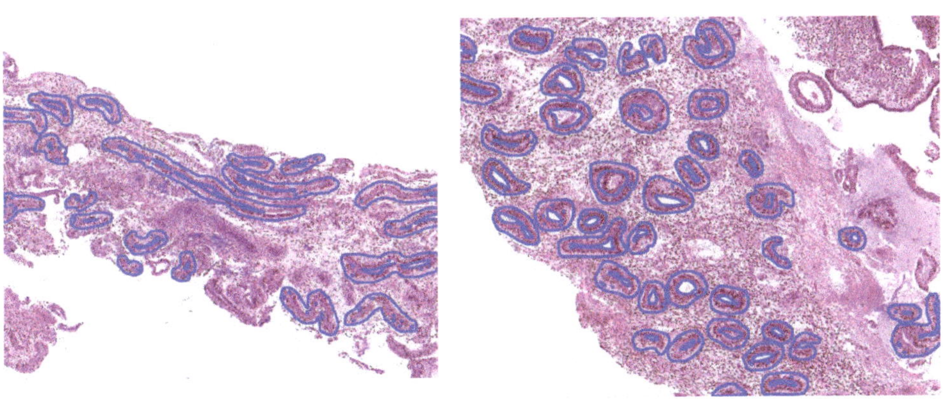

Figure 7. Example of histology image with detected endometrial glands.

6.2. Metric-Based Evaluation Results of Endometrial Sample

The size, density of the nucleus, and histograms of these measurements in the endometrial sample were chosen as objective metrics, which can be applied for the receptivity assessment. The size of the nucleus in the stroma tissue is equal to the blueish area of the HE-stained image. Squared pixel values are translated to squared micro-meters. Our investigation has shown that the stromal cell nucleus in the endometrial sample is of a size ranging from 0.005 to 0.68 μm^2 in the post-receptive stage. The nucleus size from the pre-receptive stage varies from 0.005–0.90 μm^2, and in the receptive stage, from 0.005–0.67 μm^2. The histogram of the nucleus size is shown in Figure 8, where the rational number of nuclei is given on the vertical axis, and the size of the nucleus is set aside on the horizontal axis. The black color curve represents the receptive stage, the red dashed line represents the pre-receptive values, and the post-receptive stage values are presented with the blue curve. The histogram suggests that the nucleus is bigger in the post-receptive stage when they are compared with the nuclei from other stages.

Figure 9 represents the rational histograms of the stromal cell's nucleus derived using (a) a 30 μm grid, (c) a 50 μm grid, (b) at the 30 μm range from endometrial glands, and (d) at the 50 μm range from endometrial glands. The number of grid cells is given on the vertical axis, and the number of stromal nuclei is shown on the horizontal axis. The histograms show that the highest nucleus density is higher in the receptive samples. Moreover, more nuclei can be detected next to the endometrial glands (these being the nuclei of stromal cells): for instance, on average, up to 12 nuclei can be detected next to the glands and, on average, 4 in all tissue areas.

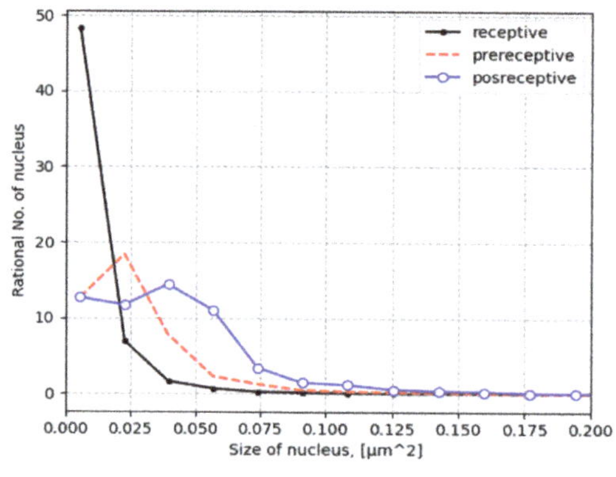

Figure 8. Histogram of the stromal cell nucleus size.

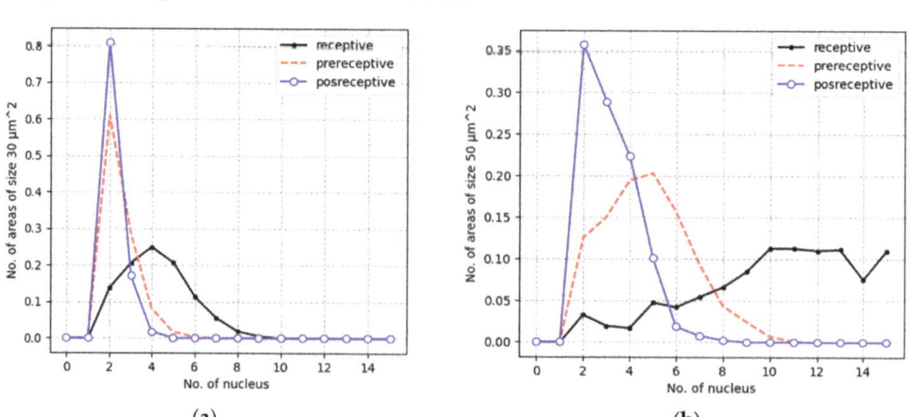

Figure 9. *Cont.*

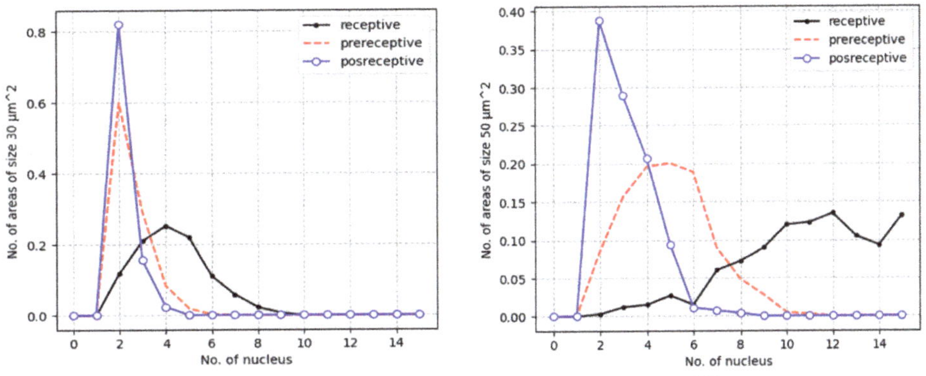

(c) (d)

Figure 9. The rational histograms of the stromal cell's nucleus are derived using (**a**) a 30 µm grid, (**c**) a 50 µm grid, (**b**) at the 30 µm range from endometrial glands, and (**d**) at the 50 µm range from endometrial glands, where the black color curve represents the receptive stage, the red dashed line represents pre-receptive values, and the post-receptive stage values are presented with the blue curve.

7. Discussion

For the purpose of the assessment of receptive and nonreceptive endometrial stages, we proposed a metric-driven approach, which is based on an image segmentation model and evaluation of nucleus size and density. Utilizing a customized dataset obtained through collaboration with Tartu University and the Lithuanian University of Health Sciences, the proposed technique and three additional deep architectures were tested. There are several issues that can induce misdetection and misclassification. The quality of the image collection used to segment the endometrial glands has a direct influence on the accuracy of the segmentation. It should be noted that various specialists may annotate the identical whole-slide picture of an endometrial biopsy differently due to differences in opinion on the borders of the glands. The accurate segmentation of endometrial tissue is a difficult task that requires several years of practice to master if it is conducted manually. Furthermore, histological image aberrations, uneven biopsy slide lighting, and image noise can all contribute to erroneous segmentation of endometrial glands.

The minimum DPI (dots per inch) for input images is important for our endometrium segmentation model's accuracy. Higher resolution generally leads to better results. However, the computational resources should be considered. The selection of image size is influenced by the desired balance between image resolution and processing speed. In our research, we selected an image resolution of 4 pixels per 1 µm. The ensemble-based method's attained detection accuracy comes at the expense of processing time. Since the ensemble technique is based on three deep neural networks, it takes three times longer to provide predictions. On a GPU graphics card, three separate segmentation models were trained and tested. The Nvidia RTX4090 with 24 GB of internal RAM was utilized. The identical custom training dataset and hyperparameters were used to train all three neural networks. To train the U-Net autoencoder that consists of 7.7 trainable parameters, less than 22 h is needed. The training of residual U-Net (21.6 trainable parameters) required up to 50 h. On average, 29 h are needed to train the U-Net++ (9.1 trainable parameters) segmentation network. In total, it took 105 h (less than 5 days) to train all ensemble-based segmentation models. Several strategies can be employed to potentially improve the overall performance when all three models demonstrate poor outcomes. The proposed endometrial assessment method can be used for a deeper analysis of images. By using the metric-driven approach, we could objectively demonstrate that the receptive endometrium had a higher density of stromal cell nuclei next to the endometrial glands compared to the pre- or post-receptive phases. This is in accordance with the generally applied pathohistological dating criteria that describe increasing stromal edema in the post-receptive endometrium as the fluids push the stromal cells further apart. An interesting additional finding is the smaller stromal cell size in the receptive stage compared to the pre- and post-receptive stages. The pathohistologist is normally incapable of routinely measuring the stromal cell sizes, which are very small. Ensemble methods enhance histology image segmentation by combining predictions from multiple models. This combination leads to higher accuracy, capturing intricate tissue details. It also boosts robustness, making segmentation more reliable despite image noise or staining variations. The ensemble further controls overfitting to specific training data, enhancing its ability to handle new histology images. These advantages make ensemble segmentation a positive choice for digital pathology tasks like cell classification, tumor analysis, and tissue composition studies. The next step would be the application of an automatic algorithm that is capable of evaluating the differences between endometrial samples that are in the receptive stage and not. The endometrial gland's structure and size changes during the menstrual cycle and glands from post-receptive samples are different from pre-receptive glands. A computer-aided receptiveness forecasting method should be developed for further use in this practical application.

8. Conclusions

For computer vision and AI researchers, the automated segmentation, recognition, and assessment of endometrial tissues remains a difficult task. In this work, we suggest using a metric-driven approach based on ensembles to automatically differentiate endometrial glands using group predictions. In order to create a training and testing dataset that is more statistically significant and to lower the computing resource needs, we also suggest an image processing phase. We used a dataset amassed during actual clinical practice to construct our experimental research. The suggested ensemble-based technique showed comparatively high endometrial gland identification accuracy. The ensemble-based model outperformed other designs, including U-Net, ResNet34-UNet, and U-Net++, with higher Dice score (0.95) and IoU (0.90) values. The metric-driven approach highlighted that the nuclei density is higher in the receptive samples. Endometrial stromal cell nuclear size and cell-to-cell distance are potential candidate criteria for the metric-driven automated evaluation of the endometrial phase. Moreover, more nuclei can be detected next to endometrial glands than in other parts of the tissue. Future studies will focus on the segmentation of more endometrial cells and/or structures, such as stroma and blood vessels. The current dataset will also be augmented with new whole-slide images of endometrial biopsies and expert-based annotations in order to build a better and more precise segmentation algorithm.

Author Contributions: Conceptualization, V.R., A.S. and E.D.; methodology, A.K.-G.; software, V.R.; validation, A.M. and R.B.; formal analysis, A.S.; investigation, V.R.; resources, M.S. and A.M.; writing—original draft preparation, V.R.; writing—review and editing, all authors; visualization, A.K.-G.; supervision, E.D. All authors have read and agreed to the published version of the manuscript.

Funding: This research was funded by the Estonian Research Council (grant PRG1076), Enterprise Estonia (grant no EU48695 and grant ReadUteru RE.5.02.22-0193), and also received funding from the Research Council of Lithuania (grant no 31V-72) and Horizon Europe (NESTOR, grant no. GA101120075).

Institutional Review Board Statement: This study was approved by the Research Ethics Committee of the University of Tartu, Estonia (No. 340T-12).

Informed Consent Statement: This study was conducted in accordance with the Declaration of Helsinki, and the protocol was approved by the Research Ethics Committee of the University of Tartu, Estonia (approval date 19 April 2021, No. 340/T-12). The scanned endometrial tissue slides of the anonymized participants were obtained from the beREADY test laboratory (www.beready.ee, accessed on 24 June 2024), Competence Centre on Health Technologies (CCHT), Tartu, Estonia).

Data Availability Statement: The data presented in this study are available on request from the corresponding author. The data are not publicly available due to ethical issues.

Conflicts of Interest: The authors declare no conflicts of interest.

References

1. World Health Organization (WHO). *International Classification of Diseases, 11th Revision (ICD-11)*; WHO: Geneva, Switzerland, 2018.
2. Cox, C.M.; Thoma, M.E.; Tchangalova, N.; Mburu, G.; Bornstein, M.J.; Johnson, C.L.; Kiarie, J. Infertility prevalence and the methods of estimation from 1990 to 2021: A systematic review and meta-analysis. *Hum. Reprod. Open* **2022**, *2022*, hoac051. [CrossRef] [PubMed]
3. Wyns, C.; De Geyter, C.; Calhaz-Jorge, C.; Kupka, M.S.; Motrenko, T.; Smeenk, J.; Bergh, C.; Tandler-Schneider, A.; Rugescu, I.A.; Goossens, V. ART in Europe, 2018: Results generated from European registries by ESHRE. European IVF Monitoring Consortium (EIM), for the European Society of Human Reproduction and Embryology (ESHRE). *Hum. Reprod. Open* **2022**, *2022*, hoac022. [CrossRef] [PubMed]
4. Raudonis, V.; Paulauskaite-Taraseviciene, A.; Sutiene, K.; Jonaitis, D. Towards the automation of early-stage human embryo development detection. *BioMed Eng. OnLine* **2019**, *18*, 120. [CrossRef] [PubMed]
5. Giménez, C.; Conversa, L.; Murria, L.; Meseguer, M. Time-Lapse Imaging. Morphokinetic analysis of In Vitro Fertilization outcomes. *Fertil. Steril.* **2023**, *120*, 218–227. [CrossRef] [PubMed]
6. Doroftei, B.; Ilie, O.-D.; Anton, N.; Armeanu, T.; Ilea, C. A Mini-Review Regarding the Clinical Outcomes of In Vitro Fertilization (IVF) Following Pre-Implantation Genetic Testing (PGT)-Next Generation Sequencing (NGS) Approach. *Diagnostics* **2022**, *12*, 1911. [CrossRef] [PubMed]
7. Wang, W.; Vilella, F.; Alama, P.; Moreno, I.; Mignardi, M.; Isakova, A.; Pan, W.; Simon, C.; Quake, S.R. Single-cell transcriptomic atlas of the human endometrium during the menstrual cycle. *Nat. Med.* **2020**, *26*, 1644–1653. [CrossRef] [PubMed]
8. Giudice, L.C. Multidimensional transcriptomic mapping of human endometrium at single-cell resolution. *Nat. Med.* **2020**, *26*, 1513–1514. [CrossRef] [PubMed]
9. Suhorutshenko, M.; Kukushkina, V.; Velthut-Meikas, A.; Altmäe, S.; Peters, M.; Mägi, R.; Krjutškov, K.; Koel, M.; Codoñer, F.M.; Martinez-Blanch, J.F.; et al. Endometrial receptivity revisited: Endometrial transcriptome adjusted for tissue cellular heterogeneity. *Hum. Reprod.* **2018**, *33*, 2074–2086. [CrossRef] [PubMed]
10. Altmäe, S.; Koel, M.; Võsa, U.; Adler, P.; Suhorutšenko, M.; Laisk-Podar, T.; Kukushkina, V.; Saare, M.; Velthut-Meikas, A.; Krjutškov, K.; et al. Meta-signature of human endometrial receptivity: A meta-analysis and validation study of transcriptomic biomarkers. *Sci. Rep.* **2017**, *7*, 10077. [CrossRef]
11. Koel, M.; Krjutškov, K.; Saare, M.; Samuel, K.; Lubenets, D.; Katayama, S.; Einarsdottir, E.; Vargas, E.; Sola-Leyva, A.; Lalitkumar, P.G.; et al. Human endometrial cell-type-specific RNA sequencing provides new insights into the embryo-endometrium interplay. *Hum. Reprod. Open* **2022**, *2022*, hoac043. [CrossRef]
12. Simón, C.; Gómez, C.; Cabanillas, S.; Vladimirov, I.; Castillón, G.; Giles, J.; Boynukalin, K.; Findikli, N.; Bahçeci, M.; Ortega, I.; et al. A 5-year multicentre randomized controlled trial comparing personalized, frozen and fresh blastocyst transfer in IVF. *Reprod. Biomed. Online* **2020**, *41*, 402–415. [CrossRef]
13. Toson, B.; Simon, C.; Moreno, I. The Endometrial Microbiome and Its Impact on Human Conception. *Int. J. Mol. Sci.* **2022**, *23*, 485. [CrossRef] [PubMed]
14. Moreno, I.; Garcia-Grau, I.; Perez-Villaroya, D.; Gonzalez-Monfort, M.; Bahçeci, M.; Barrionuevo, M.J.; Taguchi, S.; Puente, E.; Dimattina, M.; Lim, M.W.; et al. Endometrial microbiota composition is associated with reproductive outcome in infertile patients. *Microbiome* **2022**, *10*, 1. [CrossRef] [PubMed]
15. Noyes, R.W.; Hertig, A.T.; Rock, J. Dating the endometrial biopsy. *Obstet. Gynecol. Surv.* **1950**, *5*, 561–564. [CrossRef]
16. Murdoch, T.A.; Veras, E.F.T.; Mazur, T.M.; Kurman, R.J. *Diagnosis of Endometrial Biopsies and Curettings. A Practical Approach*, 3rd ed.; Springer: Berlin/Heidelberg, Germany, 2019.
17. Alfer, J.; Fattahi, A.; Bleisinger, N.; Krieg, J.; Behrens, R.; Dittrich, R.; Beckmann, M.W.; Hartmann, A.; Classen-Linke, I.; Popovici, R.M. Endometrial Dating Method Detects Individual Maturation Sequences During the Secretory Phase. *Vivo* **2020**, *34*, 1951–1963. [CrossRef] [PubMed]
18. Chen, G.D.; Pang, T.T.; Li, P.S.; Zhou, Z.X.; Lin, D.X.; Fan, D.Z.; Guo, X.L.; Liu, Z.P. Early pregnancy vitamin D and the risk of adverse maternal and infant outcomes: A retrospective cohort study. *BMC Pregnancy Childbirth* **2020**, *20*, 465. [CrossRef]
19. Fouad, S.; Randell, D.; Galton, A.; Mehanna, H.; Landini, G. Unsupervised morphological segmentation of tissue compartments in histopathological images. *PLoS ONE* **2017**, *12*, e0188717. [CrossRef]
20. Haque, I.R.I.; Neubert, J. Deep learning approaches to biomedical image segmentation. *Inform. Med. Unlocked* **2020**, *18*, 100297. [CrossRef]
21. Gondim, P.H.C.C.; Limirio, P.H.J.O.; Rocha, F.S.; Batista, J.D.; Dechichi, P.; Travençolo, B.A.N.; Backes, A.R. Automatic Segmentation of Bone Canals in Histological Images. *J. Digit. Imaging* **2021**, *34*, 678–690. [CrossRef]
22. Graham, S.; Vu, Q.D.; Raza, S.E.A.; Azam, A.; Tsang, Y.W.; Kwak, J.T.; Rajpoot, N. Hover-Net: Simultaneous segmentation and classification of nuclei in multi-tissue histology images. *Med. Image Anal.* **2019**, *58*, 101563. [CrossRef]
23. Priego-Torres, B.M.; Sanchez-Morillo, D.; Fernandez-Granero, M.A.; Garcia-Rojo, M. Automatic segmentation of whole-slide H&E stained breast histopathology images using a deep convolutional neural network architecture. *Expert Syst. Appl.* **2020**, *151*, 113387. [CrossRef]

24. Ali, H.; Haq, I.U.; Cui, L.; Feng, J. MSAL-Net: Improve accurate segmentation of nuclei in histopathology images by multiscale attention learning network. *BMC Med. Inform. Decis. Mak.* **2022**, *22*, 90. [CrossRef] [PubMed]
25. Ronneberger, O.; Fischer, P.; Brox, T. U-Net: Convolutional Networks for Biomedical Image Segmentation. In Proceedings of the Medical Image Computing and Computer-Assisted Intervention—MICCAI 2015, Munich, Germany, 5–9 October 2015; Navab N., Hornegger, J., Wells, W.M., Frangi, A.F., Eds.; Springer International Publishing: Cham, Switzerland, 2015; pp. 234–241.
26. Zhou, Z.; Siddiquee, M.M.R.; Tajbakhsh, N.; Liang, J. UNet++: Redesigning Skip Connections to Exploit Multiscale Features in Image Segmentation. *IEEE Trans. Med. Imaging* **2019**, *39*, 1856–1867. [CrossRef] [PubMed]

applied sciences

MDPI

Review

Integrating Artificial Intelligence for Academic Advanced Therapy Medicinal Products: Challenges and Opportunities

Cristobal Aguilar-Gallardo * and Ana Bonora-Centelles

Unidad de Terapias Avanzadas, Instituto Investigación Sanitaria La Fe, Av. Fernando Abril Martorell, 106, 46026 Valencia, Spain
* Correspondence: cristobal_aguilar@iislafe.es

Abstract: Cell and gene therapies represent promising new treatment options for many diseases, but also face challenges for clinical translation and delivery. Hospital-based GMP facilities enable rapid bench-to-bedside development and patient access but require significant adaptation to implement pharmaceutical manufacturing in healthcare infrastructures constrained by space, regulations, and resources. This article reviews key considerations, constraints, and solutions for establishing hospital facilities for advanced therapy medicinal products (ATMPs). Technologies like process analytical technology (PAT), continuous manufacturing, and artificial intelligence (AI) can aid these facilities through enhanced process monitoring, control, and automation. However, quality systems tailored for product quality rather than just compliance, and substantial investment in infrastructure, equipment, personnel, and multi-departmental coordination, remain crucial for successful hospital ATMP facilities and to drive new therapies from research to clinical impact.

Keywords: bioprocess; advanced therapy medicinal products (ATMPs); artificial intelligence (AI); cell and gene therapies; bench-to-bedside delivery; personalized medicine; GMP facilities; quality systems

1. Introduction

Advanced therapy medicinal products (ATMPs) like cell and gene therapies are innovative treatment approaches that modify patients' genes, cells, or tissues to treat disease. 'Academic advanced therapy' in the context of ATMPs refers to those developed within academic institutions, including medical centers and hospital environments. This approach contrasts with industrial ATMP development, focusing on pioneering innovative treatments and bridging the gap between basic research and clinical application. Academic institutions play a crucial role in the translational process, emphasizing a blend of scientific discovery and practical healthcare outcomes. These centers convert laboratory discoveries into viable therapies, integrating innovative treatment development within academic research frameworks, distinct from commercial pharmaceutical manufacturing [1]. However, ATMPs remain experimental, requiring an initial translation from laboratories to clinical trials to demonstrate safety and efficacy. The personalized nature of many ATMPs, using autologous or allogenic patient cells, adds manufacturing complexity compared to traditional pharmaceuticals. Each patient-specific batch must be rapidly produced in small quantities and under stringent aseptic conditions. Strict guidelines like good manufacturing practices (GMPs) are essential for ensuring quality. The implementation of GMPs is mandatory to secure approval from regulatory agencies for the production and use of ATMPs.

Traditionally, pharmaceutical companies have possessed the infrastructure and expertise to manufacture therapies for clinical trials under GMPs. However, the personalized nature of most autologous/allogenic ATMPs has required academic medical centers to develop their own in-house GMP facilities, to enable bench-to-bedside translation and patient access within the same institution. However, constructing GMP facilities within hospitals faces considerable constraints. Here, we review the key challenges academic medical centers must address in establishing ATMP manufacturing, as well as emerging solutions to facilitate the clinical translation of innovative new therapies.

This article aims to explore the multifaceted role of artificial intelligence techniques such as machine learning and computer vision in the ATMP manufacturing revolution. It seeks to provide a global view of the current state of AI integration, specifically the application of subfields such as natural language processing and predictive modelling, carrying out a detailed search for information on the benefits that these technologies provide and the challenges entailed, particularly in relation to GMP compliance and optimization of hospital ATMP facilities. Through this exploration, this paper will illuminate the dynamic interplay between specialized AI applications and ATMP manufacturing, highlighting how this integration of specific capabilities such as automated image analysis and adaptive control can advance the field, while ensuring safety, effectiveness, and regulatory compliance.

2. Advantages of On-Site Hospital Facilities

Having GMP facilities located directly within academic hospitals provides major advantages for producing autologous/allogenic ATMPs. Proximity allows cell-based therapies to be rapidly manufactured on-site and delivered directly to patients. This avoids risks associated with transporting fragile cell products long distances between external manufacturing sites and hospitals [2]. This closeness not only preserves the integrity of cellular products but also simplifies logistics, reducing both the costs and risks associated with transporting products over long distances. Furthermore, the alignment of manufacturing with clinical schedules allows for flexible batch planning, accommodating rapid changes due to production dynamics or patient needs [3,4]. On-site facilities also enable the smooth translation of therapies from laboratory discovery to clinical trials. Once safety has been established in early phase studies, hospital facilities can continue providing patient access through expanded access programs.

One of the major disadvantages faced by hospital facilities is limited space. Hospitals must integrate cleanrooms and manufacturing equipment into existing infrastructure not designed for production. Facilities must be strategically designed to make optimal use of available space. The use of isolators and closed systems can limit the need for larger cleanrooms [5,6]. Careful planning allows the creation of multi-product facilities that segregate therapies like viral vectors or gene-modified cells. Despite space restrictions, on-site locations remain ideal for the frequent manufacturing of personalized cell therapies requiring rapid delivery in small batches [3].

2.1. Implementing GMPs in Hospitals

While proximity provides clear advantages, implementing pharmaceutical manufacturing and GMPs within healthcare settings also poses challenges. Hospital staff are generally unfamiliar with the extensive GMP documentation, training in bioprocesses, and oversight required for clinical cell and gene therapy production [7]. Quality systems within healthcare focus on ensuring optimal medical services, whereas pharmaceutical GMPs aim to guarantee consistent product quality and safety [8]. Extensive GMP training and ongoing specialized personnel education are essential to bridge this gap.

The manufacturing of autologous/allogenic ATMPs integrates key hospital units, as depicted in Figure 1, to streamline the entire production and administration process. A clinical research and clinical trials unit spearheads the development of clinical research projects, ensuring meticulous research support and data integrity. Close to this is the hematology department, which is crucial for patient management in cell-based therapies, covering diagnosis, pre-treatment assessments, and collaboration for ATMP application. Notably, the transplantation unit within this department specializes in the preparatory and follow-up care for stem cell therapy [9]. Research areas like translational research and process development bridge the gap between laboratory research and clinical application, facilitated by innovative research fields such as biomarker identification cell therapy and genetic engineering. The apheresis unit plays a vital role in the initial collection of cellular materials, ensuring expert handling of apheresis and patient care. In the sphere of product preparation, the pharmacy department is pivotal for the final formulation and storage of ATMPs, maintaining optimal conditions until clinical use. At the heart of manufacturing is the GMP facility, encompassing a comprehensive spectrum from manufacturing to quality assurance, as well as adhering to strict documentation and compliance standards. The synergy among these units, as visualized in Figure 1, is essential for the construction, qualification, validation, and maintenance of GMP facilities. This coordinated approach ensures that hospital activities, including the handling of biological samples and adherence to GMP requirements, maintain product quality throughout all manufacturing phases. Continuous communication across these units fosters an awareness of GMP regulations, which is crucial for staff members not typically versed in pharmaceutical standards [3,10].

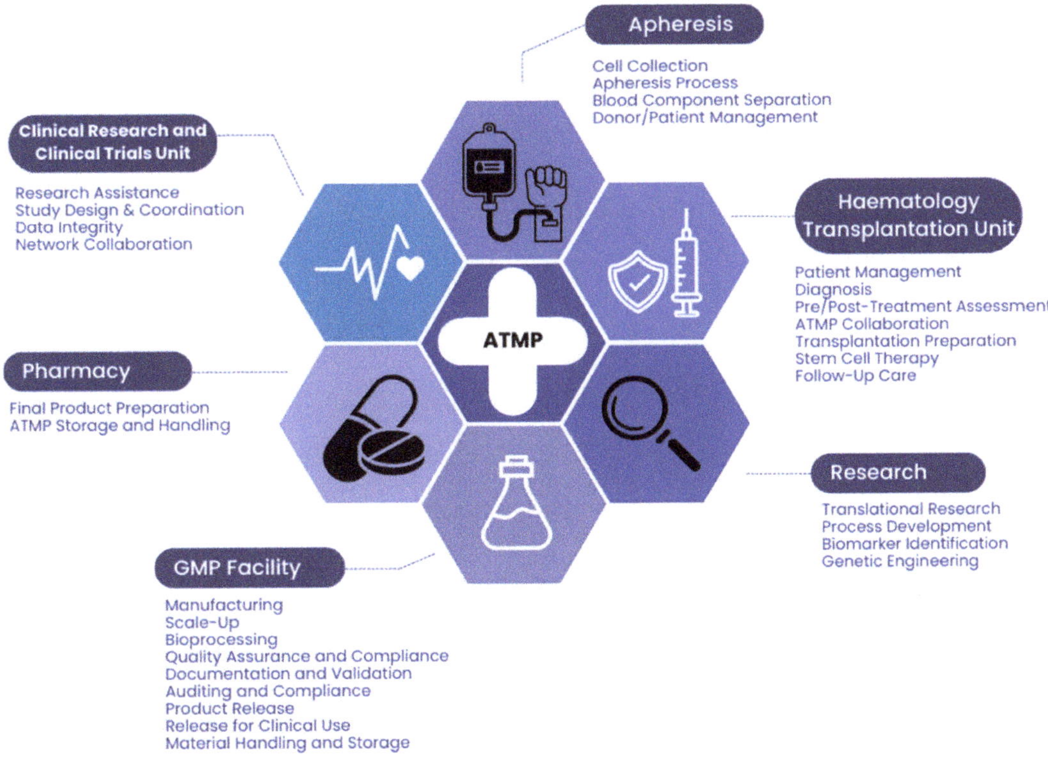

Figure 1. Presents a cohesive overview of the operational framework surrounding advanced therapy medicinal products (ATMPs). At the core of the illustration is the 'ATMP', with surrounding nodes representing various specialized units. Each hospital unit is integral to the ATMP development and application process, highlighting the collaborative nature of this advanced medicinal ecosystem.

Quality system adaptation in hospitals, specifically focusing on product quality, safety, and efficacy, is key to implementing GMPs in hospitals. Excessive procedures solely for regulatory compliance can impede operations. A risk-based approach (RBA) in hospitals can concentrate quality efforts on critical factors affecting products and patients [8]. This method facilitates translating ATMPs to clinical practice, while ensuring compliance with pharmaceutical manufacturing standards within complex hospital environments [3,11,12]. This approach helps to identify priority areas where the quality system can be optimized without compromising product quality or patient safety in any case. This enables hospitals to avoid unnecessary regulatory procedures that are solely for the sake of regulatory compliance and that do not contribute to operational efficiency or patient care. This balanced approach ensures that, while regulatory standards are fully met, the primary emphasis remains on safeguarding patient health and ensuring the efficacy of ATMPs. In essence, adapting a quality system using RBA perspectives is not only about meeting regulatory requirements but also about enhancing the quality of healthcare delivery in the challenging and dynamic environment of hospitals [13].

2.2. Investment in Infrastructure and Personnel

Significant investment in infrastructure, equipment, and personnel is essential when establishing in-house GMP facilities [14]. Constructing, qualifying, and maintaining pharmaceutical cleanrooms requires extensive capital. Specialized manufacturing and monitoring equipment suited for cell processing must be purchased and qualified. The costs of infrastructure, alongside expenses for consumables and testing, highlight the value of efficient facility designs that maximize productivity.

Recruiting personnel with appropriate backgrounds in cell therapy process development, GMP manufacturing, quality control, quality assurance, and regulatory experience is crucial but challenging given this field's novelty. Finding personnel with experience in clinical cell bioprocessing is not always simple. Staff availability can limit capacity, so manufacturing strategies maximizing operator productivity can enable hospitals to meet clinical demand within personnel constraints [5]. Extensive planning and financial investment are critical for establishing the necessary infrastructure, staff, training, and multi-departmental coordination for hospital ATMP facilities, to effectively transition new therapies from research to clinical application. This transition is especially pertinent when integrating emerging technologies like AI, where financial considerations are paramount. The study by Harrison et al. underscored the importance of economical scalability in cell therapy manufacturing, highlighting the potential of small-scale microfactories as a cost-effective approach before progressing to larger-scale macrofactories [15,16]. This model calls for careful economic assessment, particularly in automating processes to enhance efficiency and reduce costs, while maintaining quality control and managing the variability in donor cell characteristics. This strategy of balancing innovation with sustainability can serve as a template for AI integration in ATMP manufacturing, and it may even promote and facilitate clinical integration [17,18]. Infrastructure, equipment, and personnel training represent substantial investments, especially for smaller-scale academic facilities involved in the production of CAR-T cells, a type of ATMP. These upfront investments are pivotal due to the high costs associated with CAR-T cell manufacturing, which can reach approximately USD 400,000 per therapy production. However, integrating AI in this process offers a promising opportunity to reduce these costs. AI's ability to analyze and interpret data can significantly improve the efficiency and cost-effectiveness of CAR-T cell production by automating the multi-step manufacturing process, allowing comprehensive data collection. Such automation not only directly lowers high manufacturing costs but also aids in optimizing logistics and scaling production. Moreover, AI technologies could assist in identifying suitable patients for therapy, monitoring therapy progression, and predicting treatment responses. However, creating an AI-based CAR-T cell therapy system also raises challenges such as data privacy, data security, and the requirement to integrate AI systems into existing workflows. Ultimately, reducing contamination incidents and batch failures through AI can boost usable outputs, with forecasts suggesting that the total cost of goods may decrease by up to 18%, thus enhancing process sustainability. These benefits cannot be realized until there are verifiable use cases, combined with increased maturity in major capabilities such as blockchain technology and digitalization, highlighting the clear economic incentives and reduction in barriers to AI adoption of ATMP manufacturing [19,20].

Additionally, it is a fact that decentralized manufacturing has emerged as a crucial strategy in the cell and gene therapy arena, not just revolutionizing production landscapes but also addressing staffing and training challenges. Thus, a decentralized model refers to distributing production across multiple hospital nodes, while on-site facilities refer to the presence of manufacturing capabilities within each individual hospital. This decentralized paradigm complements on-site facilities by enabling production to occur in smaller, dispersed facilities across locations, rather than consolidated in one large, centralized facility. The decentralized network model allows hospitals to reap the benefits of on-site production, while distributing resources and sharing expertise across nodes. Through dispersing production across multiple locations, this inherently meets the demand for personalized treatments. The pivotal role of automation in this new paradigm complements the indispensable expertise of trained human operators, ensuring the management of process variability and adherence to stringent quality standards within 'smart cell factories'. This approach synergizes with the need for highly skilled personnel in cell therapy process development, GMP manufacturing, and regulatory compliance. It also aligns with the integration of AI and other emerging technologies, which are essential for economical scalability, as discussed in the study by Harrison et al. Decentralized manufacturing not only enhances operator productivity but also democratizes the value chain, generating socioeconomic benefits through job creation. Additionally, it offers a strategic framework for academic facilities involved in CAR-T cell production, addressing the substantial upfront investments in infrastructure and training. Incorporating AI into decentralized systems promises to reduce manufacturing costs, optimize logistics, and scale production, while ensuring data privacy and security. This model presents a sustainable solution, balancing innovation with efficiency, as well as setting a template for future advancements in ATMP manufacturing [21].

3. Enhancing Hospital Facilities with New Technologies

Emerging technologies present opportunities to enhance the capabilities of hospital ATMP facilities within ever-present space, time, cost, and personnel constraints. Process analytical technology (PAT) is a pivotal advancement employing advanced in-line monitoring and process control to optimize manufacturing [22]. By continuously analyzing physicochemical parameters like pH, dissolved oxygen, and temperature—as well as metabolites and nutrient concentrations, such as glucose and glutamine, and byproduct concentrations, such as lactate and ammonia—bioreactors can be automatically controlled, decreasing manual operations [23,24]. This approach is complemented by the application of advanced sensory technologies, particularly fluorescent optical sensors, as highlighted in recent research [25]. These sensors are instrumental for real-time monitoring, enabling the quantification of analytes of interest during bioprocessing. This capability for early detection is crucial for identifying deviations from method parameters, facilitating timely countermeasures and ensuring consistency in individualized batches. The integration of PAT with state-of-the-art sensory technologies underscores the increase in biomanufacturing efficiency for enhanced control methods in the complex cellular manufacturing environments of cell and gene therapy. Automated cell counting and viability analysis and product concentration reduces delays when waiting for quality control results before proceeding to the next manufacturing step. PAT enables real-time process adjustments and consistency between individualized batches [26]. Building upon the principles of PAT, a recent study [27] made significant strides toward enhancing the capabilities of in-line monitoring and process optimization in biomanufacturing. This research introduced a pioneering automated method for creating Raman spectroscopy models using Python and Bayes optimization. This innovation represents a significant leap in the field, dramatically improving the accuracy of models and simplifying the complexities associated with monitoring a diverse range of compounds. The study's approach notably broadened the scope of detectable compounds in cell cultures. It successfully constructed models for almost every amino acid and extended this capability to components traditionally elusive to Raman spectroscopy, such as metal ions, oxygen, and carbon dioxide. This expansion in the range of detectable compounds is pivotal, as it enhances our understanding of cell culture environments and allows for more precise control over the manufacturing process. Highlighting the precision of this method, the study's models, particularly for glucose concentration, demonstrated remarkable accuracy, with a correlation coefficient (R^2) of

0.93 and a root mean square error of 0.23. Such precision in monitoring is critical in the biomanufacturing sector, where the maintenance of optimal culture conditions directly influences product quality and yield. Moreover, the method's ability to model various compounds, including those indicative of stress markers like BiP and oxidative glutathione, opens up new possibilities for monitoring a wide array of culture characteristics. This capability is instrumental for real-time monitoring and feedback control, ensuring the continuous adaptation and optimization of culture conditions. It aligns directly with the objectives of PAT, whose fundamental focus is to maintain consistency and quality across batches through real-time process adjustments. The integration of this method with advanced AI technologies further underscores its potential. Exploiting the power of AI, this approach can create more comprehensive and precise models for a broad spectrum of parameters, extending beyond traditional medium components and metabolites. This synergy between Raman spectroscopy modelling and AI technologies provides sophisticated and efficient monitoring and control mechanisms in biopharmaceutical manufacturing, aligning with the industry's move towards more automated, precise, and intelligent process management systems.

Continuous manufacturing, producing therapies in an uninterrupted flow rather than individual batches, shows promise for integration into hospital facilities. One example that has been demonstrated is interrupted cell culture production of viral vectors [28,29], as well as perfusion systems that enable constant harvesting of cellular products [30]. Ongoing downstream processing steps are also being integrated, to develop end-to-end production. Compared to batch manufacturing, continuous processes require smaller equipment footprints, allowing hospitals to increase productivity within the given space constraints. The verification and validation methods enabled by PAT support can ensure quality control in real time. The research by Williams et al. [31] exemplified the profound impact of PAT in biopharmaceutical manufacturing, particularly in the optimization of cell and gene therapy processes. Their study employed the Ranger system, a novel refractometry-based PAT, which demonstrated its efficacy in real-time monitoring of metabolic activity within HEK293T cell cultures during the production of lentiviral vectors. This system's ability to rapidly discern the relationship between bioreactor pH and culture metabolic activity, and to adjust the pH accordingly, resulted in a notable 1.8-fold increase in metabolic activity compared to an unoptimized process. However, it also revealed a particular aspect of cellular response: increased metabolic activity did not correspond to increased lentiviral vector production, highlighting the complexity of these biological systems and the importance of sophisticated process control. Furthermore, through metabolic flux modelling, Williams et al. uncovered how low-pH environments caused a significant metabolic shift in cells, redirecting cellular resources from growth towards managing environmental stress and adverse conditions. These insights underscore the capacity of PAT, not only in enhancing process efficiency, but also for enriching our understanding of the underlying biological mechanisms, thus contributing to a continuous improvement in quality control and process optimization in real time [31].

Artificial intelligence (AI) and machine learning (ML) have the potential to facilitate and enhance the analysis of the vast amount of data generated during PAT monitoring and throughout manufacturing steps [20,32]. By detecting patterns and correlations, AI models can identify critical bioprocess parameters, predict deviations, and determine potential actions, aiding biotechnologist personnel. Intelligent algorithms can also support the automation of elements of batch record reviewing, equipment maintenance, prevention campaigns, and contamination risk analysis. AI-based automation of cell and gene therapy manufacturing, sample tracking, and environmental monitoring of the cleanroom will increase hospital facilities' consistency and oversight. Recent research has exemplified AI's aptitude for tackling personalized medicine's intricacies. Schmitt et al.'s study described predictive machine learning algorithms that can anticipate individual patient-specific therapy response rates based on biomarker and genomic data analysis [19]. Meanwhile, Li et al., [33] discussed an AI digital platform that automates cell therapy production tracking and shows enhanced consistency between autologous batches. This concept is in line with advanced AI-powered microfluidic technology, which has significantly enhanced both fundamental biological research and translational clinical diagnosis. The implementation of AI in microfluidic technology, as highlighted in a recent study, enables the processing of the large-scale data obtained in high-throughput assays. These AI models can analyze multimodal datasets including images, videos, electric signals, and sequences from microfluidic devices. They offer the capability not only to collect data, but to understand and interpret it, ultimately facilitating fundamental and translational research in fields like single-cell genomics, cell signaling, and cell type discovery. Beyond mere planning, real-time learning systems, as demonstrated in microfluidics, can dynamically optimize continuous bioreactor parameters, adjusting to variability between patient cell samples. This capability is especially crucial in single-cell biology, where AI models extract cellular features from various modalities and use deep learning algorithms for more intuitive data processing and uncovering hidden connections among data. These advancements in AI model development tailored for single-cell biology signify a new era, where AI not only enhances data processing and feature extraction, but also aids in interpreting the underlying structure of big data in cell analysis, including cell counting, sorting, and classification. The integration of AI into cell therapy manufacturing, as explored by Li et al., [33] has led to the creation of an automated high-throughput genome editing platform that revolutionizes the consistency and efficiency of producing autologous batches. This cutting-edge platform leverages AI to streamline the gene editing process in mammalian cells, radically transforming the traditional labor-intensive methods into a rapid, high-throughput, and error-minimized operation. The pivotal achievement of this innovation is the chromatin accessibility enabled learning model (CAELM), an AI learning model that accurately predicts the efficiency of cytosine base editors (CBEs). By integrating both chromatin accessibility and sequence information, CAELM offers a profound enhancement in predicting in situ base editing outcomes [33].

This advanced model stands out for its precision and reliability, surpassing existing predictive tools like BE-Hive in its correlation with actual base editing efficiencies. The strength of CAELM is evident in its Pearson's correlation values, which range from 0.42 to 0.87, demonstrating a high level of predictive accuracy critical for the development of genome editing-based therapeutics. This transformative approach not only accelerates the scientific research in base editing, but also permits more accurate and efficient therapeutic applications, marking a significant step in the intersection of AI and biomedicine [33,34].

4. Scaling Gene and Cell Therapy ATMPs from Research to the Clinic with AI

Gene and cell therapies show immense potential as advanced medicinal therapies, but scaling initial proof-of-concepts into robust clinical processes poses difficulties and limitations. The sensitivity of living systems means research protocols often fail when directly applied at the larger volumes required for patient treatments. Healthcare centers developing gene therapy ATMPs must optimize this scale-up, to progress from early studies to clinical manufacturing. AI and real-time metabolomics analysis can allow enhanced process understanding, to bridge the research-to-clinic scale-up gap.

During initial studies, gene delivery mechanisms and editing efficiency are evaluated at laboratory scale. However, small-scale conditions rarely translate directly to the larger volumes required for patient doses. Cell growth kinetics, vector productivity, and other critical quality attributes commonly diverge during scale-up. Extensive empirical optimization trials have traditionally been needed to adapt processes to clinical scale. AI technologies offer tools to accelerate scale-up by revealing key biological factors affected by production volume. ML algorithms integrating multivariate data can identify patterns linking process parameters to cell health across scales [35]. This model-driven approach rapidly highlights stress factors impairing growth or productivity when scaling up batches. AI control systems can then automatically optimize dynamic feeding, pH, dissolved oxygen, and other bioreactor parameters based on continuous metabolite monitoring.

Cellular metabolism provides integral indicators of the biological effects of gene engineering and culture environment. High-throughput metabolomics profiling coupled with AI analysis elucidates metabolic phenotypes and clarifies discrepancies between research and clinical protocols. Tracking key metabolites and pathways disrupted during scale-up highlights target areas for process improvements. For instance, glutamine limitation or build-up of lactate may only occur above certain volumes. AI modelling can integrate multi-omics datasets with process data to reveal the metabolic shifts responsible for reduced clinical-scale productivity. This understanding enables tailored nutrient supplementation or gene modifications, to restore a favorable metabolism. Additionally, real-time biosensors monitoring metabolites allow adaptive AI control systems to dynamically optimize nutrients and parameters throughout production. Maintaining cultures in ideal metabolic regimes enhances process robustness during scale-up.

5. Analysis of the Role and Potential Impact of AI in Academic ATMP Manufacturing, with Additional Details on the Key Advantages AI Can Provide

5.1. Process Monitoring

The personalized nature of autologous ATMPs results in inherent variability between patient cell samples used for manufacturing. This variability in starting material can propagate through the process, making achieving consistency between individualized batches challenging. Conventional bioprocess monitoring typically relies on manual and periodic offline sample analysis. AI enables improved real-time process oversight through advanced sensor instrumentation coupled with intelligent algorithms continuously analyzing data for patterns predictive of critical quality attributes.

Multivariate AI models imply that machine learning algorithms can integrate data streams from arrays of in-line sensors and bioreactors probe analyzers, to identify interrelationships between bio-parameters and product quality. This higher-resolution view allows slight process deviations to be detected earlier and corrections to be made through automated feedback control, rather than periodic and manual sampling. Thus, AI process monitoring provides complete tracking and mapping of the multidimensional course of cell bioproduction. ML techniques can also incorporate spectroscopic [36], imaging, and other process data, to build predictive models of final product critical quality attributes such as identity, purity, and potency [37]. This real-time predictive capability facilitates standardized quality and reduced variability within and between batches, as well as reduced batch failures.

In the exploration of AI's impact on ATMP production, we can observe distinct advantages and challenges, as outlined in Table 1. Enhanced process monitoring and the automation of manufacturing tasks are among the key benefits, leading to increased efficiency and reduced workload for biotechnologists. Moreover, AI's dynamic control and adaptability allow fine-tuning cell culture conditions, thus ensuring batch consistency, which is critical for patient-specific treatments. On the other hand, issues such as data security concerns and the requirement for specialized personnel present noteworthy obstacles, potentially hindering AI's integration.

A further analysis is presented in Table 2 of the ATMP production process with and without AI integration. It is evident that AI integration significantly enhances process monitoring and manufacturing efficiency, offering a more sophisticated approach to data management, which traditional methods lack. The enhanced quality and consistency afforded by AI contribute to better control of product integrity; nonetheless, there are higher investment and costs required for implementing such advanced technologies. The need for personnel training and expertise remains an essential consideration to fully realize the potential of AI in this field.

Table 1. Advantages and disadvantages of AI in ATMP production.

Advantages of AI in ATMP Production	Disadvantages of AI in ATMP Production
Enhanced Process Monitoring	**Data Security Concerns**
Real-time oversight and data analysis for maintaining consistency and quality.	Risks associated with patient data privacy and data integrity in AI systems.
Automation of Manufacturing Tasks	**High Initial Investment**
Increases efficiency, precision, and scalability, reducing the workload of biotechnologists.	Significant upfront costs for AI integration and infrastructure development.
Dynamic Control and Adaptability	**Limited Data in Early Development**
AI systems can adjust to the variability in patient cell samples, optimizing batch consistency.	AI models may lack accuracy in early stages due to insufficient data for machine learning.
Improved Data Management	**Requirement for Specialized Personnel**
Effective handling of large datasets, enhancing process comprehension and decision-making.	Need for staff with expertise in AI and bioprocessing, who can be scarce.
Systems Biology Integration	**Regulatory Challenges**
AI aids in understanding complex biological relationships, enhancing predictive medicine.	Ambiguity in regulatory compliance for emerging AI applications in healthcare.

Table 2. Comparison of ATMP production with and without AI integration.

Aspect of ATMP Production	With AI Integration	Without AI Integration
Process Monitoring	Enhanced real-time monitoring and analysis using AI algorithms.	Relies on manual and periodic offline sample analysis.
Manufacturing Efficiency	Higher efficiency and scalability due to automation and dynamic control.	Less efficient, often limited by manual operations and static processes.
Data Management	Advanced handling of large and complex datasets, facilitating better decision-making.	Traditional data management, potentially leading to slower and less informed decisions.
Quality and Consistency	Improved product quality and batch consistency through predictive models and real-time adjustments.	Potential variability and quality issues due to lack of real-time monitoring and control.
Investment and Costs	Higher initial investment but potential long-term cost savings through efficiency and reduced error rates.	Lower initial costs but potentially higher long-term operational expenses.
Personnel Training and Expertise	Requires staff trained in AI and data science.	Relies more on traditional bioprocessing skills.

5.2. Automation

The manufacturing of ATMPs involves numerous supplementary operations beside the bioprocess itself, including supply chain management, sample tracking, the changeover between batches, contamination control, equipment maintenance, regulatory compliance adherence, quality control, batch record reviewing, and data management. AI enables automation of many tasks, to enhance precision and consistency, increase efficiency, allow scalability according to production demands, improve cost-effectiveness, and reduce biotechnology personnel workloads. Robotic process automation can replicate and mimic administrative and repetitive activities like data entry, basic data manipulation, and report generation. ML algorithms can schedule planned equipment calibration, preventive maintenance, and cleaning procedures based on the runtime. Cleanroom environmental monitoring data analyzed by AI models can provide alerts on contamination risks and suggest corrective actions, to avoid batch losses or disruptions to production.

Automated microscopy employing computer vision techniques permits precise characterization of cells. The searching of batch records by an AI makes use of natural language processing and provides appropriate results related to valuable data. Augmented reality helps operators carry out critical manual operations, in order to minimize mistakes. Multi-faceted AI-driven automation can be used to address the spatial and staffing limitations that academic ATMP facilities often experience. Flexible cell-factories able to manufacture multiple individualized therapies in accordance with the specific requirements of a healthcare center can also be encompassed within ML methods, instead of following large-scale production. With intelligent automation, workforces can become more productive using limited staffing, while facilities can be made more efficient.

5.3. Dynamic Control

Adaptive bioprocess control systems are critical for ATMP manufacturing, given the inevitable variability between patient cell samples. Traditional bioreactors rely on feedback and control loops tracking setpoint values [38,39]. However, the optimal parameters and tolerances may differ for each autologous batch's unique biologic characteristics. AI allows more advanced control schemes that continuously recalculate in real time the ideal setpoint based on multivariate analysis. ML algorithms can discover relationships between sensor data, bioprocess parameters, and critical quality attributes of the products in bioreactors. Through this approach, a prediction model of the final product's quality can guide dynamic adjustments of process variables in real time, leading to maximized batch consistency and robustness.

Hybrid AI strategies combine mechanistic first-principles models of cell growth and metabolism with data-driven ML models that capture the existing variability in the data. These models are commonly used for research and learning purposes, to gain insights into the intrinsic behavior of biological systems. Thus, adaptive model predictive control integrates these models to continuously re-optimize process parameters based on current state measurements of the process. Thus, as more batches are produced, semi-supervised ML can improve the controller model. AI control systems are particularly well-suited for handling the high variability and lack of expertise that are frequently experienced during early ATMP process development and technology transfer, because of their capacity for self-learning. The capability of AIs in handling complexity allows flexible and sophisticated adaptive control, especially when dealing with the specific needs of tailored batches [40].

5.4. Data Management

ATMP manufacturing fundamentally relies on synthesizing various databases, starting from the clinical status of the incoming patient sample and ending with the final product testing results. The correlation between clinical indicators and production factors can have an impact on product quality and treatment outcomes. Traditional data infrastructure faces challenges due to the vast amount of data produced. This data comes from various sources: sensors in process arrays, omics analyses, and electronic records. Additionally, the need to track and trace this data adds to the complexity, creating stress and pressure on existing systems. In this regard, AI can provide tools suited for managing and handling heterogeneous structured, unstructured, and semi-structured data. ML is efficient for identifying imperceptible patterns and correlations within massive datasets. AI can integrate electronic batch records, processing data, laboratory results, clinical data, and other sources into contextualized knowledge that enhances process comprehension. Well-known techniques such as natural language processing permit mining unstructured textual records. AI can enhance data management through dimensionality reduction, noise filtering, missing data imputation, and real-time data cleansing, to consolidate relevant information from discordant sources and that is apparently unrelated into usable and applicable models, guiding decision making and controlling adjustments to optimize each personalized batch. Thus, the integration of AI's multifaceted capabilities, including knowledge contextualization, data mining, dimensionality reduction, and real-time data management, highlights its strengths for advancing process understanding and facilitating optimal real-time decision-making for the production of personalized gene therapy ATMPs.

5.5. Systems Biology and AI

The aim of systems biology is developing complex models that integrate data from multiple disciplines, in order to explain complex biologic relationships or transactions. This is contrary to the reductionist approach of the twentieth century that gave insight into some areas but not in full regarding the comprehension of complexities and interpretation of non-structured elements. In addition to other methods, systems and network biology offer a unique approach to analyze multi-omics data. This method integrates various data types to uncover new patterns and behaviors in complex molecular and cellular networks. It does this by utilizing machine learning (ML) algorithms, which helps in understanding these complex biological systems more effectively. Network biology empowered by AI is important for describing the associations within normal and dysfunctional phenotypes. It aspires to clearer, explicit, and deterministic models, in order to further predictive, preventive, and personalized medicine. The large volume of multi-omics data makes functional integration impracticable manually, necessitating advanced analytics like network analysis, Bayesian methods, and multivariate techniques—now powered by AI.

5.6. Advanced Control Systems Leveraging AI

Recently, bioreactors have employed automatic proportional-integral-derivative (PID) control for parameters like temperature, while others require manual regulation [41]. The progress in control strategies, optimization algorithms, and software systems has been significant. Contemporary bioreactors often incorporate SCADA systems requiring a human–machine interface [42,43]. Newer systems are starting to implement adaptive model-based controllers, providing two key advantages: (i) optimizing constraints and control signal ranges; (ii) dynamically adjusting actions based on control outcomes and system changes. Their strength is in continuously recalculating the optimal next steps during operation. The development of distributed control systems in communication protocols is gradually progressing. The combination of increased computing power and a wider array of algorithms now allows the implementation of iterative control techniques. This employs an extensive pool of data obtained during monitoring and a deeper understanding of cell culture behavior, facilitating the creation of more precise and sensitive AI-driven models using systems that integrate ML algorithms, computer vision, and the other AI techniques described above. Basically, AI plays a central role in managing the variability and complexity within the ambit of ATMP manufacturing. It is undeniable that AI can greatly benefit academic ATMP production, but previously it required proficient control over different facets. As previously discussed, AI can enhance process monitoring, automation, control, and data integration for personalized therapies. However, implementing AI in this sector clearly demands rigorous oversight of technology capabilities, data accuracy, personnel competencies, and regulatory adherence.

A cross-functional understanding of AI maturity is crucial. Models like the Artificial Intelligence Optimization Team's [40,44,45] AI maturity level characterization model allow an organization to evaluate its current AI proficiencies across manufacturing categories, identifying gaps [46]. This assessment enables strategic roadmaps for developing capabilities required for AI tools. Rather than algorithm development, the focus is on integrating AI into operational functions. Structured maturity evaluation also tracks progress over time.

AI depends on quality data [47] and data integrity, which are critical for patient information. Systems that ensuring privacy and effective data governance are essential before launching any AI initiatives. Data security vulnerabilities require specific and exhaustive risk analysis, as well as controls for AI/ML applications. For instance, the authentication of data provenance, quality, and security as just as important a qualifier for infrastructure. AI models continue to stay in line with changing processes by constantly curating and maintaining data. High-quality data and its integrity are crucial in AI implementation in a clinical environment as this entails sensitive patients' information. As the basis of any health AI-driven initiative, it is essential to establish strong systems, which will also guarantee privacy safety and management procedures. AI and machine learning apps that deal with medical data contain a high level of data security vulnerabilities, which require comprehensive risk assessment and customized controls specific for AI/ML in medicine.

However, within the scope of processes controlled by AI, especially the initial steps such as academic ATMP process development, this may be considered a disadvantage of applying ML techniques. The batches of data mined and collected from industries such as pharmaceuticals manufacturing can train and improve numerous ML models. Nevertheless, when the number of batches is limited, such as in academic production, the quality of training a better model becomes limited.

Therefore, in this scenario, ML algorithms may not be able to take all possible scenarios into consideration, resulting in inaccuracies in application. Under such circumstances, predictions become inaccurate, there is less adaptability to changing conditions, adaptability is low, and the insight into underlining processes is minimal, since this depends on insufficient data. Consequently, in order to improve the effectiveness of ML applications, it is imperative to increase the quantity of manufacturing batches or find alternative means to increase data collection. One available alternative is consolidation of a Healthcare center network established to, not only to improve health outcomes among patients, but also enhance ATMP quality. Within this network of hospitals, various nodes would collaborate by exchanging information and sharing expertise, to advance ATMP manufacturing without compromising on quality and safety.

Focusing on data sharing between the nodes in a network via the implementation and usage of blockchain technology for secure data sharing can enable an encrypted system for data distribution, which can be a tool for information exchange that is suitable for being validated by regulatory agencies. This immutable and private process would ensure that both raw or processed data are available for ML analysis and enhanced cell processing. This innovative application of blockchain's immutable and private framework could not only enhance data security but also update the process of data sharing, ensuring accuracy and integrity in the handling of sensitive data across the network [48–50].

Reskilling biotechnologist staff to implement augmented intelligence, while managing additional risks, is critical. AI success requires personnel fluent in its applications and limitations, especially for regulated manufacturing. Cross-functional collaboration between biotechnologists and AI experts can promote effective adoption of AI and ML. Thus, institutional cybersecurity defense requires a deep bench of talent specialized in AI/ML data risks. Specialized personnel combining computational proficiency with bioprocessing expertise remain scarce yet essential for overseeing responsible AI adoption. Most researchers lack formal data science training, while data analysts are often detached from manufacturing realities. Fostering collaborative groups between bioengineers, computer scientists, and clinicians could promote the development of truly tailored systems. Academic curriculums must also evolve, integrating statistics and bioinformatics skills with traditional knowledge. Some leading educational institutions have already implemented introductory data science courses into cell and gene therapy majors. For current personnel, institutions could offer continuing education programs through partnerships with technical universities (https://www.theattcnetwork.co.uk, accessed on 14 January 2024). Proactive reskilling builds the competencies needed to securely apply AI towards enhancing ATMP translation, rather than simply reducing costs. Therefore, investment in people and expertise is crucial, along with cutting-edge technology.

Regulatory authorities encourage AI when the benefits are demonstrated with proper GMP governance. However, ambiguity exists around emerging applications. Continuous communication, documented risk management, and a focus on enhancing quality help ensure compliance. Ultimately, AI for ATMPs requires synchronized integration across technology, data, people, regulation, and health care objectives—comprehensive management of this convergence would allow a controlled evolution toward more intelligent manufacturing [51].

Furthermore, a focus on product quality improvement must be a priority in AI integration. However, if appropriately designed and adjusted, AI systems can make processes more efficient, less prone to error, and consistent, thus improving product quality and safety. This is a proactive approach that guarantees compliance, while ensuring the healthcare system provides safe and quality services to patients.

Achieving the successful implementation of AI in relation to the manufacturing of ATMPs relies on the synchronous integration of various spheres. These areas include the implementation of cutting-edge technological solutions in healthcare, responsible data management, health practitioner cooperation, strict regulation compliance, and the alignment of AI strategies with other academic and public health players. Proper management of this diverse convergence is a challenge, as each requires explicit leadership, operational procedures, and well-defined roles and responsibilities that are coherent in a complex academic–hospital ecosystem [52].

In synthesizing the critical factors for the successful implementation of AI within the domain of ATMP manufacturing, we must acknowledge the intricate network of interdisciplinary collaboration. This involves the integration of advanced technological solutions, meticulous data management, healthcare professionals' engagement, adherence to rigorous regulatory frameworks, and strategic alignment with academic and public health initiatives. Managing this multifaceted convergence demands clear management, precise operational protocols, and well-articulated roles within the complex academic–hospital ecosystem. Furthermore, in the advanced control systems section, we elaborated on how these systems build upon previously described AI capabilities like process monitoring, automation, and dynamic control, to implement more sophisticated control algorithms. While those previous AI applications provided valuable data analysis, adjustments, and modelling, advanced control systems leverage that foundation to continuously recalculate optimal parameters using hybrid mechanistic and machine learning models. This enables a higher level of adaptive and model predictive control that goes beyond basic feedback loops to provide fully customized bioreactor optimization tailored to the unique characteristics of each individual batch in real time. Thus, the distinguishing features of advanced AI control were clarified compared to the other previous functionalities of AI discussed in the paper. Figure 2, 'AI in ATMP production', provides a structured visual overview of these interdependencies and outlines the dynamic roles of AI throughout the ATMP production cycle. It is presented here as a precursor to our concluding thoughts, reaffirming the transformative impact and the multifarious challenges of AI integration in advancing the field of ATMPs.

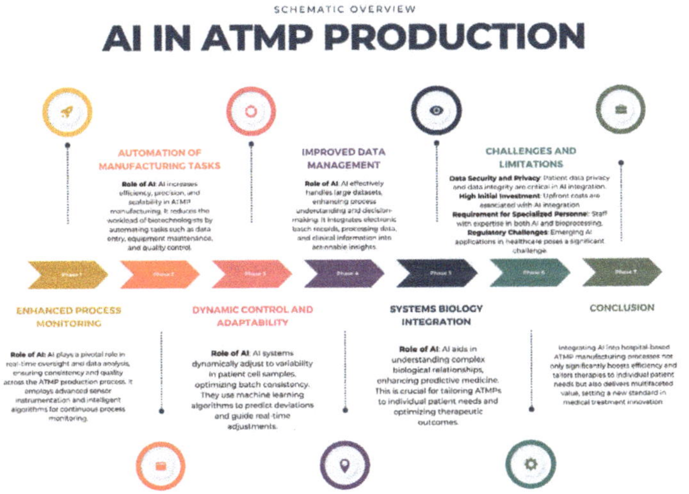

Figure 2. Visual overview of the integration of AI in ATMP production, detailing its roles, benefits, and challenges, and concluding with the potential enhancements in hospital-based ATMP efficiency and patient outcomes.

6. Conclusions

The emerging field of advanced therapy medicinal products represents a new frontier in personalized and innovative treatments, with enormous therapeutic potential. However, manufacturing customized cellular and gene therapies poses profound challenges, requiring extensive adaptation of conventional biopharmaceutical production paradigms. The intrinsic constraints of hospital-based facilities further intensify the difficulties in clinically translating these novel ATMPs. Constructing on-site modular GMP infrastructure can enable bench-to-bedside delivery but demands substantial optimization of design, quality systems, staffing, and coordination across hospital departments. While a monumental undertaking, the integration of academic research, pharmaceutical manufacturing, and clinical medicine made possible by hospital ATMP facilities can drive scientific discoveries toward direct patient impact.

Emerging technologies like process analytical monitoring, continuous production, and AI can further enhance process control, automation, and oversight, to overcome limitations. In this regard AI holds tremendous promise for allowing academic ATMP facilities to overcome constraints of limited space, staffing, patient-specific variability, and decentralized manufacturing. Intelligent algorithms can monitor processes in real time, automate ancillary tasks, enact sophisticated adaptive control, and synthesize the breadth of data involved in patient-specific production.

Early applications have demonstrated AI's utility for automated analysis and enhanced productivity. Visionary initiatives will make AI a transformational technology, ensuring these innovative personalized medicines realize their full therapeutic potential. However, fully realizing the clinical promise of personalized ATMPs ultimately relies on synergistic partnerships across disciplines, to pioneer new treatments while maintaining demanding quality standards. Improving patient outcomes should motivate explorations into AI-driven automation. Beyond operational metrics, focusing innovation on maximizing therapeutic safety and efficacy requires integrating manufacturing data with clinical databases through processes that maintain privacy safeguards.

Real-world evidence can help us understand how the quality of a cellular product impacts how it works. Using advanced analysis, connections can be made between treatment procedures and side effects, or how changes in cellular phenotype during production can affect their survival after being transplanted. By contextualizing technical data into patient impacts, development can shift from simply engineering robotic bio-factories toward purposeful design tailored for healing. Focusing on clinical outcomes can continually re-center personalized medicine innovations on whole persons rather than products. The accelerating advancement in novel biotherapeutics in hospital-based manufacturing facilities can allow continued progress in providing patients access to transformative medicines tailored to their unique needs.

Funding: This research received no external funding.

Conflicts of Interest: The authors declare no competing financial interests.

References

1. Johanna, I.; Daudeij, A.; Devina, F.; Nijenhuis, C.; Nuijen, B.; Romberg, B.; de Haar, C.; Haanen, J.; Dolstra, H.; Bremer, E.; et al. Basics of advanced therapy medicinal product development in academic pharma and the role of a GMP simulation unit. *Immuno-Oncol. Technol.* **2023**, *20*, 100411. [CrossRef]
2. Elverum, K.; Whitman, M. Delivering cellular and gene therapies to patients: Solutions for realizing the potential of the next generation of medicine. *Gene Ther.* **2020**, *27*, 537–544. [CrossRef]
3. Iancu, E.M.; Kandalaft, L.E. Challenges and advantages of cell therapy manufacturing under Good Manufacturing Practices within the hospital setting. *Curr. Opin. Biotechnol.* **2020**, *65*, 233–241. [CrossRef]
4. Bersenev, A.; Fesnak, A. Place of Academic GMP Facilities in Modern Cell Therapy. *Methods Mol. Biol.* **2020**, *2097*, 329–339. [CrossRef]
5. McGuirk, J.; Waller, E.K.; Qayed, M.; Abhyankar, S.; Ericson, S.; Holman, P.; Keir, C.; Myers, G.D. Building blocks for institutional preparation of CTL019 delivery. *Cytotherapy* **2017**, *19*, 1015–1024. [CrossRef]

6. Amini, L.; Silbert, S.K.; Maude, S.L.; Nastoupil, L.J.; Ramos, C.A.; Brentjens, R.J.; Sauter, C.S.; Shah, N.N.; Abou-El-Enein, M. Preparing for CAR T cell therapy: Patient selection, bridging therapies and lymphodepletion. *Nat. Rev. Clin. Oncol.* **2022**, *19*, 342–355. [CrossRef]
7. Abou-El-Enein, M.; Römhild, A.; Kaiser, D.; Beier, C.; Bauer, G.; Volk, H.D.; Reinke, P. Good Manufacturing Practices (GMP) manufacturing of advanced therapy medicinal products: A novel tailored model for optimizing performance and estimating costs. *Cytotherapy* **2013**, *15*, 362–383. [CrossRef]
8. Viganò, M.; Giordano, R.; Lazzari, L. Challenges of running a GMP facility for regenerative medicine in a public hospital. *Regen. Med.* **2017**, *12*, 803–813. [CrossRef]
9. Jackson, M.R. Accommodating clinical trials and other externally manufactured cellular therapy products: Challenges, lessons learned and creative solutions. *Cytotherapy* **2022**, *24*, 37–44. [CrossRef]
10. Sutherland, V.; Buffo, M.J.; Whiteside, T.L. Impact of contracted manufacturing organization protocols on operations in an aca demically based Current Good Manufacturing Practice facility. *Cytotherapy* **2022**, *24*, 32–36. [CrossRef]
11. Coppens, D.G.M.; Hoekman, J.; De Bruin, M.L.; Slaper-Cortenbach, I.C.M.; Leufkens, H.G.M.; Meij, P.; Gardarsdottir, H. Advanced therapy medicinal product manufacturing under the hospital exemption and other exemption pathways in seven European Union countries. *Cytotherapy* **2020**, *22*, 592–600. [CrossRef]
12. Priesner, C.; Hildebrandt, M. Advanced Therapy Medicinal Products and the Changing Role of Academia. *Transfus Med Hemother.* **2022**, *49*, 158–162. [CrossRef]
13. European Commission. Guidelines on Good Manufacturing Practice specific to Advanced Therapy Medicinal Products. *Eur. Comm. J.* **2017**, *4*, 1–32.
14. Digiusto, D.L.; Melsop, K.; Srivastava, R.; Tran, C.A.T. Proceedings of the first academic symposium on developing, qualifying and operating a cell and gene therapy manufacturing facility. *Cytotherapy* **2018**, *20*, 1486–1494. [CrossRef] [PubMed]
15. de Wilde, S.; Guchelaar, H.-J.; Zandvliet, M.L.; Meij, P. Clinical development of gene- and cell-based therapies: Overview of the European landscape. *Mol. Ther. Methods Clin. Dev.* **2016**, *3*, 16073. [CrossRef]
16. Chauca Strand, G.; Bonander, C.; Jakobsson, N.; Johansson, N.; Svensson, M. Assessment of the clinical and cost-effectiveness evidence in the reimbursement decisions of new cancer drugs. *ESMO Open* **2022**, *7*, 100569. [CrossRef]
17. Harrison, R.P.; Medcalf, N.; Rafiq, Q.A. Cell therapy-processing economics: Small-scale microfactories as a stepping stone toward large-scale macrofactories. *Regen. Med.* **2018**, *13*, 159–173. [CrossRef]
18. Gladwell, D.; Ciani, O.; Parnaby, A.; Palmer, S. Surrogacy and the Valuation of ATMPs: Taking Our Place in the Evidence Generation/Assessment Continuum. *Pharmacoeconomics.* **2024**, *42*, 137–144. [CrossRef]
19. Bäckel, N.; Hort, S.; Kis, T.; Nettleton, D.F.; Egan, J.R.; Jacobs, J.J.L.; Grunert, D.; Schmitt, R.H. Elaborating the potential of Artificial Intelligence in automated CAR-T cell manufacturing. *Front. Mol. Med.* **2023**, *3*, 1250508. [CrossRef]
20. Hort, S.; Herbst, L.; Bäckel, N.; Erkens, F.; Niessing, B.; Frye, M.; König, N.; Papantoniou, I.; Hudecek, M.; Jacobs, J.J.L.; et al. Toward Rapid, Widely Available Autologous CAR-T Cell Therapy—Artificial Intelligence and Automation Enabling the Smart Manufacturing Hospital. *Front. Med.* **2022**, *9*, 913287. [CrossRef]
21. Harrison, R.P.; Ruck, S.; Medcalf, N.; Rafiq, Q.A. Decentralized manufacturing of cell and gene therapies: Overcoming challenges and identifying opportunities. *Cytotherapy* **2017**, *19*, 1140–1151. [CrossRef]
22. Gerzon, G.; Sheng, Y.; Kirkitadze, M. Process Analytical Technologies—Advances in bioprocess integration and future perspectives. *J. Pharm. Biomed. Anal.* **2022**, *207*, 114379. [CrossRef]
23. Majors, B.S.; Betenbaugh, M.J.; Chiang, G.G. Links between metabolism and apoptosis in mammalian cells: Applications for anti-apoptosis engineering. *Metab. Eng.* **2007**, *9*, 317–326. [CrossRef]
24. Ahmed, S.; Chauhan, V.M.; Ghaemmaghami, A.M.; Aylott, J.W. New generation of bioreactors that advance extracellular matrix modelling and tissue engineering. *Biotechnol. Lett.* **2019**, *41*, 1–25. [CrossRef]
25. Harrison, R.P.; Chauhan, V.M. Enhancing cell and gene therapy manufacture through the application of advanced fluorescent optical sensors (Review). *Biointerphases* **2017**, *13*, 01A301. [CrossRef] [PubMed]
26. Jaccard, N.; Griffin, L.D.; Keser, A.; Macown, R.J.; Super, A.; Veraitch, F.S.; Szita, N. Automated method for the rapid and precise estimation of adherent cell culture characteristics from phase contrast microscopy images. *Biotechnol. Bioeng.* **2014**, *111*, 504–517. [CrossRef]
27. Tanemura, H.; Kitamura, R.; Yamada, Y.; Hoshino, M.; Kakihara, H.; Nonaka, K. Comprehensive modeling of cell culture profile using Raman spectroscopy and machine learning. *Sci. Rep.* **2023**, *13*, 21805. [CrossRef] [PubMed]
28. Yang, Z.; Paes, B.C.M.F.; Fulber, J.P.C.; Tran, M.Y.; Farnós, O.; Kamen, A.A. Development of an Integrated Continuous Manufacturing Process for the rVSV-Vectored SARS-CoV-2 Candidate Vaccine. *Vaccines* **2023**, *11*, 841. [CrossRef] [PubMed]
29. Payne, J.; Cronin, J.; Haer, M.; Krouse, J.; Prosperi, W.; Drolet-Vives, K.; Lieve, M.; Soika, M.; Balmer, M.; Kirkitadze, M. In-line monitoring of surfactant clearance in viral vaccine downstream processing. *Comput. Struct. Biotechnol. J.* **2021**, *19*, 1829–1837. [CrossRef] [PubMed]
30. Moreira, A.S.; Cavaco, D.G.; Faria, T.Q.; Alves, P.M.; Carrondo, M.J.T.; Peixoto, C. Advances in Lentivirus Purification. *Biotechnol. J.* **2021**, *16*, 2000019. [CrossRef]
31. Williams, T.; Kalinka, K.; Sanches, R.; Blanchard-Emmerson, G.; Watts, S.; Davies, L.; Knevelman, C.; McCloskey, L.; Jones, P.; Mitrophanous, K.; et al. Machine learning and metabolic modelling assisted implementation of a novel process analytical technology in cell and gene therapy manufacturing. *Sci. Rep.* **2023**, *13*, 834. [CrossRef]

32. Odeh-Couvertier, V.Y.; Dwarshuis, N.J.; Colonna, M.B.; Levine, B.L.; Edison, A.S.; Kotanchek, T.; Roy, K.; Torres-Garcia, W. Predicting T-cell quality during manufacturing through an artificial intelligence-based integrative multiomics analytical platform. *Bioeng. Transl. Med.* **2022**, *7*, e10282. [CrossRef]
33. Li, S.; An, J.; Li, Y.; Zhu, X.; Zhao, D.; Wang, L.; Sun, Y.; Yang, Y.; Bi, C.; Zhang, X.; et al. Automated high-throughput genome editing platform with an AI learning in situ prediction model. *Nat. Commun.* **2022**, *13*, 7386. [CrossRef]
34. Gao, Z.; Li, Y. Enhancing single-cell biology through advanced AI-powered microfluidics. *Biomicrofluidics* **2023**, *17*, 51301. [CrossRef]
35. Emerson, J.; Kara, B.; Glassey, J. Multivariate data analysis in cell gene therapy manufacturing. *Biotechnol. Adv.* **2020**, *45*, 107637. [CrossRef]
36. Kern, S.; Wander, L.; Meyer, K.; Guhl, S.; Mukkula, A.R.G.; Holtkamp, M.; Salge, M.; Fleischer, C.; Weber, N.; King, R.; et al. Flexible automation with compact NMR spectroscopy for continuous production of pharmaceuticals. *Anal. Bioanal. Chem.* **2019**, *411*, 3037–3046. [CrossRef] [PubMed]
37. Feng Báez, J.P.; George De la Rosa, M.V.; Alvarado-Hernández, B.B.; Romañach, R.J.; Stelzer, T. Evaluation of a compact composite sensor array for concentration monitoring of solutions and suspensions via multivariate analysis. *J. Pharm. Biomed. Anal.* **2023**, *233*, 115451. [CrossRef]
38. Rathore, A.S.; Mishra, S.; Nikita, S.; Priyanka, P. Bioprocess Control: Current Progress and Future Perspectives. *Life* **2021**, *11*, 557. [CrossRef]
39. Jabarivelisdeh, B.; Carius, L.; Findeisen, R.; Waldherr, S. Adaptive predictive control of bioprocesses with constraint-based modeling and estimation. *Comput. Chem. Eng.* **2020**, *135*, 106744. [CrossRef]
40. Sarker, I.H. AI-Based Modeling: Techniques, Applications and Research Issues Towards Automation, Intelligent and Smart Systems. *SN Comput. Sci.* **2022**, *3*, 158. [CrossRef] [PubMed]
41. Chevalier, M.; Gómez-Schiavon, M.; Ng, A.H.; El-Samad, H. Design and Analysis of a Proportional-Integral-Derivative Controller with Biological Molecules. *Cell Syst.* **2019**, *9*, 338–353.e10. [CrossRef]
42. Mitra, S.; Murthy, G.S. Bioreactor control systems in the biopharmaceutical industry: A critical perspective. *Syst. Microbiol. Biomanuf.* **2022**, *2*, 91–112. [CrossRef]
43. Mujawar, S.; Deshpande, A.; Gherkar, A.; Simon, S.E.; Prajapati, B. Introduction to Human-Machine Interface. In *Human-Machine Interface*; John Wiley & Sons, Ltd.: Hoboken, NJ, USA, 2023; pp. 1–23, ISBN 9781394200344.
44. Zheng, Y. Optimization of computer programming based on mathematical models of artificial intelligence algorithms. *Comput. Electr. Eng.* **2023**, *110*, 108834. [CrossRef]
45. Heaton, H.; Fung, S.W. Explainable AI via learning to optimize. *Sci. Rep.* **2023**, *13*, 10103. [CrossRef]
46. Cheng, Y.; Bi, X.; Xu, Y.; Liu, Y.; Li, J.; Du, G.; Lv, X.; Liu, L. Artificial intelligence technologies in bioprocess: Opportunities and challenges. *Bioresour. Technol.* **2023**, *369*, 128451. [CrossRef] [PubMed]
47. Arinez, J.F.; Chang, Q.; Gao, R.X.; Xu, C.; Zhang, J. Artificial Intelligence in Advanced Manufacturing: Current Status and Future Outlook. *J. Manuf. Sci. Eng.* **2020**, *142*, 110804. [CrossRef]
48. Lam, C.; van Velthoven, M.H.; Meinert, E. Developing a Blockchain-Based Supply Chain System for Advanced Therapies: Protocol for a Feasibility Study. *JMIR Res. Protoc.* **2020**, *9*, e17005. [CrossRef] [PubMed]
49. Singh, R.; Dwivedi, A.D.; Srivastava, G. Internet of Things Based Blockchain for Temperature Monitoring and Counterfeit Pharmaceutical Prevention. *Sensors* **2020**, *20*, 3951. [CrossRef] [PubMed]
50. Moosavi, J.; Naeni, L.M.; Fathollahi-Fard, A.M.; Fiore, U. Blockchain in supply chain management: A review, bibliometric, and network analysis. *Environ. Sci. Pollut. Res. Int.* **2021**. [CrossRef]
51. EMA. Multi-annual AI workplan 2023–2028 HMA-EMA Big Data Steering Group. **2023**, 1–13. Available online: https://www.ema.europa.eu/en/news/artificial-intelligence-workplan-guide-use-ai-medicines-regulation (accessed on 1 February 2024).
52. EMA. Reflection paper on the use of artificial intelligence in lifecycle medicines. *Eur. Med. Agency* **2023**, *31*, 1–17.

applied sciences

MDPI

Article

Stability of Feature Selection in Multi-Omics Data Analysis

Tomasz Łukaszuk [1], Jerzy Krawczuk [1], Kamil Żyła [2] and Jacek Kęsik [2,*]

[1] Faculty of Computer Science, Bialystok University of Technology, Wiejska 45A, 15-351 Bialystok, Poland; t.lukaszuk@pb.edu.pl (T.Ł.); j.krawczuk@pb.edu.pl (J.K.)

[2] Department of Computer Science, Faculty of Electrical Engineering and Computer Science, Lublin University of Technology, Nadbystrzycka 36B, 20-618 Lublin, Poland; k.zyla@pollub.pl

* Correspondence: j.kesik@pollub.pl

Abstract: In the rapidly evolving field of multi-omics data analysis, understanding the stability of feature selection is critical for reliable biomarker discovery and clinical applications. This study investigates the stability of feature-selection methods across various cancer types by utilizing 15 datasets from The Cancer Genome Atlas (TCGA). We employed classifiers with embedded feature selection, including Support Vector Machines (SVM), Logistic Regression (LR), and Lasso regression, each incorporating L1 regularization. Through a comprehensive evaluation using five-fold cross-validation, we measured feature-selection stability and assessed the accuracy of predictions regarding TP53 mutations, a known indicator of poor clinical outcomes in cancer patients. All three classifiers demonstrated optimal feature-selection stability, measured by the Nogueira metric, with higher regularization (fewer selected features), while lower regularization generally resulted in decreased stability across all omics layers. Our findings indicate differences in feature stability across the various omics layers; *mirna* consistently exhibited the highest stability across classifiers, while the *mutation* and *rna* layers were generally less stable, particularly with lower regularization. This work highlights the importance of careful feature selection and validation in high-dimensional datasets to enhance the robustness and reliability of multi-omics analyses.

Keywords: multi-omics; high-dimensional data; cancer genomics; feature selection; stability; L1 regularization

1. Introduction

Multi-omics is the approach whereby datasets contain multiple layers of data, which can be referred to as different "omes". Informally, names of science branches end in the suffix "-omics" (e.g., genomics in biology), which is related to the "-ome" suffix, which is used to address the objects of study of such fields (e.g., genome). Combining different "omes" (different layers of data) creates complex data that can be integrated and then analyzed to find novel associations. We can understand systems better through various omics layers that reveal supplementary sources of variability [1].

Transition to multi-omics data has opened new directions of research concerning integrated system-level approaches [2]. Multi-omics data allow the derivation of insights from highly interrelated data and facilitate multi-scale depiction of systems, including biological ones [1]. We can see such applications, among others, in the following domains: disease subtyping, biomarker prediction, treatment optimization, disease prognosis, food safety/microbial risk assessment, toxicology [3], and many more. Even culture is affected, e.g., in terms of quantitative analysis and exploration of cultural trends, which is based on news records, digitized books, social media contributions, etc. [4–6].

We also observe an increasing number of multi-omics data repositories from the following initiatives: The Cancer Genome Atlas repository, a joint effort between the National Cancer Institute and the National Human Genome Research Institute, which generated over 2.5 petabytes of genomic, epigenomic, transcriptomic, and proteomic data [7,8]; and the International Cancer Genomics Consortium repository, a global initiative to build a comprehensive catalog of mutational abnormalities in the major tumor types [9,10]. Due to the dispersion of dataset publishing spaces, indexing services have been developed, e.g., the Omics Discovery Index, that participate in the discovery and linking of public omics datasets [11,12]. Security policies have gained importance as well [13].

Multi-omics data have put new force into biomedical research, especially by allowing systematic modeling and a comprehensive understanding of mechanisms behind disease progression and associated risk management [14–16]. Naturally, we cannot imagine these applications without machine-learning (ML) and artificial-intelligence (AI) support, as deriving conclusions from these data is one of the most demanding tasks [17,18]. Recently, deep learning (DL) has gained high interest due to its performance and the capability of capturing nonlinear and hierarchical features [14,19–21].

In the field of machine learning, classification tasks, data mining, and exploration often require effective feature extraction and selection to improve model performance. Feature selection becomes particularly important in multi-omics data analysis, where the number of features (e.g., genes, proteins, metabolites) far exceeds the number of observations (samples or instances). This imbalance between the dimensionality of the data and the available observations necessitates a careful selection of features, as using all available features can lead to overfitting and reduce the model's ability to generalize.

In classification tasks, especially when dealing with datasets where the number of features exceeds the number of observations, it is not feasible for the model to make decisions based on all features; instead, it relies on a subset of features that are selected during the learning process. This subset is selected to maximize predictive power while minimizing complexity and overfitting, representing a trade-off between model accuracy and the risk of overfitting. By selecting a smaller set of relevant features, the model is better able to generalize to unseen data, but this comes at the cost of potentially losing some predictive power if too many features are excluded.

The process of selecting features as part of the model training is known as embedded feature selection and is often referred to as an "intrinsic" or "embedded" method [22]. Among the embedded methods, feature selection is most commonly performed by techniques based on the L1 norm (such as Lasso regression) and decision tree-based methods (such as Random Forest), both of which incorporate feature selection into the model-fitting process [23]. In contrast, feature selection can also be done as a separate step (prior to model training), but such an approach still often requires building a classifier on the selected features to evaluate its performance, ultimately linking the quality of feature selection with the classifier's performance.

The importance of feature selection in multi-omics data has been well recognized, and several studies have benchmarked various feature-selection methods. For instance, Li et al. [24] conducted a large-scale benchmark experiment comparing different feature-selection methods, providing valuable insights into the effectiveness of various approaches. The benchmark was based on 15 cancer datasets from TCGA [8]. According to the authors, no such benchmark was performed before their work. After literature inquiry, including [25,26], they chose the following 8 feature-selection methods (the most frequently used in context of cancer classification): T-test [27], Information gain (infor) [28], ReliefF [29], Minimum Redundancy Maximum Relevance (mRMR) [30], Recursive Feature Elimination (RFE) [31], Genetic Algorithm (GA) [32], Least Absolute Shrinkage and Selection Operator (Lasso) [33], and permutation importance of Random Forest (RF-VI) [34]. In order to assess the predictive performance, accuracy, and the AUC, the Brier test was used. Friedman's test was applied to test for differences between the dataset-specific performance measure values obtained with different methods.

Li et al. [24] concluded that feature selection is an especially important topic, as the proper selection of data features may improve prediction accuracy and reduce the complexity of machine-learning models. Based on the benchmark results, the following main statements were made: (1) RF-VI (method of embedded type [34]) and mRMR (method of filter type [30]) can be used, where it is sufficient to use only small numbers of best features; (2) Lasso (method of embedded type [33]) provides comparable or slightly better predictive performance when compared to the previously mentioned methods, although models have a noticeably bigger number of features; (3) the mRMR method is computationally expensive.

Unfortunately, the authors focused on predictive accuracy, missing another important aspect, that of stability of feature selection, which creates another gap in the research. Specifically, it remains unclear how consistent and reliable the selected features are across various classification models and datasets. To sum things up, the importance lies in the better reproducibility of findings derived from multi-omics analyses and better resiliency to minor changes in the training dataset.

The stability of feature selection is an emerging topic. Khaire and Dhanalakshmi [35] provided a review of works concerning feature-selection techniques, keeping in mind different sources of instability and the high dimensionality of data. They noted that a high correlation of features may frequently produce multiple equally optimal signatures, reducing the confidence of selected features. Up-to-date analysis and comparison of feature-selection methods were provided by Barbieri et al. [36]. They focused on comparing different stability metrics, claiming their work to be an extensive and complete review of feature-selection algorithms and their evaluation. They mention challenges like high-dimensional data, small samples, noisy and redundant features, and biased data. Metrics for selection accuracy, selection redundancy, prediction performance, algorithmic stability, selection reliability, and computational time were employed. Furthermore, Lazebnik and Rosenfeld [37] showed the shortcomings of existing stability metrics, unable to properly address data drift or non-uniformly distributed missing values. A new solution inspired by Lyapunov stability in dynamic systems was proposed. Finally, tightly targeted works also exist, such as COVID-19-oriented ones [38,39].

As we can see, much work has been devoted either to feature-selection algorithms for medical data or to the general stability of feature selection. Nevertheless, to the authors' best knowledge, no one has tried to address the stability of feature selection in the case of cancer multi-omics TCAG datasets. These aim to enrich the original work by Li et al. [24] by extending their findings to stability aspects, which seems to be valuable for the machine-learning community.

To summarize, in this paper:

- we emphasize the importance of testing feature-selection stability when assessing the quality of a classification model applied to multi-omic data;
- we empirically study the accuracy and feature-selection stability in high-dimension multi-omics data and analyze 15 datasets and 3 classification methods with embedded feature selection;
- we propose to combine accuracy with feature-selection stability for classifier evaluation.

The rest of the paper is organized as follows: in Section 2, we describe the classifiers used, feature-stability measures, in particular the measure defined by Nogueira, the datasets used, and the experimental setup, and offer a few words on the evaluation of classification models. In Section 3, we present the results of the experiments. In Section 4, we discuss the outcome we achieved, particularly within the context of the most recent literature. Finally, we conclude in Section 5.

2. Materials and Methods

2.1. Classifiers with Embedded Feature Selection

In this study, we employed classifiers with embedded feature-selection mechanisms based on the L1 norm. The L1 norm, or Lasso regularization, is particularly effective in high-dimensional settings where the number of features exceeds the number of observations, as it encourages sparsity in the feature space. The classifiers used in our analysis include Support Vector Machine (SVM), Logistic Regression (LR), and Lasso regression, each of which integrates feature selection directly within the model-training process.

Let the dataset consist of m observations O_j $(j = 1, ..., m)$. Each observation O_j is described by n features and represented as an n-dimensional feature vector $\mathbf{x}_j = [x_{j1}, ..., x_{jn}]^T$. The components x_{ji} of the vectors $\mathbf{x}_j$ are referred to as features. Each feature vector $\mathbf{x}_j$ is associated with a binary label (or class) y_j. The positive class, indicating the presence of a disease, is typically denoted by 1, while the negative class can be represented as either 0 (as used in logistic and linear regression) or -1 (as is common in Support Vector Machine models). Consequently, we can express the general-criterion function as follows:

$$\Phi_C(\mathbf{w}, \theta) = \frac{1}{m} \cdot \sum_{j=1}^{m} error(y_j, \hat{y}(\mathbf{x}_j, \mathbf{w}, \theta)) + \frac{1}{C} \sum_{i=1}^{n} |w_i|, \tag{1}$$

where $\mathbf{w} = [w_1, ..., w_n]^T \in \mathbf{R}^n$ represents the weight vector, and $\theta \in \mathbf{R}^1$ denotes the threshold of the hyperplane $H(\mathbf{w}, \theta)$. These parameters are determined during the minimization of the criterion function $\Phi_C(\mathbf{w}, \theta)$.

The criterion function in Equation (1) consists of two parts. The first term represents the loss function, which measures the difference between the true values y_j and the predicted values $\hat{y}(\mathbf{x}_j, \mathbf{w}, \theta)$. The second term is the regularization term, which penalizes the values of the model weights $\mathbf{w}$.

While the entire function needs to be minimized during training, the regularization term ensures that the model weights remain small. The hyperparameter C controls the relative importance of the two terms: a smaller value of C gives more weight to regularization (encouraging smaller weights), while a larger value of C emphasizes minimizing the loss function, allowing for higher weights. The value of C must be set prior to optimization and determines the trade-off between model fit and complexity.

Using the absolute values (the L1 norm) of the coefficients $|w_i|$ in the second regularization term has the property that during optimization, the weights not only become smaller but actually tend to become exactly zero, thus performing feature selection. In the case of the L2 norm, where squared weights are used in the regularization term w_i^2, the weights tend to go towards zero but not exactly zero. This property of L1 regularization makes it useful for high-dimensional datasets.

A lower value of C reduces the weight assigned to model errors while increasing the strength of regularization. This results in more weights being driven to zero, leading to a sparser model with fewer features. Conversely, a higher value of C increases model complexity by allowing the inclusion of more features, enabling the model to fit the training data more closely. This close fit is generally undesirable in the context of multi-omics data, where the number of features n significantly exceeds the number of observations m.

2.1.1. Support Vector Machines (SVM)

Support Vector Machines [40] are powerful supervised-learning models utilized for classification tasks. By incorporating L1 regularization, SVMs can effectively perform feature selection while constructing a hyperplane that maximizes the margin between different classes. In our experiments, we employed the linear version of the kernel. An observation x_i is classified as belonging to the positive class $y = 1$ if it is located on the positive side of the hyperplane $H(\mathbf{w}, \theta)$; otherwise, it is assigned to the negative class.

$$\hat{y}_i = sgn(\mathbf{w}^T \mathbf{x}_i + \theta) \tag{2}$$

Assuming $y_i \in \{-1, 1\}$, the error function can be expressed as a hinge loss function [41]:

$$error_i = max(0, 1 - y_i(\mathbf{w}^T \mathbf{x}_i + \theta)) \tag{3}$$

The error, or loss, is equal to 0 if the observation x_i lies on the correct side of the hyperplane according to its true label y_i.

2.1.2. Logistic Regression (LR)

Logistic Regression [42] is a widely used classifier that models the probability of a binary outcome based on one or more predictor variables. By applying L1 regularization, logistic regression can effectively perform feature selection by shrinking less informative coefficients to zero, therefore eliminating them from the model. The model prediction $\hat{y}$ is given by a logistic function, with values in the range (0, 1) interpreted as the probability that x_i belongs to the positive class $y_i = 1$, while 1-probability represents the likelihood of belonging to the negative class. The negative class, in the case of LR, is usually labeled as 0.

$$\hat{y}_i = \frac{1}{1 + e^{-(\mathbf{w}^T \mathbf{x}_i + \theta)}} \tag{4}$$

$$error_i = -log(\hat{y}_i) \; if \; y_i = 1 \; else \; - log(1 - \hat{y}_i) \tag{5}$$

2.1.3. Lasso Regression

Lasso (Least Absolute Shrinkage and Selection Operator) regression [43] is a linear regression method that incorporates L1 regularization to prevent overfitting and enhance feature selection.

$$\hat{y}_i = \mathbf{w}^T \mathbf{x}_i + \theta \tag{6}$$

$$error_i = y_i - \hat{y}_i \tag{7}$$

In our binary classification problem, where $y_i \in \{0, 1\}$, we use a threshold of 0.5 to assign the class $y_i = 1$ if $\hat{y}_i > 0.5$ and the class $y_i = 0$ otherwise.

2.2. *Feature-Selection Stability Measure*

One of the first measures used to assess stability was based on the intersection of feature sets, such as the Jaccard Index [44]. These measures allow for the evaluation of similarity between feature sets with different cardinalities, but they do not account for the total number of features and, therefore, lack a correction for chance. This correction was first introduced by Kuncheva [45], but it applied only to sets with the same cardinality. Lustgarten later extended this approach [46] to accommodate sets with different cardinalities. More recently, Nogueira and Brown [47] proposed a new feature-selection stability measure based on the frequency of selected features, which is calculated based on the Z matrix.

$$Z = \begin{bmatrix} z_{11} & z_{12} & z_{13} & \cdots & z_{1n} \\ z_{21} & z_{22} & z_{23} & \cdots & z_{2n} \\ & & \cdots\cdots\cdots & & \\ z_{k1} & z_{k2} & z_{k3} & \cdots & z_{kn} \end{bmatrix} \tag{8}$$

Each row Z_k of Z corresponds to a feature-selection subset, while the columns represent individual features. The selection frequency of a feature f is calculated as

$$p_f = \frac{1}{k} \sum_{i=1}^{k} z_{if}$$

and the unbiased sample variance of the selection of the f-th feature is given by:

$$s_f^2 = \frac{k}{k-1} p_f (1 - p_f).$$

The average number of selected features over k feature sets, denoted by $\bar{n}$, is:

$$\bar{n} = \frac{1}{k} \sum_{i=1}^{k} \sum_{f=1}^{n} z_{if}.$$

Additionally, we define the normalized average number of selected features p_n as:

$$p_n = \frac{\bar{n}}{n}.$$

Finally, the Nogueira feature-stability measure $\phi(Z)$ is defined as follows:

$$\phi(Z) = 1 - \frac{\frac{1}{n}\sum_{f=1}^{n} s_f^2}{p_n(1-p_n)} \quad (9)$$

As demonstrated by Nogueira and Brown [47], this measure satisfies all five desired properties, while other measures fail to meet some of them. For this reason, we chose to utilize this measure in our research.

1. Fully defined. It should also measure stability for subsets with different cardinalities.
2. Correction for chance. Subsets of features can share some of the features even if selected randomly.
3. Bounds. The stability $\phi(Z)$ (9) should be upper/lower bounded by constants not dependent on the overall number of features or the number of features selected.
4. Maximum stability. A measure should achieve its maximum if and only if all feature sets in Z are identical.
5. Strict monotonicity. The stability estimator $\phi(Z)$ (9) should be a strictly decreasing function of the sample variances s_f^2 of the variables Z_f (column in the matrix Z).

2.3. Datasets

In our study, we utilized the same datasets as those described in the benchmark study of feature selection by Li et al. [24], as we aimed to enhance their results by measuring feature-selection stability. Specifically, we selected the same 15 cancer datasets from The Cancer Genome Atlas (TCGA, http://cancergenome.nih.gov, accessed on 30 October 2024) [8]. The selection criteria stipulated that datasets must contain at least 100 samples, have no missing observations, include the outcome variable for TP53 mutations, and not have more than 90% of observations in a single class. From these datasets, we included four omics layers: *cnv* (CNV, copy number variation), *mirna* (miRNA, micro ribonucleic acid), *mutation*, and *rna* (RNA, ribonucleic acid). The *methylation* block was excluded due to its substantial size, which would have resulted in excessive computational times.

These datasets were also previously studied by Herrmann et al. [48], who selected 18 datasets and considered the outcome variable to be the (censored) survival time. Various prediction methods from both machine-learning and statistical approaches demonstrated the limited utility of multi-omics data for this task.

An overview of the 15 included datasets is provided in Table 1. Following Li et al. [24], we predict the presence of TP53 mutations, which have been associated with poor clinical outcomes in cancer patients [49].

2.4. Experimental Setup

For each dataset, we conducted experiments separately on individual omics features (*cnv, mirna, mutation,* and *rna*) as well as on the combined feature set. Each experiment was conducted using 5-fold cross-validation, repeated 3 times with different random seeds. For each data subset (omics layers or the combined feature set) and each classifier type (LR, SVM, Lasso), we selected the regularization parameter C prior to the cross-validation loops. This parameter was adjusted to obtain feature subsets of low, medium, and high cardinality, corresponding to approximately 7%, 30%, and 55% of the total number of observations in the datasets, respectively. Details about the algorithm for choosing the C value are described in the next paragraph. Using classifiers with fixed values for the regularization parameters C, we fitted classification models to the training data and extracted the selected features from the fitted models (those with weights $w_i \neq 0$). The selected features were saved for each split, resulting in a total of 15 subsets of features (5 folds × 3 repetitions) for each classifier and each C value across all omics in the dataset. These subsets were then utilized to calculate feature-selection stability. Additionally, for each of these runs, we computed the accuracy on the test set, as shown in Figure 1.

Table 1. Summary of the datasets used in the experiments. The "Split" column indicates the number of objects without TP53 mutations and those with the mutation, respectively. The "__ALL__" column represents the total number of available features, while the columns on the right display the number of features for each omics layer.

Name	Objects	Split 0/1	__ALL__	cnv	mirna	mutation	rna
BLCA	382	196/186	100,451	57,964	825	18,576	23,081
BRCA	735	480/255	99,475	57,964	835	17,974	22,694
COAD	191	85/106	99,520	57,964	802	18,537	22,210
ESCA	106	23/83	96,854	57,964	763	12,627	25,494
HNSC	443	136/307	97,535	57,964	793	17,247	21,520
LGG	419	224/195	90,150	57,964	645	9234	22,297
LIHC	159	115/44	91,565	57,964	776	11,820	20,994
LUAD	426	214/212	100,840	57,964	799	18,387	23,681
LUSC	418	72/346	100,891	57,964	895	18,499	23,524
PAAD	124	46/78	93,325	57,964	612	12,391	22,348
PRAD	407	359/48	91,984	57,925	585	11,701	21,769
SARC	126	78/48	91,595	57,964	778	10,000	22,842
SKCM	249	210/39	99,815	57,964	1002	18,592	22,248
STAD	295	156/139	103,365	57,964	787	18,580	26,027
UCEC	405	261/144	103,354	57,447	866	21,052	23,978

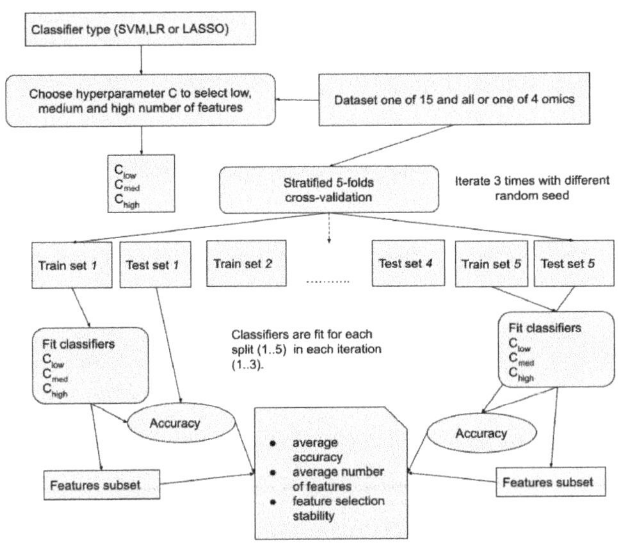

Figure 1. Experimental setup. For each omics layer and all omics, 5-fold stratified cross-validation was repeated 3 times. Each of 3 classifiers was trained using three different C values (C_{low}, C_{med} and C_{high}). For each classifier, both feature selection stability and accuracy were calculated.

The experiments were conducted in the Python 3.9 programming environment. In most cases, including procedures for generating training and test dataset splits as well as the classification methods, implementations from the `scikit-learn` [50] library were utilized. Detailed implementation information is provided in the source code available in the

GitHub repository (https://github.com/tlukaszuk/feature-selection-stability-on-multi-omics-data (accessed on 26 November)).

An important part of our computational procedure was selecting the value of parameter C to ensure that the classifier utilizes the desired number of features. It should be noted, however, that in practice, it is not possible to select C to produce a classifier model that uses exactly the desired number of features. The number of features used by the classifier is influenced by the subset of data on which it is fitted. Nonetheless, it can be expected that classifier models fitted on similarly large subsets of the same dataset, with the same C value, will use a comparable number of features. In practice, we may find that these feature counts do not vary by more than 5%.

Based on the above, the determination of parameter C is achieved by taking as input the type of classifier (LR, SVM, or Lasso), the desired number of features nf for the fitted classifier model, and the dataset $D = \{\mathbf{x}_j, y_j\}$ (or its omics layer). The computational procedure employs a gradual narrowing of the range of C values, training successive classifier models and checking the resulting feature subset size. This process continues until a classifier model is obtained that, for the tested parameter $C = C_{opt}$, uses approximately the desired number of features nf (within a tolerance of 5%). The value C_{opt} is then returned as the determined C value, ensuring that classifier models fitted on similarly large subsets of the same dataset D will use approximately nf features.

In our computational procedure, the determination of C-parameter values is performed separately for each dataset and its subsets containing features from a single omics layer. For each dataset, we first define the desired numbers of features nf_{low}, nf_{med} and nf_{high} that the classification models should utilize. These feature counts correspond to approximately 7%, 30%, and 55% of the 80% of the total number of observations (to match the size of the training split used during 5-fold cross-validation).

The C-parameter selection is carried out independently for each classifier type (SVM, LR, Lasso), and each desired feature count nf_{low}, nf_{med}, nf_{high}. Additionally, a random 80% split of the observation set is used during the C-parameter determination procedure to reflect the training set size employed in the main computational workflow.

As a result, different sets of C-parameter values (low, med, and high) are used for each classifier and each dataset or its omics subsets.

2.5. Evaluation of the Classification Models

Classification accuracy is a metric that measures how often a model correctly classifies instances in a dataset. It is calculated as the ratio of correctly predicted instances to the total number of instances. High accuracy indicates that the model's predictions closely match the actual labels, which is generally desirable.

Classification accuracy is a widely used evaluation metric. However, for unbalanced datasets, where one class has significantly more observations than the other, classification accuracy can be misleading. High accuracy values may not reflect good model quality, as the model might only perform well for the majority class. In our study, several datasets are unbalanced. To address this, we use balanced classification accuracy, which accounts for the number of observations in each class in the evaluated sample. Throughout this paper, any reference to classification accuracy refers specifically to balanced classification accuracy.

In the computational procedure, we used 5-fold cross-validation, where 4/5 of the observations were used to fit the classifier model, and the remaining 1/5 were used for evaluation. The training and evaluation process was repeated multiple times, each with a different split between training and testing, following cross-validation guidelines. From our perspective, when evaluating a classifier, it is more important to consider the classification accuracy on the test subset as an unbiased estimate, reflecting the expected performance on new observations when the models are applied in practice.

The second parameter we present from our experiments is the stability of feature selection, expressed using the Nogueira measure (Equation (9)). This stability was evaluated based on the compositions of feature subsets selected by classifier models trained on 15 dataset splits (using 3 repetitions of 5-fold cross-validation) as shown in Figure 1. A higher stability value indicates greater reproducibility of the feature subset compositions and stronger independence of the classifier model from variations in the training set, which is beneficial in practical applications.

Recognizing that both feature-selection stability and classification accuracy are crucial for assessing the quality of a predictive model, we propose combining these two parameters into a single metric using a weighted harmonic mean F_β.

$$F_\beta = \frac{1+\beta}{\frac{1}{acc} + \frac{\beta}{fss}} \tag{10}$$

where acc denotes the classification accuracy value, and fss denotes the feature-selection stability value obtained for the tested classifier model. The parameter β is a weighting factor that determines the contribution of feature-selection stability to the F_β metric. The relative impact of the two evaluation metrics, feature-selection stability, and classification accuracy, on the calculation of F_β is controlled by the value of β. A β value of 1 indicates an equal contribution from both metrics. Values of $\beta > 1$ increase the weight of feature-selection stability in assessing model quality, while values of $0 < \beta < 1$ place greater emphasis on classification accuracy. The appropriate choice of β depends on the specific problem and the relative importance of each evaluation metric.

3. Results

This section presents and discusses the results obtained from our experiments. The focus of this presentation will be on the three aspects investigated: classification accuracy, feature-selection stability, and our proposed metric, which combines classification accuracy and feature-selection stability into a single parameter.

Given the large number of datasets used in this study, we will not present the results for each dataset individually. Instead, we will report averaged values and standard deviations for each type and kind of classifier studied, with a breakdown by omics layer. This approach will allow for more general conclusions to be drawn.

The classification accuracy values for the examined methods across different omics layers are detailed in Table 2 and Figure 2. The results are categorized by three ranges of the regularization parameter C (low, med, high).

It can be observed that for virtually every omics layer, the highest classification accuracy is achieved with classifiers of med-complexity. This suggests that moderate model complexity, defined by the number of features used, is optimal for achieving accuracy. Increasing or decreasing the number of features leads to a decline in classification accuracy.

Regarding the classification accuracy values, the highest results were seen with the *__ALL__* (0.721–0.745) and *rna* (0.723–0.744) layers, while the lowest results were observed with the *mutation* layer (0.605–0.617).

Table 2. Classification accuracy values (means and standard deviations) on the test part of the dataset achieved for the examined classification methods in the three ranges of C parameter values (low, med, high).

Classifier	Omics Layer __ALL__	cnv	mirna	mutation	rna
SVM_low	0.724 ± 0.061	0.663 ± 0.070	0.686 ± 0.065	0.612 ± 0.063	0.729 ± 0.059
SVM_med	**0.743 ± 0.061**	0.678 ± 0.064	0.685 ± 0.063	0.616 ± 0.056	**0.740 ± 0.062**
SVM_high	0.721 ± 0.066	0.661 ± 0.069	0.655 ± 0.061	**0.605 ± 0.062**	0.723 ± 0.064
LR_low	0.723 ± 0.062	0.661 ± 0.070	0.685 ± 0.066	0.612 ± 0.065	0.728 ± 0.060
LR_med	0.739 ± 0.064	0.677 ± 0.066	0.685 ± 0.063	0.615 ± 0.058	0.738 ± 0.065
LR_high	0.728 ± 0.063	0.668 ± 0.065	0.661 ± 0.060	**0.606 ± 0.058**	0.728 ± 0.065
Lasso_low	0.727 ± 0.057	0.684 ± 0.070	0.684 ± 0.064	0.608 ± 0.063	0.732 ± 0.056
Lasso_med	**0.745 ± 0.062**	0.690 ± 0.059	0.696 ± 0.059	0.617 ± 0.058	**0.743 ± 0.060**
Lasso_high	0.742 ± 0.061	0.681 ± 0.069	0.678 ± 0.064	**0.606 ± 0.058**	**0.744 ± 0.059**

The best results are highlighted in green, while the weakest results are highlighted in red.

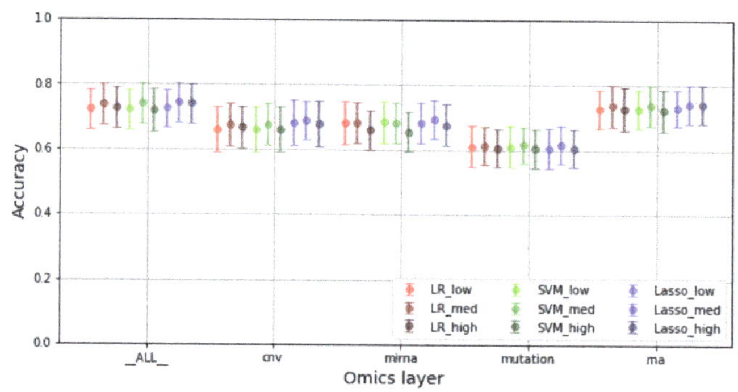

Figure 2. Classification accuracy values on the test part of the dataset achieved for the examined classification methods in the three ranges of C parameter values. The central dots represent the mean values calculated from the results across 15 datasets and 15 spits of each dataset. The vertical lines represent the standard deviation values.

Among the classifiers evaluated, the SVM model exhibited the highest overall accuracy at the med range of C with an accuracy of 0.743, while the weakest performance was observed for the mutation layer in the high range, with an accuracy of 0.605. The LR model exhibited slightly lower accuracy compared to SVM. However, similar to SVM, its best performances (0.739 and 0.738) were achieved in the med range. The achieved peak accuracies of 0.745 in the med range for the overall dataset and 0.743 for the *rna* omics layer, highlighting its effectiveness in this configuration. It is also worth noting that the differences in classification accuracy across classifier types (SVM, LR, Lasso) in corresponding configurations are minimal.

The stability of feature selection values, as measured by the Nogueira metric, is summarized in Table 3 and Figure 3 for the examined classification methods across different ranges of the regularization parameter C (low, med, high).

Table 3. The values of feature-selection stability (means and standard deviations), as measured by the Nogueira metric, obtained for the classification methods across three ranges of C parameter values (low, med, high).

Classifier	Omics Layer				
	__ALL__	cnv	mirna	mutation	rna
SVM_low	0.482 ± 0.086	0.449 ± 0.079	0.597 ± 0.091	0.420 ± 0.093	0.470 ± 0.085
SVM_med	0.396 ± 0.035	0.381 ± 0.039	0.470 ± 0.047	0.398 ± 0.045	0.387 ± 0.035
SVM_high	0.353 ± 0.033	0.364 ± 0.030	0.372 ± 0.046	0.363 ± 0.036	0.345 ± 0.033
LR_low	0.479 ± 0.082	0.453 ± 0.080	0.590 ± 0.087	0.419 ± 0.093	0.464 ± 0.089
LR_med	0.397 ± 0.035	0.385 ± 0.041	0.472 ± 0.045	0.401 ± 0.050	0.390 ± 0.034
LR_high	0.384 ± 0.033	0.372 ± 0.031	0.394 ± 0.041	0.383 ± 0.028	0.376 ± 0.037
Lasso_low	0.470 ± 0.089	0.447 ± 0.080	0.589 ± 0.080	0.424 ± 0.093	0.462 ± 0.091
Lasso_med	0.401 ± 0.044	0.376 ± 0.042	0.488 ± 0.033	0.399 ± 0.050	0.395 ± 0.037
Lasso_high	0.376 ± 0.033	0.368 ± 0.030	0.409 ± 0.041	0.374 ± 0.036	0.366 ± 0.030

The best results are highlighted in green, while the weakest results are highlighted in red.

Among the classifiers evaluated, the SVM demonstrated varying stability, with the highest stability for the *mirna* layer at the low C range, achieving a value of 0.597. However, stability decreased significantly in the high C range, with an overall stability score of only 0.353, indicating reduced reliability in feature selection. The LR exhibited consistent performance, particularly at the low C range, where the stability for the *mirna* layer reached 0.590. Stability values for LR were generally lower in the med and high ranges, reflecting a consistent but less robust feature selection across the parameter spectrum. The Lasso regression also showed strong stability at the low C range, with the highest value of 0.589 for the *mirna* layer. However, similar to the other methods, stability diminished in the higher parameter ranges, especially noted with a score of 0.366 for the *rna* layer in the high range. Overall, the low C range consistently yielded better feature-selection stability across all classifiers, highlighting the trade-off between model complexity and stability in multi-omics data analysis.

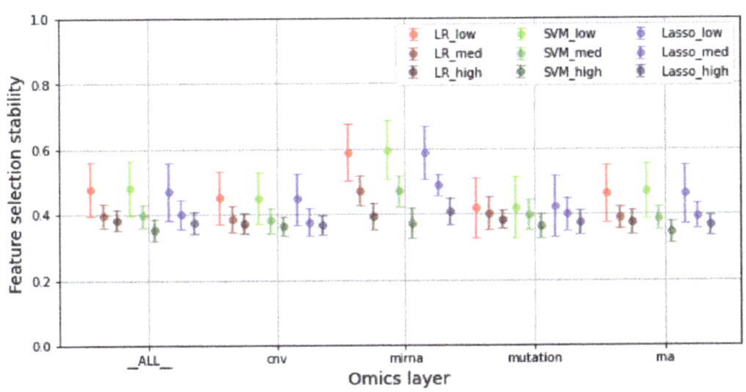

Figure 3. The values of feature-selection stability, according to the Nogueira measure, obtained for the tested classification methods across three ranges of C parameter values. The central dots represent the mean values calculated from the results across 15 datasets. The vertical lines represent the standard deviation values.

The weighted harmonic mean F_β of classification accuracy and feature-selection stability values, achieved for the examined classification methods across different ranges of the regularization parameter C (low, med, high), is summarized in Table 4. This measure provides a balanced assessment of both performance metrics, with equal weighting assigned ($\beta = 1$).

Table 4. Values (means and standard deviations) of the weighted harmonic mean F_β of classification accuracy and feature-selection stability achieved for the examined classification methods in the three ranges of C parameter values (low, med, and high). The values presented in the table were determined for $\beta = 1$, indicating equal weighting of classification accuracy and feature-selection stability.

Classifier	Omics Layer				
	__ALL__	cnv	mirna	mutation	rna
SVM_low	0.578 ± 0.096	0.528 ± 0.062	0.637 ± 0.093	0.495 ± 0.092	0.570 ± 0.094
SVM_med	0.515 ± 0.049	0.485 ± 0.049	0.553 ± 0.043	0.482 ± 0.054	0.507 ± 0.048
SVM_high	0.473 ± 0.044	0.466 ± 0.036	0.471 ± 0.040	0.452 ± 0.044	0.465 ± 0.044
LR_low	0.575 ± 0.093	0.530 ± 0.063	0.632 ± 0.090	0.494 ± 0.093	0.565 ± 0.097
LR_med	0.515 ± 0.050	0.488 ± 0.050	0.555 ± 0.041	0.483 ± 0.059	0.509 ± 0.049
LR_high	0.502 ± 0.051	0.475 ± 0.039	0.490 ± 0.037	0.468 ± 0.043	0.495 ± 0.051
Lasso_low	0.570 ± 0.099	0.535 ± 0.065	0.632 ± 0.091	0.496 ± 0.093	0.565 ± 0.099
Lasso_med	0.520 ± 0.059	0.484 ± 0.048	0.572 ± 0.046	0.482 ± 0.057	0.515 ± 0.052
Lasso_high	0.498 ± 0.046	0.475 ± 0.037	0.507 ± 0.039	0.461 ± 0.046	0.489 ± 0.045

The best results are highlighted in green, while the weakest results are highlighted in red.

Among the classifiers, the LR achieved the highest overall weighted harmonic mean in the low C range, with a value of 0.575, indicating strong performance in both classification accuracy and feature-selection stability. The best stability was recorded for the *mirna* layer, reaching 0.632, which highlights the robustness of LR in this context. The SVM also performed well in the low C range, with a weighted harmonic mean of 0.578, demonstrating solid classification accuracy, particularly for the *mirna* layer at 0.637. However, performance decreased in the med and high ranges, suggesting that increasing model complexity adversely affects the balance between accuracy and stability. The Lasso regression exhibited similar trends, with the best overall performance in the low C range at 0.570 and notable stability for the *mirna* layer at 0.632. As with the other methods, a decline in performance was observed as C increased, particularly evident in the high C range, where Lasso achieved the lowest score of 0.498. Overall, the results indicate that lower values of C tend to yield better balances between classification accuracy and feature selection stability across all classifiers, emphasizing the importance of model tuning in multi-omics analyses.

Figure 4 presents a summary of the F_β values obtained for the three different β-weight values. In each case, the less-complex models (low, using fewer features) exhibit higher F_β values, even when the contribution of classification accuracy is weighted five times higher than feature-selection stability.

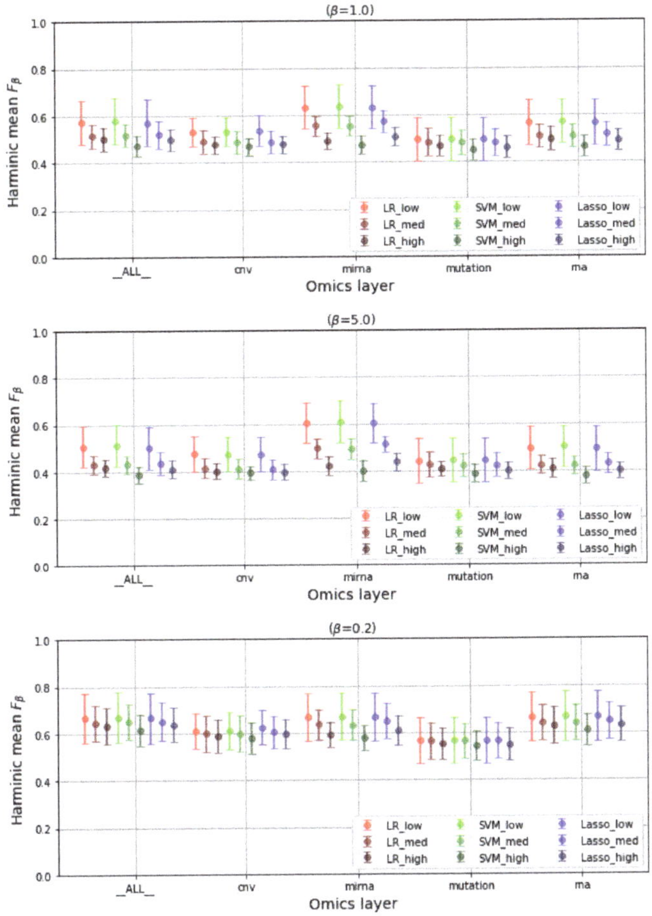

Figure 4. Values of the weighted harmonic mean F_β of classification accuracy and feature selection stability achieved for the tested classification methods in the three ranges of C parameter values. The central dots represent the mean values calculated from the results across 15 datasets. The vertical lines represent the standard deviation values. In the first graph, classification accuracy and feature-selection stability have equal contributions to the harmonic mean ($\beta = 1$). In the second graph, stability is weighted 5 times more than classification accuracy ($\beta = 5$). In the third graph, classification accuracy is weighted 5 times more than feature-selection stability ($\beta = 0.2$).

4. Discussion

The aim of our work was not to precisely replicate the experiments presented in Li et al. [24] but to extend the evaluation metrics they used, focused on classification accuracy and related metrics, to include feature selection stability, which is increasingly recognized as an important evaluation parameter [22,36,51]. In our analysis, we used different feature-selection and classification methods than Li et al. [24] but applied them to the same datasets. We achieved similar classification accuracy values. Additionally, we demonstrated that when considering both classification accuracy and feature-selection stability, a model with different parameters can be identified as the best. Classification accuracy (or its derivative) remains a crucial parameter for evaluating the quality of a classification model, but incorporating feature-selection stability provides a more comprehensive assessment.

In our analysis, the classification accuracy across individual omic layers and the combined feature set did not exhibit significant variations. This stability in accuracy may be attributed to the inherent biological nature of cancer, which manifests across multiple omics layers. The consistent representation of cancer-related pathways and processes in genomic, transcriptomic, proteomic, and metabolomic data suggests that key signals for classification are preserved across these diverse data types. This highlights the interconnectedness of biological systems in cancer pathology and reinforces the notion that integrating multi-omics data can offer a more comprehensive understanding of the disease.

Furthermore, the robust performance across different omics layers underscores the potential of comprehensive multi-omics approaches for effective biomarker discovery. It also suggests that cancer characteristics are sufficiently prominent across all omics layers, resulting in similar predictive power. However, this consistency warrants further investigation into whether certain omics layers contribute disproportionately to classification outcomes. Such insights could inform future studies on optimal feature selection and model training in multi-omics research.

Our future work could focus on extending the validation of the presented method to high-dimensional datasets beyond the medical domain, such as those found in fields like finance, social sciences, or environmental studies. This would help to evaluate the generalizability and robustness of the method in various contexts. Additionally, developing a comprehensive framework for the automated assessment of feature-selection stability in multi-omics data is another promising direction. This framework could integrate multiple stability metrics, incorporate machine-learning algorithms tailored to different omics types, and provide visualization tools to aid in interpreting stability outcomes. Such advancements would enhance the usability and effectiveness of stability assessments in complex, high-dimensional datasets, ultimately contributing to more reliable and reproducible feature-selection processes across diverse scientific disciplines.

In concluding the discussion, it is essential to acknowledge the limitations of the presented research. We take into consideration only four omic layers, which may not capture the full complexity of biological systems. In reality, there are additional omic layers, such as methylation, which can provide valuable insights. By excluding these layers, the analysis may overlook critical interactions and regulatory mechanisms that could influence the results. Future studies should aim to include a broader range of omic layers to provide a more holistic understanding and to better reflect the intricacies of multi-omics datasets.

5. Conclusions

In conclusion, this study underscores the importance of evaluating both classification accuracy and feature-selection stability in multi-omics data analysis. By employing a range of classifiers, including Support Vector Machine, Logistic Regression, and Lasso regression, we demonstrated that the choice of regularization parameter C significantly impacts both performance metrics. Our findings indicate that lower values of C consistently yield a better balance between classification accuracy and feature selection stability, particularly for Logistic Regression and Lasso regression.

The integration of the Nogueira feature-stability measure and the weighted harmonic mean of accuracy and stability offers a comprehensive approach to assess the reliability of feature selection in multi-omics contexts. The insights gained from our analysis highlight the necessity for careful model tuning and validation to improve the robustness of biomarker discovery processes in cancer research.

Overall, this work not only contributes to the understanding of feature-selection stability but also sets the stage for future investigations aimed at enhancing predictive modeling in multi-omics studies. By prioritizing stability alongside accuracy, researchers can develop more reliable models that facilitate advancements in precision medicine and the effective treatment of complex diseases.

Author Contributions: Conceptualization, T.Ł. and J.K. (Jerzy Krawczuk); methodology, T.Ł. and J.K. (Jerzy Krawczuk); software, T.Ł. and J.K. (Jerzy Krawczuk); validation, T.Ł., J.K. (Jerzy Krawczuk),

K.Ż. and J.K. (Jacek Kęsik); formal analysis, T.Ł. and J.K. (Jerzy Krawczuk); investigation, T.Ł. and J.K. (Jerzy Krawczuk); resources, T.Ł. and J.K. (Jerzy Krawczuk); data curation, T.Ł. and J.K. (Jerzy Krawczuk); writing—original draft preparation, T.Ł., J.K. (Jerzy Krawczuk), K.Ż. and J.K. (Jacek Kęsik); writing—review and editing, T.Ł., J.K. (Jerzy Krawczuk), K.Ż. and J.K. (Jacek Kęsik); visualization, T.Ł. and J.K. (Jerzy Krawczuk); supervision, T.Ł. and J.K. (Jacek Kęsik). All authors have read and agreed to the published version of the manuscript.

Funding: The APC was funded by the Lublin University of Technology Scientific Fund.

Institutional Review Board Statement: Not applicable.

Informed Consent Statement: Not applicable.

Data Availability Statement: The data and codes to reproduce the results in the paper are available publicly on GitHub: https://github.com/tlukaszuk/feature-selection-stability-on-multi-omics-data.

Conflicts of Interest: The authors declare no conflicts of interest.

Abbreviations

The following abbreviations are used in this manuscript:

LASSO or Lasso	Least Absolute Shrinkage and Selection Operator
LR	Logistic Regression
SVM	Support Vector Machines
TCGA	The Cancer Genome Atlas

References

1. Shahrajabian, M.H.; Sun, W. Survey on multi-omics, and multi-omics data analysis, integration and application. *Curr. Pharm. Anal.* **2023**, *19*, 267–281. [CrossRef]
2. Subramanian, I.; Verma, S.; Kumar, S.; Jere, A.; Anamika, K. Multi-omics data integration, interpretation, and its application. *Bioinform. Biol. Insights* **2020**, *14*, 1177932219899051. [CrossRef] [PubMed]
3. Canzler, S.; Schor, J.; Busch, W.; Schubert, K.; Rolle-Kampczyk, U.E.; Seitz, H.; Kamp, H.; von Bergen, M.; Buesen, R.; Hackermüller, J. Prospects and challenges of multi-omics data integration in toxicology. *Arch. Toxicol.* **2020**, *94*, 371–388. [CrossRef] [PubMed]
4. Michel, J.B.; Shen, Y.K.; Aiden, A.P.; Veres, A.; Gray, M.K.; Team, G.B.; Pickett, J.P.; Hoiberg, D.; Clancy, D.; Norvig, P.; et al. Quantitative analysis of culture using millions of digitized books. *Science* **2011**, *331*, 176–182. [CrossRef]
5. Albuquerque, U.P.; Cantalice, A.S.; Oliveira, E.S.; de Moura, J.M.B.; Dos Santos, R.K.S.; da Silva, R.H.; Brito-Júnior, V.M.; Ferreira-Júnior, W.S. Exploring large digital bodies for the study of human behavior. *Evol. Psychol. Sci.* **2023**, *9*, 385–394. [CrossRef]
6. Kęsik, J.; Żyła, K.; Montusiewicz, J.; Miłosz, M.; Neamtu, C.; Juszczyk, M. A methodical approach to 3d scanning of heritage objects being under continuous display. *Appl. Sci.* **2022**, *13*, 441. [CrossRef]
7. Wang, Z.; Jensen, M.A.; Zenklusen, J.C. A practical guide to the cancer genome atlas (TCGA). In *Statistical Genomics: Methods and Protocols*; Humana Press: New York, NY, USA, 2016; pp. 111–141.
8. NIH, TCGA Program. Available online: https://www.cancer.gov/ccg/research/genome-sequencing/tcga (accessed on 30 October 2024).
9. Zhang, J.; Bajari, R.; Andric, D.; Gerthoffert, F.; Lepsa, A.; Nahal-Bose, H.; Stein, L.D.; Ferretti, V. The international cancer genome consortium data portal. *Nat. Biotechnol.* **2019**, *37*, 367–369. [CrossRef]
10. ICGC Data Repository. Available online: https://docs.icgc-argo.org/docs/data-access/icgc-25k-data (accessed on 30 October 2024).
11. Perez-Riverol, Y.; Bai, M.; da Veiga Leprevost, F.; Squizzato, S.; Park, Y.M.; Haug, K.; Carroll, A.J.; Spalding, D.; Paschall, J.; Wang, M.; et al. Discovering and linking public omics data sets using the Omics Discovery Index. *Nat. Biotechnol.* **2017**, *35*, 406–409. [CrossRef]
12. Omics DI Homepage. Available online: https://www.omicsdi.org/ (accessed on 30 October 2024).
13. Kozieł, G. Information security policy creating. *Actual Probl. Econ.* **2011**, *126*, 376–380.
14. Kang, M.; Ko, E.; Mersha, T.B. A roadmap for multi-omics data integration using deep learning. *Briefings Bioinform.* **2022**, *23*, bbab454. [CrossRef]
15. He, X.; Liu, X.; Zuo, F.; Shi, H.; Jing, J. Artificial intelligence-based multi-omics analysis fuels cancer precision medicine. *Semin. Cancer Biol.* **2023**, *88*, 187–200. [CrossRef]
16. Chakraborty, S.; Sharma, G.; Karmakar, S.; Banerjee, S. Multi-OMICS approaches in cancer biology: New era in cancer therapy. *Biochim. Biophys. Acta (BBA)-Mol. Basis Dis.* **2024**, *1870*, 167120. [CrossRef] [PubMed]
17. Alkhateeb, A.; Rueda, L. *Machine Learning Methods for Multi-Omics Data Integration*; Springer: Berlin/Heidelberg, Germany, 2023.
18. Ahmed, Z.; Wan, S.; Zhang, F.; Zhong, W. Artificial intelligence for omics data analysis. *BMC Methods* **2024**, *1*, 4. [CrossRef]

19. Wekesa, J.S.; Kimwele, M. A review of multi-omics data integration through deep learning approaches for disease diagnosis prognosis, and treatment. *Front. Genet.* **2023**, *14*, 1199087. [CrossRef] [PubMed]
20. Leng, D.; Zheng, L.; Wen, Y.; Zhang, Y.; Wu, L.; Wang, J.; Wang, M.; Zhang, Z.; He, S.; Bo, X. A benchmark study of deep learning-based multi-omics data fusion methods for cancer. *Genome Biol.* **2022**, *23*, 171. [CrossRef]
21. Labory, J.; Bottini, S. The multiomics revolution in the era of deep learning: Allies or enemies? In *Artificial Intelligence for Medicine*; Elsevier: Amsterdam, The Netherlands, 2024; pp. 201–216.
22. Pes, B. Ensemble feature selection for high-dimensional data: A stability analysis across multiple domains. *Neural Comput. Appl.* **2020**, *32*, 5951–5973. [CrossRef]
23. Łukaszuk, T.; Krawczuk, J. Importance of feature selection stability in the classifier evaluation on high-dimensional genetic data *PeerJ* **2024**, *12*, e18405. [CrossRef]
24. Li, Y.; Mansmann, U.; Du, S.; Hornung, R. Benchmark study of feature selection strategies for multi-omics data. *BMC Bioinform.* **2022**, *23*, 412. [CrossRef]
25. Momeni, Z.; Hassanzadeh, E.; Abadeh, M.S.; Bellazzi, R. A survey on single and multi omics data mining methods in cancer data classification. *J. Biomed. Inform.* **2020**, *107*, 103466. [CrossRef]
26. Al-Tashi, Q.; Abdulkadir, S.J.; Rais, H.M.; Mirjalili, S.; Alhussian, H. Approaches to multi-objective feature selection: A systematic literature review. *IEEE Access* **2020**, *8*, 125076–125096. [CrossRef]
27. Peck, R.; Devore, J. Statistics: The exploration and analysis of data. *Cengage Learn.* **2011**, *464465*, 516–519.
28. Gao, L.; Ye, M.; Lu, X.; Huang, D. Hybrid method based on information gain and support vector machine for gene selection in cancer classification. *Genom. Proteom. Bioinform.* **2017**, *15*, 389–395. [CrossRef] [PubMed]
29. Kononenko, I.; Šimec, E.; Robnik-Šikonja, M. Overcoming the myopia of inductive learning algorithms with RELIEFF. *Appl. Intell.* **1997**, *7*, 39–55. [CrossRef]
30. Peng, H.; Long, F.; Ding, C. Feature selection based on mutual information criteria of max-dependency, max-relevance, and min-redundancy. *IEEE Trans. Pattern Anal. Mach. Intell.* **2005**, *27*, 1226–1238. [CrossRef]
31. Guyon, I.; Weston, J.; Barnhill, S.; Vapnik, V. Gene selection for cancer classification using support vector machines. *Mach. Learn.* **2002**, *46*, 389–422. [CrossRef]
32. Oreski, S.; Oreski, G. Genetic algorithm-based heuristic for feature selection in credit risk assessment. *Expert Syst. Appl.* **2014**, *41*, 2052–2064. [CrossRef]
33. Tibshirani, R. The lasso method for variable selection in the Cox model. *Stat. Med.* **1997**, *16*, 385–395. [CrossRef]
34. Breiman, L. Random forests. *Mach. Learn.* **2001**, *45*, 5–32. [CrossRef]
35. Khaire, U.M.; Dhanalakshmi, R. Stability of feature selection algorithm: A review. *J. King Saud Univ.-Comput. Inf. Sci.* **2022**, *34*, 1060–1073. [CrossRef]
36. Barbieri, M.C.; Grisci, B.I.; Dorn, M. Analysis and comparison of feature selection methods towards performance and stability. *Expert Syst. Appl.* **2024**, *249*, 123667. [CrossRef]
37. Lazebnik, T.; Rosenfeld, A. A new definition for feature selection stability analysis. *Ann. Math. Artif. Intell.* **2024**, *92*, 753–770. [CrossRef]
38. Mohtasham, F.; Pourhoseingholi, M.; Hashemi Nazari, S.S.; Kavousi, K.; Zali, M.R. Comparative analysis of feature selection techniques for COVID-19 dataset. *Sci. Rep.* **2024**, *14*, 18627. [CrossRef]
39. Hayet-Otero, M.; Garcia-Garcia, F.; Lee, D.J.; Martínez-Minaya, J.; España Yandiola, P.P.; Urrutia Landa, I.; Nieves Ermecheo, M.; Quintana, J.M.; Menéndez, R.; Torres, A.; et al. Extracting relevant predictive variables for COVID-19 severity prognosis: An exhaustive comparison of feature selection techniques. *PLoS ONE* **2023**, *18*, e0284150. [CrossRef] [PubMed]
40. Cortes, C. Support-Vector Networks. *Mach. Learn.* **1995**, *20*, 273–297. [CrossRef]
41. Bartlett, P.L.; Wegkamp, M.H. Classification with a Reject Option using a Hinge Loss. *J. Mach. Learn. Res.* **2008**, *9*, 1823–1840.
42. Hosmer, D.W., Jr.; Lemeshow, S.; Sturdivant, R.X. *Applied Logistic Regression*; John Wiley & Sons: Hoboken, NJ, USA, 2013.
43. Ranstam, J.; Cook, J.A. LASSO regression. *J. Br. Surg.* **2018**, *105*, 1348. [CrossRef]
44. Saeys, Y.; Abeel, T.; Van de Peer, Y. Robust feature selection using ensemble feature selection techniques. In *Machine Learning and Knowledge Discovery in Databases, Proceedings of the European Conference, ECML PKDD 2008, Antwerp, Belgium, 15–19 September 2008*; Proceedings, Part II 19; Springer: Berlin/Heidelberg, Germany, 2008; pp. 313–325.
45. Kuncheva, L. A stability index for feature selection. In Proceedings of the Artificial Intelligence and Applications, AIAP'07, Innsbruck, Austria, 12–14 February 2007; ACTA Press: Anaheim, CA, USA, 2007; pp. 390–395.
46. Lustgarten, J.; Gopalakrishnan, V.; Visweswaran, S. Measuring stability of feature selection in biomedical datasets. In Proceedings of the AMIA Annual Symposium Proceedings, San Francisco, CA, USA, 14–18 November 2009; American Medical Informatics Association: Bethesda, MD, USA, 2009; Volume 2009, pp. 406–410.
47. Nogueira, S.; Sechidis, K.; Brown, G. On the stability of feature selection algorithms. *J. Mach. Learn. Res.* **2018**, *18*, 1–54.
48. Herrmann, M.; Probst, P.; Hornung, R.; Jurinovic, V.; Boulesteix, A.L. Large-scale benchmark study of survival prediction methods using multi-omics data. *Briefings Bioinform.* **2021**, *22*, bbaa167. [CrossRef]
49. Wang, X.; Sun, Q. TP53 mutations, expression and interaction networks in human cancers. *Oncotarget* **2017**, *8*, 624. [CrossRef]
50. Pedregosa, F.; Varoquaux, G.; Gramfort, A.; Michel, V.; Thirion, B.; Grisel, O.; Blondel, M.; Prettenhofer, P.; Weiss, R.; Dubourg, V.; et al. Scikit-learn: Machine Learning in Python. *J. Mach. Learn. Res.* **2011**, *12*, 2825–2830.

51. Kalousis, A.; Prados, J.; Hilario, M. Stability of feature selection algorithms: A study on high-dimensional spaces. *Knowl. Inf. Syst.* **2007**, *12*, 95–116. [CrossRef]

applied sciences

MDPI

Article

A Novel Prognostic Model for Gastric Cancer with EP_Dis-Based Co-Expression Network Analysis

Yalan Xu [1], Hongyan Zhang [1,*], Dan Cao [2], Zilan Ning [1], Liu Zhu [1] and Xueyan Liu [1]

1 College of Information and Intelligence, Hunan Agricultural University, Changsha 410128, China; coco@stu.hunau.edu.cn (Y.X.); zilanning@hunau.edu.cn (Z.N.); zhuliu@stu.hunau.edu.cn (L.Z.); liuxueyan@stu.hunau.edu.cn (X.L.)

2 College of Science, Central South University of Forestry and Technology, Changsha 410004, China; caodan@csuft.edu.cn

* Correspondence: hongyan_zhang@hunau.edu.cn; Tel.: +86-139-7313-6716

Abstract: Ferroptosis is a regulated form of cell death that involves iron-dependent lipid peroxidation. Ferroptosis-related genes (FRGs) play an essential role in the tumorigenesis of gastric cancer (GC), which is one of the most common and lethal cancers worldwide. Understanding the prognostic significance of FRGs in GC can shed light on GC treatment and diagnosis. In this study, we proposed a new gene co-expression network analysis method, namely EP-WGCNA. This method used Euclidean and Pearson weighted distance (EP_dis) to construct a weighted gene co-expression network instead of the Pearson's correlation coefficient used in the original WGCNA method. The aim was to better capture the interactions and functional associations among genes. We used EP-WGCNA to identify the FRGs related to GC phenotype and applied bioinformatics methods to select the FRGs associated with the prognosis (P-FRGs) of GC patients. Firstly, we screened the FRGs that were differentially expressed based on the TCGA and GTEx databases. Then, we selected the P-FRGs using EP-WGCNA, Cox regression, and Kaplan–Meier analysis. The prognostic model based on P-FRGs-Cox (*ALB, BNIP3, DPEP1, GLS2, MEG3, PDK4, TF*, and *TSC22D3*) was constructed on the TCGA-GTEx dataset. According to the median risk score, all patients in the TCGA training dataset and GSE84426 testing dataset were classified into a high- or low-risk group. GC patients in the low-risk group showed higher survival probability than those in the high-risk group. The time-dependent receiver operating characteristic (timeROC) showed that EP-WGCNA-Cox predicted 0.77 in the training set and 0.64 in the testing set for the 5-year survival rate of GC patients, which was better than traditional WGCNA-Cox (P-WGCNA-Cox). In addition, we validated that the P-FRGs were significantly differentially expressed in the adjacent non-tumor gastric tissues and tumor tissues by immunohistochemical staining from the Human Protein Atlas (HPA) database. We also found that the P-FRGs were enriched in tumorigenic pathways by enrichment analysis. In conclusion, our study demonstrated that EP-WGCNA can mine the key FRGs related to the phenotype of GC and is superior to the P-WGCNA. The EP-WGCNA-Cox model based on P-FRGs is reliable in predicting the survival rate of GC patients and can provide potential biomarkers and therapeutic targets for GC.

Keywords: gastric cancer; prognosis; ferroptosis; EP-WGCNA

1. Introduction

Gastric cancer (GC) is a prevalent and deadly malignancy worldwide. According to the recent statistics from the GLOBOCAN database, it ranks fifth in incidence and fourth in mortality in the world [1]. Surgery is the primary and most effective treatment for GC patients, which can significantly improve their survival rate [2]. However, the survival rate remains constrained by low early diagnosis rate [3] and poor postoperative recovery [4]. Therefore, there is an urgent need to identify novel biomarkers for GC screening, diagnosis, prognosis, and therapy. Biomarkers are molecules that can facilitate disease screening, diagnosis, characterization, and monitoring [5], and they are more convenient and economical than the direct measurement of the final clinical endpoint in clinic [6]. Effective biomarkers can assist in finding optimal individualized treatment approaches for GC patients.

Ferroptosis is a novel form of programmed cell death that depends on iron and involves free lipid peroxidation and plasma membrane rupture. Unlike apoptosis, cell necrosis, and autophagy, ferroptosis has distinct features and mechanisms [7]. Its main characteristics are shown in two aspects: cell morphology and cellular component. Ferroptosis leads to smaller mitochondria, increased membrane density, and a ridge reduction in cells. Ferroptosis also increases lipid peroxidation and reactive oxygen species (ROS) in cells. The main mechanism of ferroptosis is to catalyze the highly expressed unsaturated fatty acids on the cell membrane under the action of ferric or ester oxygenase. This results in lipid peroxidation, thus inducing cell death. In addition, ferroptosis decreases the expression of the antioxidant system (glutathione GSH and glutathione peroxidase 4-GPX4) [7]. Many studies have revealed that ferroptosis-related genes (FRGs) are potential prognostic biomarkers for cancer. For example, Sun et al. [8] constructed a ferroptosis-related risk score (FRRS) using random forest and principal component analysis on 1328 samples and 36 FRGs. They validated the FRRS in three independent datasets and showed that it could predict the prognosis and immunotherapy response of lung adenocarcinoma patients. Similarly, Mou et al. [9] identified 25 FRGs and methylation genes that correlated with the survival of renal clear cell carcinoma patients using bioinformatics methods. Moreover, Zhu et al. [10] reported that a low expression of two FRGs was associated with poor outcomes of adrenocortical carcinoma patients. However, the role of these FRGs in GC prognosis remains unclear.

Weighted gene co-expression network analysis (WGCNA) is a widely used and powerful network analysis method for identifying key genes in tumor datasets. It organizes genes with similar functions and regulatory mechanisms into common modules and explores the relationship between these modules and biological processes. WGCNA analysis is based on two assumptions: (1) Genes with similar expression patterns may have co-regulation, functional relevance or be in the same pathway; (2) Gene networks follow a scale-free distribution. Based on these two points, we can divide gene networks into different modules according to expression similarity and then identify hub genes [11]. WGCNA has been widely used in the predicting research of cancer prognosis-related genes. However, the classical WGCNA methods usually measure linear similarity between genes based on the Pearson correlation coefficient (denoted as P-WGCNA). This measure can only capture the local variable trends between two gene expression levels and may lose some necessary information for complex structured datasets. Therefore, Ning et al. [12] proposed a new similarity measure method—EP_dis—that combined Euclidean distance and Pearson distance by a weighted method. EP_dis captures both global spatial correlation and local variation trend between data points. Based on this, we consider using EP_dis as a method to measure gene similarity and construct a gene co-expression network (EP-WGCNA) to capture more intrinsic relationships between gene expression levels. A smaller EP_dis represents a stronger similarity between the two genes.

In summary, we focused on the GC dataset as the research object and utilized the EP-WGCNA-Cox to predicted prognosis-related ferroptosis genes (P-FRGs). We comprehensively analyzed the function and biological significance of P-FRGs from multiple perspectives. We used timeROC [13] to assess the predictive performance of the prognostic model, GO functional enrichment analysis [14] to analyze gene function enrichment, literature report to validate the findings, and immunohistochemical staining in the Human Protein Atlas (HPA) database to confirm the gene expression.

2. Materials and Methods

2.1. Data Source and Preprocessing

We downloaded RNA sequencing data (HTSeq-Counts) of 407 GC samples (adjacent non-tumor: 32, tumor: 375) and corresponding clinical data from the TCGA database (TCGA-STAD, https://xenabrowser.net/datapages (accessed on 25 April 2022)). To balance the number of tumor and non-tumor tissue samples, we also downloaded gene expression data of 174 normal gastric tissue samples from the GTEx database (https://xenabrowser.net/datapages (accessed on 30 April 2022)) and combined them with the adjacent non-tumor tissue samples [15]. We used this combined dataset of TCGA-GTEx as the training set (all data were generated by Illumina platform). For validation, we used the GSE84426 dataset from the GEO database. On 12 August 2022, we downloaded 564 FRGs from the FerrDB database [16]. We extracted probe information from the annotation file to annotate the genes for both TCGA and GTEx data. Then, we classified the tumor and non-tumor tissues based on clinical information. We merged the tumor, non-tumor, and normal tissues by gene names. We normalized the sequencing depth and removed batch effects. This resulted in a new dataset, with sample name as row name and gene name as column name, including 581 GC samples (normal: 206, tumor: 375) and 57,793 genes. Table 1 shows the clinical pathological features of patients in TCGA-STAD and GSE84426. Some patients had incomplete clinical data, so not all information is shown in Table 1.

Table 1. Clinical characteristics of the GC patients included in this study.

Characteristics		TCGA-STAD (n = 375)	GSE84426 (n = 76)
Age	≤65	164 (43.73%)	22 (28.95%)
	>65	208 (55.47%)	54 (71.05%)
Gender	Male	239 (63.73%)	54 (71.05%)
	Female	136 (36.27%)	22 (28.95%)
Stage	I	36 (9.60%)	–
	II	69 (18.40%)	–
	III	95 (25.33%)	–
	IV	22 (5.87%)	–
T stage	T1	14 (3.73%)	0
	T2	51 (13.60%)	3 (3.95%)
	T3	109 (29.07%)	25 (32.90%)
	T4	59 (15.73%)	48 (63.15%)
N stage	N0	67 (17.87%)	9 (11.84%)
	N1	65 (17.33%)	33 (43.42%)
	N2	50 (13.33%)	33 (43.42%)
	N3	45 (12.00%)	1 (1.32%)
M stage	M0	213 (56.80%)	–
	M1	12 (3.20%)	–
Survival status	Alive	230 (61.33%)	41 (53.95%)
	Dead	145 (38.67%)	34 (44.74%)

Some patients had incomplete clinical data, so the table did not show information for all patients.

We used R (version 4.2.1) language to filter out genes with low expression in the TCGA-GTEx dataset (quantitative analysis was performed by count-per-million first, and then those whose gene value was less than 1 were filtered out) and conducted a Trimmed Mean of M-values (TMM) normalization of the data. Next, we screened the differentially expressed genes (DEGs) in the dataset using empirical Bayesian estimation and exact test based on the negative binomial model, with $|logFC| > 1$ and padj < 0.05 as screening criteria. We obtained the padj using the Benjamini–Hochberg (BH) method. Finally, we took the genes shared by DEGs and FRGs and noted them as DE-FRGs.

2.2. Co-Expression Network Analysis—P-WGCNA and EP-WGCNA

In this study, the classical P-WGCNA construction was implemented directly using a series of functions provided by the WGCNA package in R language, while the improved EP-WGCNA was implemented by self-coding based on the related functions in the WGCNA package. The main implementation steps of the two are as follows:

(1) Calculate the similarity matrix S_{ij}. Based on the P-WGCNA method, the elements in the similarity matrix are composed of Pearson linear correlation coefficients between gene i and gene j, that is , $(S_{ij})^{unsigned} = cor(i,j)$; and based on the EP-WGCNA method, the elements are composed of EP_dis between gene i and gene j, that is, $S_{ij} = EP\_dis(i,j)$.

(2) Define the adjacency matrix $A_{ij} = |S_{ij}|^{\beta}$, that is, perform power law operation on the similarity. In order to make the connection between genes in the network follow a scale-free distribution, select the soft threshold β according to the scale-free network model index R^2; β is represented in code by softPower. The code implemented by the two methods in this step:

```
#P-WGCNA
Adjacency = adjacency (datExpr, power=softPower);
#calculate the adjacencies, datExpr represents gene expression matrix
```

```
#EP-WGCNA
Adjacency = adjacency.fromSimilarity (EP_dis, power=softPower)
#calculate the adjacencies based on EP_dis
```

(3) Construct a topological overlap matrix TOM_{ij}.

(4) Calculate the distance matrix disTOM $= 1 - TOM_{ij}$, construct a hierarchical clustering tree, and use the dynamic pruning algorithm to obtain gene modules. The minimum number of genes in the module is set to 30. Then, merge similar modules with a merge threshold of 0.2.

(5) Calculate the correlation coefficient between gene module feature genes and phenotypes (denoted as ME) to identify significant modules. The P-WGCNA used Pearson correlation coefficients, and the EP-WGCNA used EP_dis [12]. The larger the ME value of a module, the more related it is to the phenotype. This study selected modules with $|\text{ME}| > 0.8$ as significant modules.

2.3. Prognostic Model Construction and Validation

We used univariate and multivariate Cox regression analyses [17] to identify the P-FRGs. Based on the P-FRGs, we constructed a Cox regression model of prognostic hazard ratios on the training set. The expression values of the P-FRGs were the expressions of corresponding genes in TCGA-GTEx. We used the overall survival time and status of GC patients in TCGA as our response variables. To quantify the risk for each patient, we calculated the risk score based on the standardized expression level (g_i) as follows:

$$\text{Risk Score} = \sum_{i=1}^{N} g_i \times a_i \quad (1)$$

where N is the number of genes and a_i is the coefficient from Cox regression analysis. We dichotomized the patients into high- and low-risk groups based on whether their risk score was above or below the median value. Subsequently, we conducted Kaplan–Meier (KM) analysis [17] to assess the survival outcomes between the two groups. We also used timeROC to evaluate the predictive ability of the prognostic model for the 5-year survival rate of patients. In addition, we validated the prognostic model in an external dataset, GSE84426.

2.4. GO Enrichment Analysis

Gene ontology (GO) enrichment analysis was used to analyze the gene function of P-FRGs, including biological process (BP), cellular component (CC), and molecular function

(MF). The GO pathway with a p-value and false discovery rate (FDR) below 0.05 was selected and recorded for further analysis.

2.5. Immunohistochemical Staining from the HPA Database

The Human Protein Atlas (HPA, https://www.proteinatlas.org/ (accessed on 15 February 2023)) database examined the expression of each protein in detail in 64 cell lines, 48 normal human tissues, and 20 tumor tissues using highly specific antibodies and immunoassay techniques (Western blotting, immunofluorescence, and immunohistochemistry). It provides information on the tissue and cellular distribution of 26,000 human proteins. In this study, we used the HPA database to explore the expression of P-FRGs in GC.

2.6. Statistical Analysis

Fisher's exact test with p-values adjusted by the BH method was used to compare gene expression between tumor tissues and non-tumorous tissues. Univariate and multivariate Cox regression analyses were conducted to identify the independent factors related to survival time and survival status. The overall survival between different groups was compared by Kaplan–Meier analysis with the Log-rank test. If not specified above, a p-value below 0.05 was considered statistically significant. All statistical analyses were performed with R software (version 4.2.1).

3. Results

3.1. Phenotypic Related Genes Were Identified by P-WGCNA and EP-WGCNA

Following the differential expression analysis, total number of 11,606 DEGs were identified. To reduce the computational complexity of gene co-expression network analysis, we selected the top 30% of genes based on their absolute median deviation. Subsequently, we organized the data into a data matrix with rows as samples (581) and columns as genes (3000) and used it as the input matrix for both the P-WGCNA and EP-WGCNA.

As shown in Figure 1A,B, when performing weighted gene co-expression network analysis based on P-WGCNA, 13 gene modules were obtained by dynamic cutting, and 8 modules were obtained after merging; when performing network analysis based on EP-WGCNA, 7 gene modules were obtained by dynamic cutting, and 5 modules were obtained after merging. The correlation between each module and GC phenotype is shown in Figure 1C,D, where different colors on the y-axis represent different modules, and two phenotypes of normal people and GC patients are listed on the x-axis. Modules with a correlation greater than 0.8 with the phenotype were selected as significant modules. The significant modules and the number of genes in each module identified based on P-WGCNA were blue (1233) and pink (481), with a total of 1714 genes. However, the genes identified based on EP-WGCNA were brown (865), blue (575), and grey (613), with a total of 2053 genes. To find out the DE-FRGs in the significant modules identified by both algorithms, we intersected each module with 564 FRGs. As shown in Figure 1E,F, there were 39 DE-FRGs identified by P-WGCNA, and 44 DE-FRGs were identified by EP-WGCNA.

3.2. Selection of Ferroptosis-Related Genes Associated with Patient Prognosis

We performed univariate and multivariate Cox regression analysis to evaluate the association between the DE-FRGs identified by P-WGCNA and EP-WGCNA and the prognosis of GC patients, using their survival time and status as dependent variables. We used a p-value < 0.1 for univariate analysis and a p-value < 0.05 for multivariate analysis as the screening criteria. Among the DE-FRGs identified by P-WGCNA, nine P-FRGs were identified, including *ALB*, *AR*, *BNIP3*, *CBS*, *CDC25A*, *FABP4*, *MEG3*, *MYB* and *PDK4* (Supplementary Materials Table S1), while among the DE-FRGs identified by EP-WGCNA, eight P-FRGs were identified, including *ALB*, *BNIP3*, *DPEP1*, *GLS2*, *MEG3*, *PDK4*, *TF* and *TSC22D3*, as shown in Table 2. The complete results of Cox regression analysis based on P-WGCNA and EP-WGCNA screened genes are presented in Supplementary Materials Tables S2 and S3. Then, we used Log-rank test (with Log-rank $p < 0.05$ as the screening criterion) and Kaplan–Meier (KM) curve analysis to examine the correlation between these P-FRGs and the overall survival of GC patients. We found that all of them were significantly associated with the overall survival. In Figure 2 are the KM curves of the eight P-FRGs screened by EP-WGCNA-Cox. Among these genes, *ALB, BNIP3, DPEP1, FABP4, MEG3, PDK4, TF* and *TSC22D3* demonstrated significantly higher survival time in the low expression group than in the high expression group, while *GLS2* had significantly higher survival time in the high expression group than in the low expression group. The KM curves of the nine P-FRGs screened by P-WGCNA-Cox are presented in Supplementary Materials Figure S1.

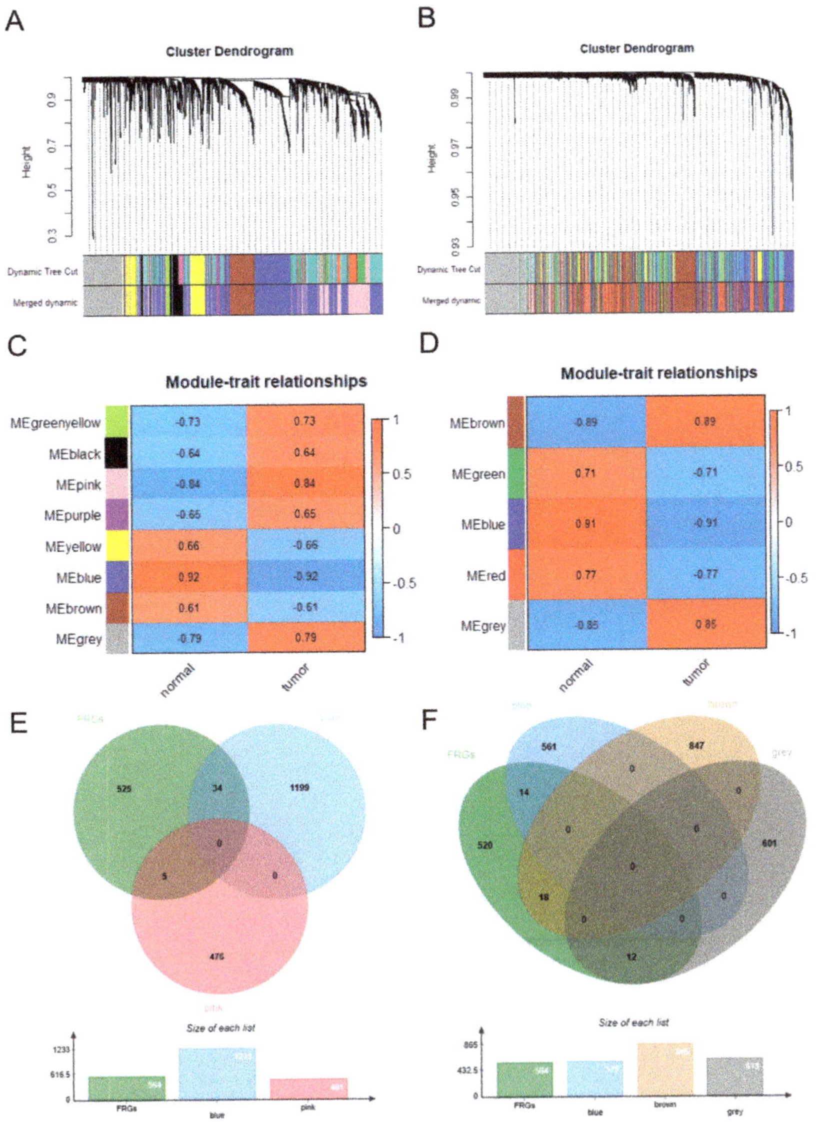

Figure 1. (**A**,**B**): Gene clustering tree and module division based on P-WGCNA and EP-WGCNA methods, respectively. The dynamic tree cut represents the module divided by the original calculation and the merged dynamic represents the merged result; (**C**,**D**): The correlation between each module

and GC phenotype based on P-WGCNA and EP-WGCNA methods, respectively. Red indicates that the module is positively correlated with GC phenotypes, and blue indicates that the module is negatively correlated with GC phenotypes. The greater the absolute value of the number, the stronger the correlation; (**E**,**F**): The number of DE-FRGs contained in significant modules identified based on P-WGCNA and EP-WGCNA methods, respectively. Green represents the ferroptosis-related genes, other colors represent the module colors selected, and numbers represent the number of genes contained in each module.

Table 2. Univariate and multivariate regression analysis of the correlation between overall survival of GC patients and DE-FRGs identified by EP-WGCNA (p-value < 0.05).

Characteristics	Univariate Analysis		Multivariate Analysis	
	Hazard Ratio (95% CI)	***p* Value**	**Hazard Ratio (95% CI)**	***p* Value**
ALB	1.464 (1.051–2.041)	0.024	1.413 (1.005–1.987)	0.047
BNIP3	1.363 (0.979–1.899)	0.047	1.049 (0.737–1.492)	0.022
DPEP1	1.296 (0.933–1.800)	0.012	1.568 (1.076–2.284)	0.019
GLS2	0.821 (0.591–1.140)	0.039	1.286 (0.908–1.823)	0.012
MEG3	1.454 (1.045–2.023)	0.026	1.573 (1.095–2.259)	0.026
PDK4	1.825 (1.302–2.559)	<0.001	1.505 (1.077–2.102)	0.014
TF	1.530 (1.098–2.131)	0.012	1.300 (0.919–1.837)	0.038
TSC22D3	1.407 (1.011–1.959)	0.043	1.017 (0.695–1.487)	0.023

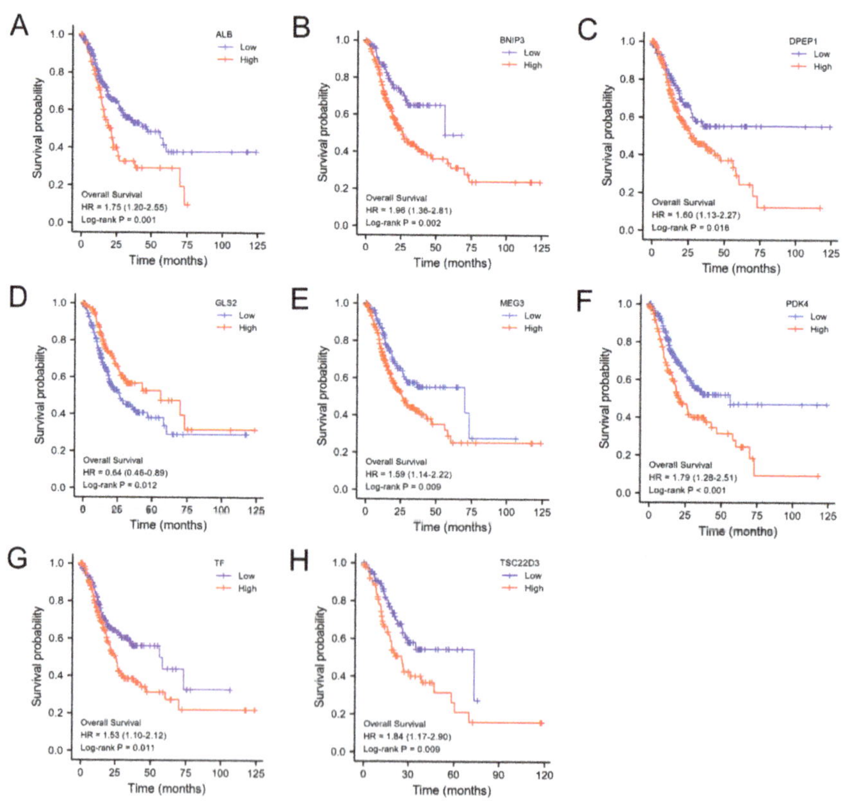

Figure 2. Relationship between P-FRGs identified by EP-WGCNA-Cox and overall survival of GC patients. Blue represents the low expression group and red represents the high expression group. (**A**) *ALB*. (**B**) *BNIP3*. (**C**) *DPEP1*. (**D**) *GLS2*. (**E**) *MEG3*. (**F**) *PDK4*. (**G**) *TF*. (**H**) *TSC22D3*.

3.3. Prognostic Model Construction and Validation

Using P-WGCNA-Cox and EP-WGCNA-Cox, nine P-FRGs and eight P-FRGs were identified, respectively. Then, risk score models were established on the training set TCGA-STAD using the following formulas:

P-WGCNA-Cox:

$$\begin{aligned} \text{RiskScore} &= g(ALB) \times 0.07 + g(AR) \times 0.03 + g(CBS) \times 0.07 \\ &+ g(CDC25A) \times 0.03 + g(BNIP3) \times 0.06 \\ &+ g(FABP4) \times 0.05 + g(MEG3) \times 0.11 + g(MYB) \times (-0.07) \\ &+ g(PDK4) \times 0.02 \end{aligned} \quad (2)$$

EP-WGCNA-Cox:

$$\begin{aligned} \text{RiskScore} &= g(ALB) \times 0.05 + g(BNIP3) \times 0.05 + g(DPEP1) \times 0.01 \\ &+ g(GLS2) \times (-0.18) + g(MEG3) \times 0.08 \\ &+ g(PDK4) \times 0.04 + g(TF) \times 0.08 + g(TSC22D3) \times 0.01 \end{aligned} \quad (3)$$

Based on the median risk score of P-WGCNA-Cox and EP-WGCNA-Cox models, 375 GC cases were classified into a high-risk group (n = 187) and a low-risk group (n = 188), as depicted in Figure 3A,B. The KM curves showed that the overall survival rate of the low-risk group was significantly higher compared to that of the high-risk group ($p < 0.05$) for both methods. The timeROC curve showed that for the 5-year survival rate of GC patients, the prognostic model constructed by P-WGCNA-Cox predicted 0.69 (Figure 3C), while the prognostic model constructed by EP-WGCNA-Cox predicted 0.77 (Figure 3D), indicating that the EP-WGCNA-Cox model had a better performance in predicting the survival rate of GC patients.

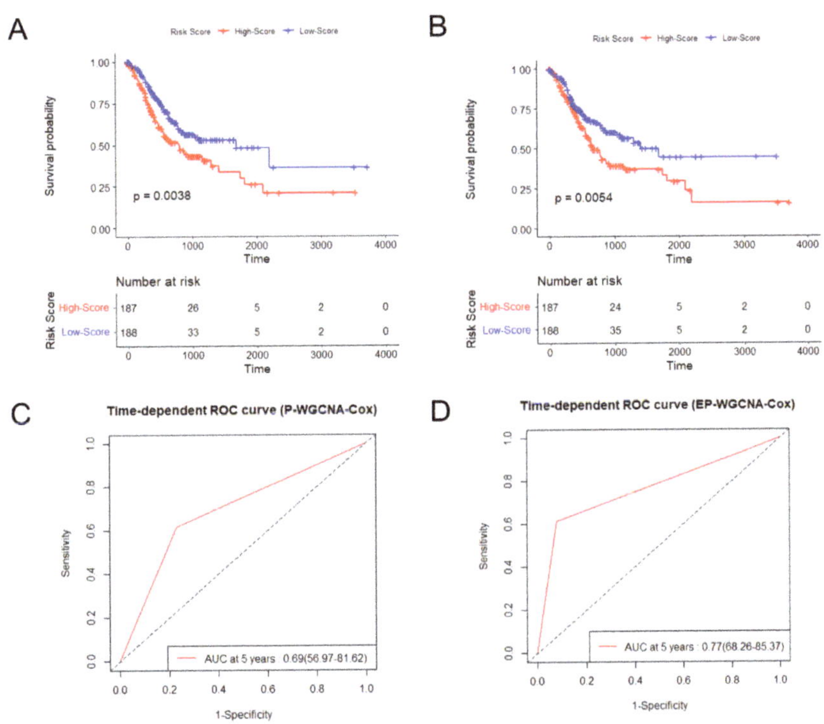

Figure 3. P-WGCNA-Cox and EP-WGCNA-Cox prognostic models were constructed on TCGA-STAD. (**A**,**B**): KM curves of overall survival of GC patients in the P-WGCNA-Cox and EP-WGCNA-Cox prognostic

models in the high and low risk groups; (**C**,**D**): timeROC curve of 5-year survival in GC patients predicted by P-WGCNA-Cox and EP-WGCNA-Cox prognostic models.

To assess the robustness of the prognostic model, the risk score for each patient in the validation set GSE84426 was calculated using the same formulas employed in the training set. Similar to the classification in the training set, the patients in the validation set were divided into a high-risk group (n = 37) and a low-risk group (n = 38), and the KM curve showed that the overall survival rate of the GC low-risk group was also significantly higher than that of the high-risk group ($p < 0.05$) (Figure 4A,B). The timeROC analysis showed that the AUC of the P-WGCNA-Cox was 0.59 at 5 years (Figure 4C). On the other hand, the AUC of the EP-WGCNA-Cox was 0.64 at 5 years (Figure 4D). This results indicate that the prognostic model constructed by EP-WGCNA-Cox had a good reliability.

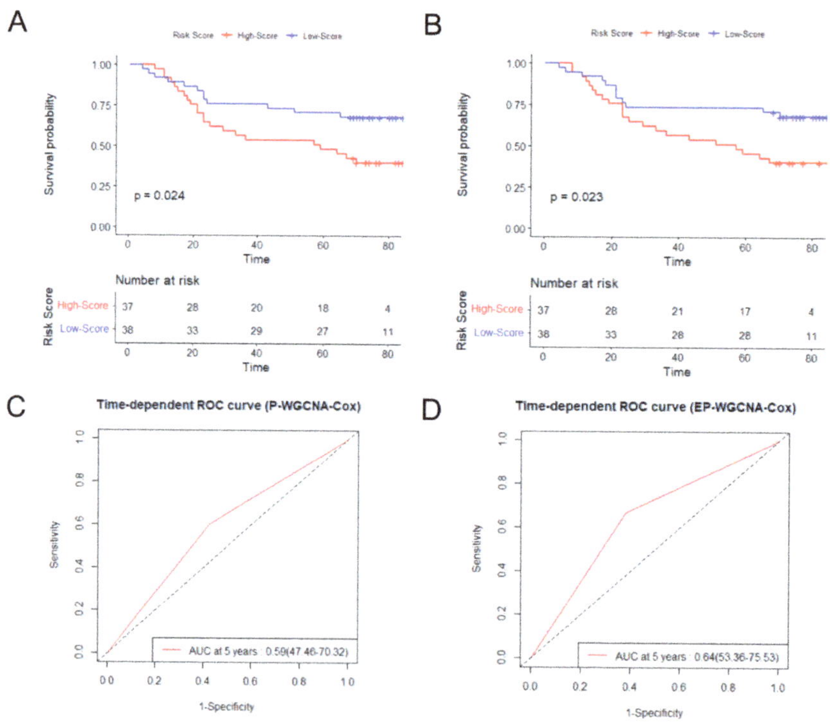

Figure 4. P-WGCNA-Cox and EP-WGCNA-Cox prognostic models were constructed on GSE84426. (**A**,**B**): KM curves of overall survival of GC patients in the P-WGCNA-Cox and EP-WGCNA-Cox prognostic models in the high and low risk groups; (**C**,**D**): timeROC curve of 5-year survival in GC patients predicted by P-WGCNA-Cox and EP-WGCNA-Cox prognostic models.

3.4. GO Enrichment Analysis

We performed GO enrichment analysis on the eight P-FRGs identified by EP-WGCNA-Cox to explore their gene function; the specific enrichment results are shown in Table 3. In terms of BP, the significantly enriched pathways included reactive oxygen species metabolic process (GO:0072593), cellular response to metal ion (GO:0071248), cellular response to inorganic substance (GO:0071241), cellular response to iron ion (GO:0071281), transferrin transport (GO:0033572), ferric iron transport (GO:0015682) and cellular iron ion homeostasis (GO:0006879). In terms of CC, these genes were significantly enriched in blood microparticle (GO:0072562), integral component of mitochondrial outer membrane

(GO:0031307), intrinsic component of mitochondrial outer membrane (GO:0031306), platelet alpha granule lumen (GO:0031093) and platelet alpha granule (GO:0031091). In terms of MF, the significantly enriched pathways were ferric iron binding (GO:0008199), oxygen binding (GO:0019825), antioxidant activity (GO:0016209), hydrolase activity, acting on carbon-nitrogen bonds (GO:0016810) and iron ion binding (GO:0050662).

Table 3. Partial results of GO enrichment analysis of P-FRGs.

Ontology	ID	Description	*p*-Value	FDR
BP	GO:0072593	reactive oxygen species metabolic process	6.73×10^5	0.009
BP	GO:0071248	cellular response to metal ion	0.002	0.041
BP	GO:0071241	cellular response to inorganic substance	0.002	0.046
BP	GO:0071281	cellular response to iron ion	0.003	0.046
BP	GO:0033572	transferrin transport	0.011	0.050
BP	GO:0015682	ferric iron transport	0.012	0.050
BP	GO:0006879	cellular iron ion homeostasis	0.019	0.022
CC	GO:0072562	blood microparticle	8.12×10^4	0.034
CC	GO:0031307	integral component of mitochondrial outer membrane	0.006	0.038
CC	GO:0031306	intrinsic component of mitochondrial outer membrane	0.006	0.038
CC	GO:0031093	platelet alpha granule lumen	0.020	0.043
CC	GO:0031091	platelet alpha granule	0.027	0.048
MF	GO:0008199	ferric iron binding	0.003	0.033
MF	GO:0019825	oxygen binding	0.010	0.034
MF	GO:0016209	antioxidant activity	0.024	0.039
MF	GO:0016810	hydrolase activity, acting on carbon-nitrogen bonds	0.034	0.048

3.5. Immunohistochemical Staining

We searched the immunohistochemical images of P-FRGs from the HPA database. In the HPA database, the quantity of cells stained is greater than 75%, indicating significant differential expression. In accordance with the degree of staining and the quantity of stained cells, it was found that *ALB*, *BNIP3*, *DPEP1*, *GLS2*, *PDK4*, *TF*, and *TSC22D3* were significantly differentially expressed in the adjacent non-tumor gastric tissues and tumor tissues (Figure 5). According to the information provided by the database, immunostaining was performed with following antibodies: *ALB* (HPA031025), *BNIP3* (CAB011676), *DPEP1* (HPA009426), *GLS2* (HPA038608), *PDK4* (HPA056731), *TF* (HPA001527) and *TSC22D3* (CAB034364). No immunohistochemical images of *MEG3* were found.

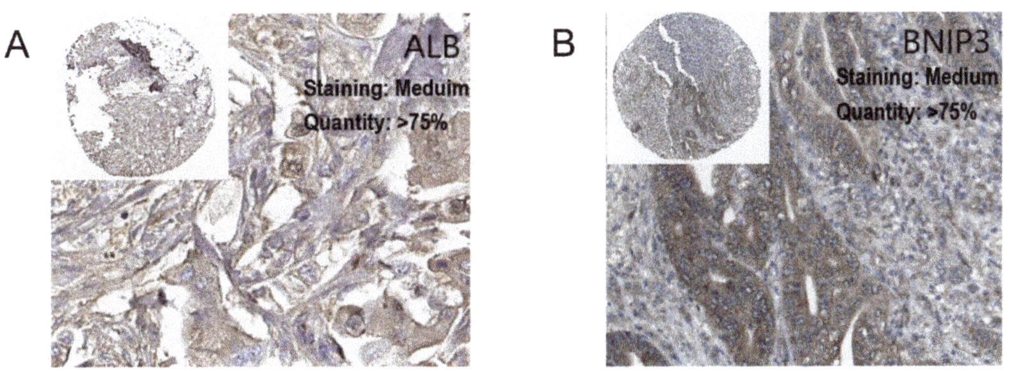

Figure 5. *Cont.*

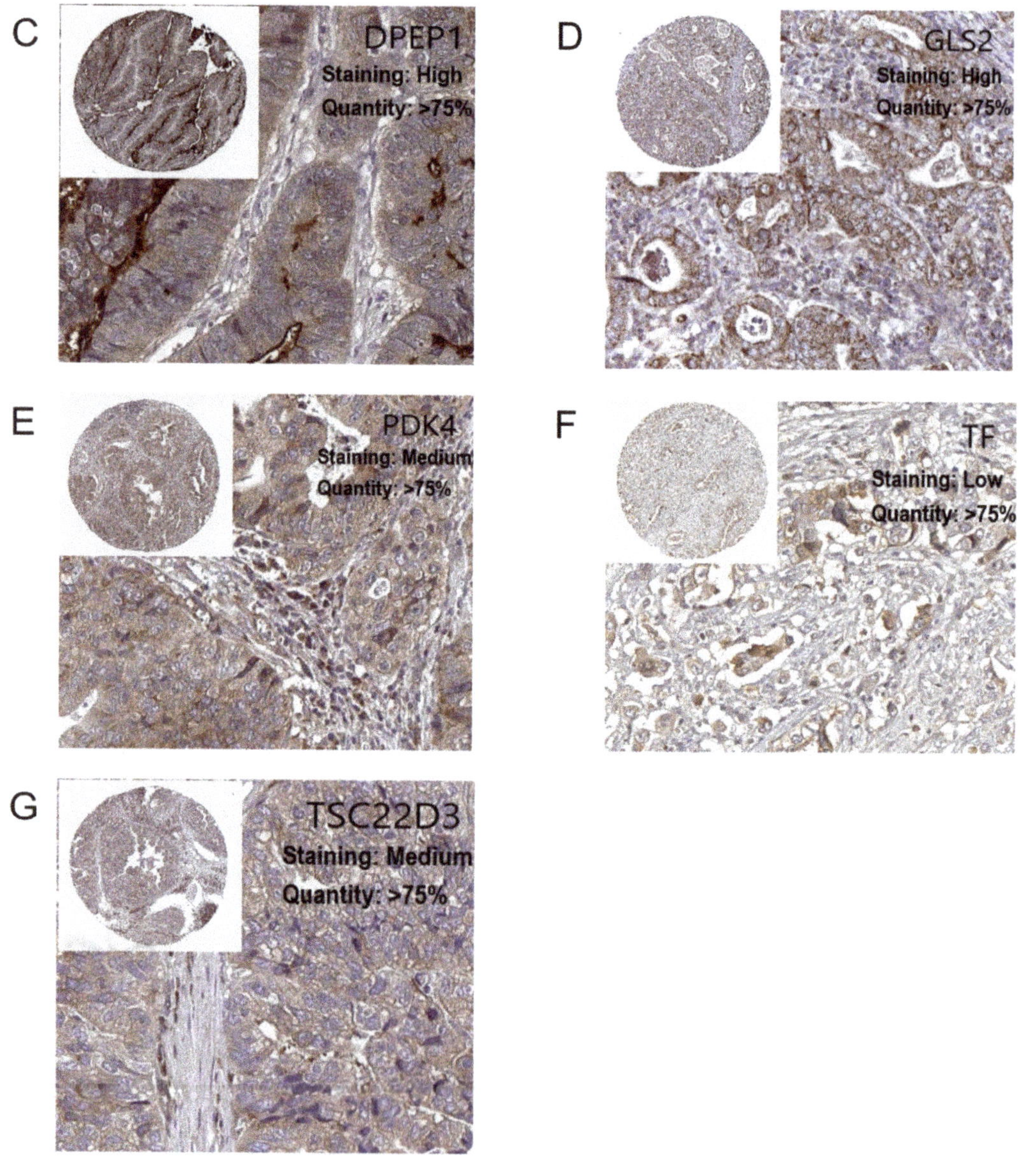

Figure 5. The expression characteristics of 7 P-FRGs in GC. (**A**) *ALB*. (**B**) *BNIP3*. (**C**) *DPEP1*. (**D**) *GLS2*. (**E**) *PDK4*. (**F**) *TF*. (**G**) *TSC22D3*.

4. Discussion

The current incidence and mortality rates of gastric cancer (GC) are on the rise, with a concerning trend of increasing proportions and younger age of onset [18]. Researchers have found that iron metabolism is altered in GC cells, making iron vital for their growth and survival [19]. This finding offers a new perspectives for GC prevention and treatment, as well as opportunities for studying FRGs in GC. However, GC datasets usually have large samples and high dimensions, making it challenging to identify FRGs that directly impact patient outcomes from these datasets. Therefore, the selection of relevant and informative genes becomes crucial. Eliminating irrelevant, redundant, and noisy genes can reduce the computational burden of the classifier and enhance their accuracy. Additionally, this gene selection process facilitates the validation of selected genes in molecular biology experiments [20].

In this study, we used P-WGCNA and EP-WGCNA to select genes that are closely related to phenotype. Then, we further used univariate and multivariate Cox regression analyses and KM curves to calculate the correlation between these genes and GC prognosis. Then, we identified nine P-FRGs (*ALB, AR, BNIP3, CBS, CDC25A, FABP4, MEG3, MYB* and *PDK4*) based on P-WGCNA-Cox. Eight P-FRGs (*ALB, BNIP3, DPEP1, GLS2, MEG3, PDK4, TF*, and *TSC22D3*) were identified based on EP-WGCNA-Cox. Risk scoring models based on nine and eight P-FRGs were constructed, respectively. The KM curve showed that the survival rate of the low-risk group divided based on the median risk score was significantly higher than that of the high-risk group. TimeROC showed that the prognostic model constructed by P-FRGs based on the EP-WGCNA-Cox method was reliable and superior to P-WGCNA-Cox in predicting the 5-year survival of patients, which was also verified in the validation set GSE84426. In addition, we used GO functional enrichment analysis and the HPA database to further study the eight P-FRGs. It was found that eight P-FRGs were significantly enriched in ferric iron binding (GO: 0008199), blood microparticle (GO: 0072562), reactive oxygen species metabolic process (GO: 0072593) and so on. Relevant studies have shown that these pathways are important factors in the occurrence and development of GC and the occurrence of ferroptosis [21–23]. According to the degree of immunohistochemical staining and the quantity of stained cells staining from HPA, seven P-FRGs (*ALB, BNIP3, DPEP1, GLS2, PDK4, TF*, and *TSC22D3*) were significantly differentially expressed in the adjacent non-tumor gastric tissues and tumor tissues.

In the past, clinical characteristics such as age, TNM stages, and some serum markers were commonly used to predict the prognosis of GC patients. However, due to individual differences, these single factors may not provide sufficient accuracy or effectiveness in improving treatment options [24]. With the development of molecular biology and genomics, researchers have found that cancer is a genetic disease and have proposed therapies targeting specific genes [25]. Ferroptosis has been proven to be closely related to the proliferation, invasion, metastasis, and drug resistance of GC [26], but its connections to the prognosis of GC patients remains unclear. In this context, we constructed a new prognostic model (EP-WGCNA-Cox) based on eight FRGs and found it is more reliable in predicting the survival rate of GC patients than P-WGCNA-Cox. In addition, compared with other studies, the EP-WGCNA-Cox model also has some advantages. For example, Huang et al. [27] and Zhang et al. [28] found the 5-year survival rate of GC patients was 0.668 and 0.713, respectively, using LASSO-Cox. Wang et al. [29] constructed a three-FRG risk score to predict the survival rate of GC patients by P-WGCNA-Cox and the AUC was 0.611, which is lower than our P-WGCNA-Cox result. This is likely due to the additional dataset, GTEX, included in our training process. Mao et al. [30] used P-WGCNA-LASSO-Cox to construct an 18-gene signature and it predicted that the 5-year survival rate was 0.726, while our EP-WGCNA-Cox result was 0.77. This indicates that EP-WGCNA can be mined for key genes and EP-WGCNA-Cox is reliable in predicting the survival rate of GC patients.

Referring to the literature reports, among the eight P-FRGs screened based on EP-WGCNA, *ALB* (Albumin) has a variety of important physiological functions, including maintaining blood colloid osmotic pressure between blood vessels and tissues, binding and participating in the transport of various small molecule substances, detoxification and reprocessing of metabolic products, inhibiting platelet aggregation and anticoagulation, etc., which are of great significance in the life process. Recent studies have shown that postoperative *ALB* expression is an effective prognostic factor for elderly GC patients [31], and the ratio of C-reactive protein to *ALB* can predict poor local prognosis for late-stage GC patients [32]. In addition, *ALB* expression is also closely related to the occurrence and development of endometrial cancer [33], liver cancer [34] and osteosarcoma [35]. *BNIP3*

(BCL2 Interacting Protein 3) polymorphism is highly correlated with GC patients' disease susceptibility and clinicopathological characteristics [36], and histidine deficiency promotes GC mitochondrial autophagy by mediating *BNIP3* promoter demethylation via lncRNA *PVT1*, thereby inhibiting GC cell proliferation [37]. *GLS2* (Glutaminase 2) overexpression can significantly inhibit GC cell proliferation and migration and enhance GC cell apoptosis by upregulating cystathionine gamma-lyase 3 expression [38]. *MEG3* (Maternally Expressed 3, non-coding protein) has been proven to be related to the primary tumor site of GC [39] and may be a susceptibility factor for the development of lung cancer, colorectal cancer, and GC [40]. Studies have shown that *PDK4* (Pyruvate Dehydrogenase Kinase 4) has been identified as a potential candidate diagnostic biomarker and therapeutic target for GC patients [41], *TF* (Transferrin) has been shown to be highly expressed in GC and associated with poor prognosis of GC patients [42], and *TSC22D3* (TSC22 Domain Family Member 3) is considered to be involved in the GC iron death-related key competitive endogenous RNA network [43]. *DPEP1* (Dipeptidase 1) has been shown to be an important regulator of single-pathway iron death and to cause kidney disease development by altering cellular iron transport [44], and it is also related to leukemia [45], hepatoblastoma [46], osteoarthritis [47] and colon cancer resistance [48]; however, *DPEP1*'s relationship with GC patient prognosis is less studied. Based on this chapter's research, *DPEP1* may be a new research direction for GC.

This study has several limitations that need to be acknowledged. Firstly, datasets are all from public databases, and as such the results should be validated through in vitro and vivo experiments. Secondly, we relied on the HPA database to explore the expression of P-FRGs. Furthermore, the immunohistochemical image of *MEG3* is not available, and this should be validated via alternative experiments, such as RT-PCR and Western blot.

5. Conclusions

In conclusion, the EP-WGCNA proposed in this paper can mine the key FRGs related to the prognosis of GC patients and is superior to the P-WGCNA. The EP-WGCNA-Cox model, based on *ALB, BNIP3, DPEP1, GLS2, MEG3, PDK4, TF* and *TSC22D3,* is reliable for predicting the 5-year survival rate of GC patients. For clinical use, P-FRGs can be measured to monitor the development of GC. In the follow-up research process, the EP-WGCNA proposed in this paper can be extended to the prognostic gene prediction of other types of cancers. By utilizing gene expression from various cancer types, it is possible to explore the differences and commonalities between different cancers. In addition, the research results of this paper can be further explored using techniques such as RT-PCR and Western blot.

Supplementary Materials: The following supporting information can be downloaded at: https://www.mdpi.com/article/10.3390/app13127108/s1, Figure S1: Relationship between P-FRGs identified by P-WGCNA-Cox and overall survival of GC patients, blue represents the low expression group and red represents the high expression group. (A) *ALB*. (B) *AR*. (C) *BNIP3*. (D) *CBS*. (E) *CDC25A*. (F) *FABP4*. (G) *MEG3*. (H) *MYB*. (I) *PDK4*.; Table S1: Univariate and multivariate regression analysis of the correlation between overall survival of GC patients and DE-FRGs identified by P-WGCNA (p-value < 0.05); Table S2: Univariate and multivariate regression analysis of the correlation between overall survival of GC patients and DE-FRGs identified by P-WGCNA; Table S3: Univariate and multivariate regression analysis of the correlation between overall survival of GC patients and DE-FRGs identified by EP-WGCNA; Ref. [20].

Author Contributions: Conceptualization, H.Z., Z.N. and Y.X.; methodology, H.Z., Z.N., D.C. and Y.X.; software, Y.X. and L.Z.; validation, H.Z., Z.N. and D.C.; formal analysis, Y.X., L.Z. and X.L.; investigation, H.Z. and Y.X.; resources, H.Z. and Z.N.; data curation, Y.X., L.Z. and X.L.; writing—original draft preparation, H.Z., D.C., Y.X. and L.Z.; writing—review and editing, H.Z., D.C., Z.N., L.Z. and X.L.; visualization, H.Z. and Y.X.; supervision, H.Z.; project administration, H.Z.; funding acquisition, H.Z. and D.C. All authors have read and agreed to the published version of the manuscript.

Funding: This research was funded by Natural Science Foundation of Hunan Province, grant number 2021JJ30351, the Scientific Research Fund of Hunan Provincial Education Department, grant number No. 21C0133 and the Key Research and Development Program of Hunan Province, grant number 2020NK2033.

Institutional Review Board Statement: Not applicable.

Informed Consent Statement: Not applicable.

Data Availability Statement: The datasets analyzed during the current study are available in the TCGA repository, TCGA-STAD, the GTEX repository, Normal Tissue Expression and the GEO database repository, GSE84426.

Conflicts of Interest: The authors declare no conflict of interest.

Abbreviations

The following abbreviations are used in this manuscript:

FRGs	Ferroptosis-related genes
GC	Gastric Cancer
WGCNA/P-WGCNA	Weighted gene co-expression network analysis based on Pearson
EP_dis	Euclidean and Pearson weighted distance
EP-WGCNA	Construction of weighted gene co-expression network based on EP_dis
P-FRGs	Ferroptosis-related Genes associated with the prognosis of patients
TCGA	The Cancer Genome Atlas
GTEx	Genotype-Tissue Expression
GEO	Gene Expression Omnibus
timeROC	Time-dependent Receiver Operating Characteristic
HPA	Human Protein Atlas
DEGs	Differentially expressed genes
DE-FRGs	Differentially expressed ferroptosis-related genes
TMM	Trimmed Mean of M-values
ME	The correlation coefficient between gene module feature genes and phenotypes
KM	Kaplan–Meier
GO	Gene ontology
BP	Biological process
CC	Cellular component
MF	Molecular function
FDR	False discovery rate

References

1. Sung, H.; Ferlay, J.; Siegel, R.L.; Laversanne, M.; Soerjomataram, I.; Jemal, A.; Bray, F. Global Cancer Statistics 2020: GLOBOCAN Estimates of Incidence and Mortality Worldwide for 36 Cancers in 185 Countries. *CA Cancer J. Clin.* **2021**, *71*, 209–249. [CrossRef] [PubMed]
2. Kanda, M. Preoperative predictors of postoperative complications after gastric cancer resection. *Surg. Today* **2020**, *50*, 3–11. [CrossRef] [PubMed]
3. Eusebi, L.H.; Telese, A.; Marasco, G.; Bazzoli, F.; Zagari, R.M. Gastric cancer prevention strategies: A global perspective. *J. Gastroenterol. Hepatol.* **2020**, *35*, 1495–1502. [CrossRef] [PubMed]
4. Lin, Y.; Shen, C.; Guo, X.K.; Li, Y.; Wang, D.D.; Chen, X.; Wang, Z.; Wu, K.; Tao, K.X.; Wu, C.Q. Safety evaluation of hyperthermic intraperitoneal chemotherapy in patients with local advanced gastric cancer after radical resection for prevention of peritoneal metastasis. *Zhonghua Wei Chang Wai Ke Za Zhi* **2022**, *25*, 48–55. (In Chinese) [CrossRef] [PubMed]
5. Matsuoka, T.; Yashiro, M. Biomarkers of gastric cancer: Current topics and future perspective. *World J. Gastroenterol.* **2018**, *24*, 2818–2832. [CrossRef]
6. Aronson, J.K.; Ferner, R.E. Biomarkers—A General Review. *Curr. Protoc. Pharmacol.* **2017**, *76*, 9.23.1–9.23.17. [CrossRef]
7. Mou, Y.; Wang, J.; Wu, J.; He, D.; Zhang, C.; Duan, C.; Li, B. Ferroptosis, a new form of cell death: Opportunities and challenges in cancer. *J. Hematol. Oncol.* **2019**, *12*, 34. [CrossRef]
8. Sun, S.; Guo, W.; Lv, F.; Zhang, G.; Wang, J.; Li, R.; Tan, F.; Li, N.; Xue, Q.; Gao, Y.; et al. Comprehensive Analysis of Ferroptosis Regulators in Lung Adenocarcinomas Identifies Prognostic and Immunotherapy-Related Biomarkers. *Front. Mol. Biosci.* **2021**, *8*, 587436. [CrossRef]

9. Mou, Y.; Zhang, Y.; Wu, J.; Hu, B.; Zhang, C.; Duan, C.; Li, B. The Landscape of Iron Metabolism-Related and Methylated Genes in the Prognosis Prediction of Clear Cell Renal Cell Carcinoma. *Front. Oncol.* **2020**, *10*, 788. [CrossRef]
10. Zhu, B.; Zhi, Q.; Xie, Q.; Wu, X.; Gao, Y.; Chen, X.; Shi, L. Reduced expression of ferroportin1 and ceruloplasmin predicts poor prognosis in adrenocortical carcinoma. *J. Trace Elem. Med. Biol.* **2019**, *56*, 52–59. [CrossRef]
11. Cheng, Y.; Li, L.; Qin, Z.; Li, X.; Qi, F. Identification of castration-resistant prostate cancer-related hub genes using weighted gene co-expression network analysis. *J. Cell. Mol. Med.* **2020**, *24*, 8006–8017. [CrossRef]
12. Ning, Z.; Chen, J.; Huang, J.; Sabo, U.J.; Yuan, Z.; Dai, Z. WeDIV—An improved k-means clustering algorithm with a weighted distance and a novel internal validation index. *Egypt. Inform. J.* **2022**, *4*, 1110–8665. [CrossRef]
13. Blanche, P.; Dartigues, J.; Jacqmin-Gadda, H. Estimating and Comparing time-dependent areas under receiver operating characteristic curves for censored event times with competing risks. *Stat. Med.* **2013**, *32*, 5381–5397. [CrossRef]
14. Alexa, A.; Rahnenfuhrer, J.; Lengauer, T. Improved scoring of functional groups from gene expression data by decorrelating GO graph structure. *Bioinformatics.* **2006**, *22*, 1600–1607. [CrossRef]
15. Liu, Y.; Zhang, X.; Zhang, J.; Tan, J.; Li, J.; Song, Z. Development and Validation of a Combined Ferroptosis and Immune Prognostic Classifier for Hepatocellular Carcinoma. *Front. Cell Dev. Biol.* **2020**, *8*, 596679. [CrossRef] [PubMed]
16. Zhou, N.; Bao, J. FerrDb: A manually curated resource for regulators and markers of ferroptosis and ferroptosis-disease associations. *Database* **2020**, *2020*, baaa021. [CrossRef] [PubMed]
17. Therneau, T. A Package for Survival Analysis in R. R Package Version 3.5-3. 2023. Available online: https://CRAN.R-project.org/package=survival (accessed on 15 February 2023).
18. Qu, X.; Zhao, X.; Liu, Y.; Wang, N.; Zhang, L.; Zhu, X.; Dong, Q.; Liu, J.; Shi, Y. The clinicopathological characteristics of early-onset gastric cancer and its evolutionary trends: A retrospective study. *Am. J. Cancer Res.* **2022**, *12*, 2757–2769. Available online: https://www.ncbi.nlm.nih.gov/pmc/articles/PMC9251691/ (accessed on 20 March 2023).
19. Qu, L.; He, X.; Tang, Q.; Fan, X.; Liu, J.; Lin, A. Iron metabolism, ferroptosis, and lncRNA in cancer: Knowns and unknowns. *J. Zhejiang Univ. Sci. B* **2022**, *23*, 844–862. [CrossRef]
20. Li, X. Gene Selection for Cancer Classification Using the Combination of SVM-RFE and GA. *Comput. Model. New Technol.* **2014**, *18*, 262–267.
21. Eom, J.W.; Lim, J.W.; Kim, H. Lutein Induces Reactive Oxygen Species-Mediated Apoptosis in Gastric Cancer AGS Cells via NADPH Oxidase Activation. *Molecules* **2023**, *28*, 1178. [CrossRef] [PubMed]
22. Huang, M.; Wang, Z.; Yao, L.; Zhang, L.; Gou, X.; Mo, H.; Li, H.; Hu, L.; Zhou, X. Ferric chloride induces ferroptosis in Pseudomonas aeruginosa and heals wound infection in a mouse model. *Int. J. Antimicrob. Agents* **2023**, *61*, 106794. [CrossRef]
23. Yin, Y.; Jiang, T.; Hao, Y.; Zhang, J.; Li, W.; Hao, Y.; He, W.; Song, Y.; Feng, Q.; Ma, W. Cascade catalytic nanoplatform based on ions interference strategy for calcium overload therapy and ferroptosis. *Int. J. Pharm.* **2021**, *606*, 120937. [CrossRef]
24. Ye, Y.; Dai, Q.; Li, S.; He, J.; Qi, H. A Novel Defined Risk Signature of the Ferroptosis-Related Genes for Predicting the Prognosis of Ovarian Cancer. *Front. Mol. Biosci.* **2021**, *8*, 645845. [CrossRef]
25. Hu, J.; Cao, J.; Topatana, W.; Juengpanich, S.; Li, S.; Zhang, B.; Shen, J.; Cai, L.; Cai, X.; Chen, M. Targeting mutant p53 for cancer therapy: Direct and indirect strategies. *J. Hematol. Oncol.* **2021**, *14*, 157. [CrossRef]
26. Gu, R.; Xia, Y.; Li, P.; Zou, D.; Lu, K.; Ren, L.; Zhang, H.; Sun, Z. Ferroptosis and its Role in Gastric Cancer. *Front. Cell Dev. Biol.* **2022**, *10*, 860344. [CrossRef]
27. Huang, Y.; Zhou, Y.M.; Sun, W.; Peng, P.; Zhou, L. Screening Ferroptosis Related Genes Influencing Prognosis of Gastric Adenocarcinoma Through Bioinformatics Analysis. *Acta Med. Univ. Sci. Technol. Huazhong* **2021**, *50*, 597–602. [CrossRef]
28. Zhang, J.; Zhang, N.; Fu, X.; Wang, W.; Liu, H.; McKay, M.J.; Dejkriengkraikul, P.; Nie, Y. Bioinformatic analysis of cancer-associated fibroblast related gene signature as a predictive model in clinical outcomes and immune characteristics of gastric cancer. *Ann. Transl. Med.* **2022**, *10*, 698. [CrossRef]
29. Wang, F.; Chen, C.; Chen, W.P.; Li, Z.L.; Cheng, H. Development and Validation of a Novel Ferroptosis-Related Gene Signature for Predicting Prognosis and the Immune Microenvironment in Gastric Cancer. *Biomed. Res. Int.* **2021**, *2021*, 6014202. [CrossRef] [PubMed]
30. Mao, D.; Zhou, Z.; Song, S.; Li, D.; He, Y.; Wei, Z.; Zhang, C. Identification of Stemness Characteristics Associated With the Immune Microenvironment and Prognosis in Gastric Cancer. *Front. Oncol.* **2021**, *11*, 626961. [CrossRef] [PubMed]
31. Li, X.; Shao, L.; Lu, X.; Yang, Z.; Ai, S.; Sun, F.; Wang, M.; Guan, W.; Liu, S. Risk factors for lymph node metastasis in gastric neuroendocrine tumor: A retrospective study. *BMC Surg.* **2021**, *21*, 174. [CrossRef]
32. Alkurt, E.G.; Durak, D.; Turhan, V.B.; Sahiner, I.T. Effect of C-Reactive Protein-to-Albumin Ratio on Prognosis in Gastric Cancer Patients. *Cureus* **2022**, *14*, e23972. [CrossRef] [PubMed]
33. Lei, J.; Wang, Y.; Guo, X.; Yan, S.; Ma, D.; Wang, P.; Li, B.; Du, W.; Guo, R.; Kan, Q. Low preoperative serum ALB level is independently associated with poor overall survival in endometrial cancer patients. *Future Oncol.* **2020**, *16*, 307–316. [CrossRef]
34. Fujioka-Kobayashi, M.; Schaller, B.; Mourão, C.F.A.B.; Zhang, Y.; Sculean, A.; Miron, R.J. Biological characterization of an injectable platelet-rich fibrin mixture consisting of autologous albumin gel and liquid platelet-rich fibrin (Alb-PRF). *Platelets* **2021**, *32*, 74–81. [CrossRef]
35. Pan, Q.; Lou, J.; Yan, P.; Kang, X.; Li, P.; Huang, Z. WTAP contributes to the tumorigenesis of osteosarcoma via modulating ALB in an m6A-dependent manner. *Genomics* **2023**, *20*, 110566. [CrossRef] [PubMed]

36. Lou, X.; Hu, D.; Li, Z.; Teng, Y.; Lou, Q.; Huang, S.; Zou, Y.; Wang, F. Associations of BNIP3 and DAPK1 gene polymorphisms with disease susceptibility, clinicopathologic features, anxiety, and depression in gastric cancer patients. *Int. J. Clin. Exp. Pathol.* **2021**, *14*, 633–645. Available online: https://www.ncbi.nlm.nih.gov/pmc/articles/PMC8167493/ (accessed on 15 March 2023).
37. Xin, L.; Lu, H.; Liu, C.; Zeng, F.; Yuan, Y.W.; Wu, Y.; Wang, J.L.; Wu, D.Z.; Zhou, L.Q. Methionine deficiency promoted mitophagy via lncRNA PVT1-mediated promoter demethylation of BNIP3 in gastric cancer. *Int. J. Biochem. Cell Biol.* **2021**, *141*, 106100. [CrossRef]
38. Xu, L.; Zhou, D.; Li, F.; Ji, L. Glutaminase 2 functions as a tumor suppressor gene in gastric cancer. *Transl. Cancer Res.* **2020**, *9*, 4906–4913. [CrossRef] [PubMed]
39. Soghala, S.; Harsiny, K.; Momeni, P.; Hatami, M.; Kholghi Oskooei, V.; Hussen, B.M.; Taheri, M.; Ghafouri-Fard, S. Down-regulation of LINC-ROR, HOXA-AS2 and MEG3 in gastric cancer. *Heliyon* **2022**, *8*, e11155. [CrossRef] [PubMed]
40. Wang, W.; Xiong, W.; Zheng, J.; Jin, Y.; Dong, L.; Feng, X.; Ban, Y.; Chen, B. The contribution of MALAT1 gene rs3200401 and MEG3 gene rs7158663 to the risk of lung, colorectal, gastric and liver cancer. *Pathol. Res. Pract.* **2022**, *240*, 154212. [CrossRef]
41. Zhang, Z.; Han, S.; Ouyang, S.; Zeng, Z.; Liu, Z.; Sun, J.; Kang, W. PDK4 Constitutes a Novel Prognostic Biomarker and Therapeutic Target in Gastric Cancer. *Diagnostics* **2022**, *12*, 1101. [CrossRef]
42. Chen, J.; Sun, B.; Wu, J.; Du, C. ONECUT2 Accelerates Tumor Proliferation Through Activating ROCK1 Expression in Gastric Cancer. *Cancer Manag. Res.* **2020**, *12*, 6113–6121. [CrossRef] [PubMed]
43. Jin, W.; Liu, J.; Yang, J.; Feng, Z.; Feng, Z.; Huang, N.; Yang, T.; Yu, L. Identification of a key ceRNA network associated with ferroptosis in gastric cancer. *Sci. Rep.* **2022**, *12*, 20088. [CrossRef] [PubMed]
44. Guan, Y.; Liang, X.; Ma, Z.; Hu, H.; Liu, H.; Miao, Z.; Linkermann, A.; Hellwege, J.N.; Voight, B.F.; Susztak, K. A single genetic locus controls both expression of DPEP1/CHMP1A and kidney disease development via ferroptosis. *Nat. Commun.* **2021**, *12*, 5078. [CrossRef]
45. Zhang, J.M.; Xu, Y.; Gale, R.P.; Wu, L.X.; Zhang, J.; Feng, Y.H.; Qin, Y.Z.; Jiang, H.; Jiang, Q.; Jiang, B.; et al. DPEP1 expression promotes proliferation and survival of leukaemia cells and correlates with relapse in adults with common B cell acute lymphoblastic leukaemia. *Br. J. Haematol.* **2020**, *190*, 67–78. [CrossRef] [PubMed]
46. Chen, J.; Jin, H.; Zhou, H.; Hei, X.; Liu, K. Research into the characteristic molecules significantly affecting liver cancer immunotherapy. *Front. Immunol.* **2023**, *14*, 1029427. [CrossRef]
47. Zhang, Z.; Mei, Y.; Feng, M.; Wang, C.; Yang, P.; Tian, R. The relationship between common variants in the DPEP1 gene and the susceptibility and clinical severity of osteoarthritis. *Int. J. Rheum. Dis.* **2021**, *24*, 1192–1199. [CrossRef]
48. Zeng, C.; Qi, G.; Shen, Y.; Li, W.; Zhu, Q.; Yang, C.; Deng, J.; Lu, W.; Liu, Q.; Jin, J. DPEP1 promotes drug resistance in colon cancer cells by forming a positive feedback loop with ASCL2. *Cancer Med.* **2023**, *12*, 412–424. [CrossRef]

www.ingramcontent.com/pod-product-compliance
Lightning Source LLC
Chambersburg PA
CBHW062046220926
51850CB00010B/2680

MDPI AG
Grosspeteranlage 5
4052 Basel
Switzerland
Tel.: +41 61 683 77 34

Applied Sciences Editorial Office
E-mail: applsci@mdpi.com
www.mdpi.com/journal/applsci